FORTRAN Programming and WATFIV

FORTRAN
Programming
and WATFIV

JAMES L. PARKER

MARILYN BOHL

SCIENCE RESEARCH ASSOCIATES, INC.
Chicago, Palo Alto, Toronto
Henley-on-Thames, Sydney, Paris
A Subsidiary of IBM

Figures 1.2 and 1.4 are courtesy of International
Business Machines Corporation.

The following exercises are reprinted with permission from
INTRODUCTION TO COMPUTER SCIENCE by C. W. Gear,
© 1973, Science Research Associates, Inc.: chapter 2, P.1;
chapter 5, E.2, E.3, E.4, E.5, E.6, P.1; chapter 6, E.12, P.1, P.2,
P.3, P.4: chapter 7, E.1, E.2, E.3, E.4, E.5, E.6, P.1, P.3, P.4, P.5;
chapter 8, E.6, P.3, P.4, P.5, P.6, P.7, P.8, P.9, P.10;
chapter 11, P.1, P.2.

CONTENTS

The structure of the book is particularly important to those who want to use it effectively. This preface describes the structure, ways the book may be used, and the intended audience.

THE STRUCTURE OF THE TEXT

Each chapter in this text covers one set of FORTRAN statements or a single programming topic. It is organized into four parts as shown below.

INTRO	Introduction
TUT	Tutorial Assumes only preceding tutorial sections.
REF	Reference May assume all tutorial sections and specified reference material as well.
QUEST	Questions 1. Drill exercises 2. Programming problems

The introduction to the chapter (indicated by INTRO) outlines the material covered and gives a preview of what to expect in the chapter.

The tutorial section of each chapter (indicated by TUT) presents the statements involved. Although it is aimed at the beginning programmer, those of you who are familiar with another computer language should scan this section because it contains useful facts not repeated elsewhere.

Next is a reference section (marked REF in the margin) that deals with more advanced programming concepts. You can use it to expand your knowledge of FORTRAN and to answer specific questions.

The last section of each chapter (QUEST) consists of questions divided into two types. The first are thought or drill questions intended to reinforce your knowledge of individual FORTRAN statements and their use. Answers to selected questions of this type are given in appendix A. Questions of the second type are design and programming problems. They lead to the development of complete FORTRAN or WATFIV programs. Executing and debugging

Preface

these programs is, of course, the best means of exercising, reinforcing, and applying your knowledge in specific problem-solving situations. Each question is identified by either TUT or REF to let you know whether it refers to tutorial or reference material.

The table of contents is a detailed outline of the text. The index is hierarchical so you can easily find information you need. A summary of FORTRAN and WATFIV statements is printed inside the front and back covers as a reference guide and a convenience for beginning programmers.

RECOMMENDED METHOD OF STUDY

The tutorial and reference sections of each chapter are not meant to be read consecutively. The recommended order of study is given in the following chart. It suggests one sequence you may use, but there are others. The tutorial sections need not be studied in the precise order shown. In particular, the chapter on type statements (chapter 2) may be studied at a later time if a brief explanation of default typing is provided. The tutorial section of chapter 6 may be read after the tutorial section of chapter 7, permitting greater use of IF and GO TO statements before work with arrays. The chapter on design and debugging (chapter 9) may follow the first study of the tutorial section of chapter 1. In this way, you are introduced to these techniques before beginning to write somewhat sophisticated programs.

We recommend that you read the whole book, though not necessarily in concentrated study. You can begin programming while reading just the tutorial sections. But if you learn only this material, you are at a disadvantage in the long run; you learn only a portion of FORTRAN capabilities. The reference material is designed to help you extend your knowledge of FORTRAN and use it more effectively.

The reference features make the information in the book readily accessible to the three groups it is intended to serve:

- Beginning programmers taking an introductory computer science or FORTRAN course, or any other course that includes FORTRAN
- Programmers or students learning FORTRAN as a second language
- FORTRAN programmers who want a comprehensive reference for IBM's FORTRAN G and H or for WATFIV

A TEXT FOR BEGINNING PROGRAMMERS

The text emphasizes practical FORTRAN programming. The initial tutorial sections are brief, providing only essential information and allowing the student to begin programming as soon as possible. Each tutorial section depends only on preceding tutorial sections. When you have read the tutorial material and are familiar with it, you can turn to the reference sections for answers to specific questions and to extend your programming capabilities.

This book is not meant to be a self-teaching text for the novice programmer. It can be used in connection with a beginning course in computer science or as an independent FORTRAN text. In particular, it is designed to complement C. W. Gear, *Introduction to Computer Science* (Palo Alto: Science Research

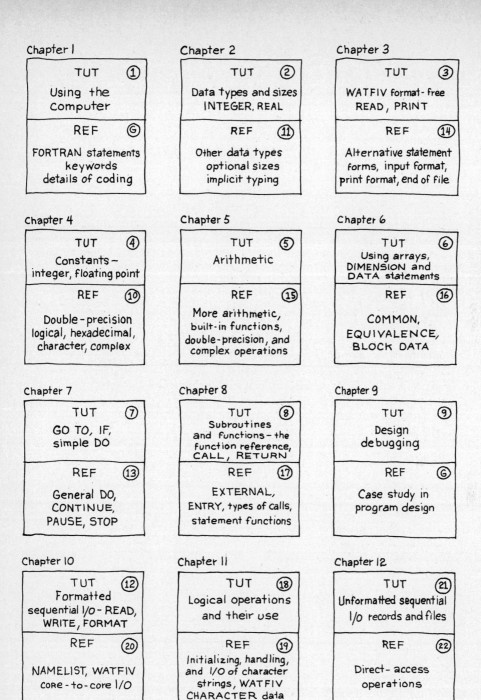

Chapter 1

TUT ①
Using the Computer

REF Ⓖ
FORTRAN statements keywords details of coding

Chapter 2

TUT ②
Data types and sizes INTEGER, REAL

REF ⑪
Other data types optional sizes implicit typing

Chapter 3

TUT ③
WATFIV format-free READ, PRINT

REF ⑭
Alternative statement forms, input format, print format, end of file

Chapter 4

TUT ④
Constants — integer, floating point

REF ⑩
Double-precision logical, hexadecimal, character, complex

Chapter 5

TUT ⑤
Arithmetic

REF ⑮
More arithmetic, built-in functions, double-precision, and complex operations

Chapter 6

TUT ⑥
Using arrays, DIMENSION and DATA statements

REF ⑯
COMMON, EQUIVALENCE, BLOCK DATA

Chapter 7

TUT ⑦
GO TO, IF, simple DO

REF ⑬
General DO, CONTINUE, PAUSE, STOP

Chapter 8

TUT ⑧
Subroutines and functions — the function reference, CALL, RETURN

REF ⑰
EXTERNAL, ENTRY, types of calls, statement functions

Chapter 9

TUT ⑨
Design debugging

REF Ⓖ
Case study in program design

Chapter 10

TUT ⑫
Formatted sequential I/O – READ, WRITE, FORMAT

REF ⑳
NAMELIST, WATFIV core-to-core I/O

Chapter 11

TUT ⑱
Logical operations and their use

REF ⑲
Initializing, handling, and I/O of character strings, WATFIV CHARACTER data

Chapter 12

TUT ㉑
Unformatted sequential I/O records and files

REF ㉒
Direct-access operations

① Recommended order of study

Ⓖ General reference material

Associates, 1973). Some exercises (indicated by § in the margin) in this text also appear in the Gear text, and references to related material in the Gear text are included when appropriate.

A SECOND LANGUAGE TEXT

The completeness and reference facility of the text are intended to help the more advanced student pick up the FORTRAN language quickly. He need only read through the tutorial sections and do the drill exercises at the ends of the chapters to obtain a working knowledge of FORTRAN. He can use the table of contents, reference sections, and index to find answers to particular questions. The structure of the text keeps all the material about given sets of operations, such as input/output, in well-identified sections of the book. This helps the experienced programmer, who usually knows the kind of information he needs.

A REFERENCE TEXT

Every effort has been made to make the text complete with respect to IBM 360/370 FORTRAN and WATFIV. It is organized so that particular facts can be located quickly. All the common built-in functions are listed. (See appendix F.) WATFIV control cards and error messages are also covered in appendixes.

Although this text is intended as a complete reference to FORTRAN G and H and WATFIV, it does not replace the type of documentation generally identified as a programmer's guide. Such a guide contains much information that is totally system-dependent—job control statements, calling sequences, and the like. This type of information, which is not appropriate to this text, is normally available at a computer installation.

ACKNOWLEDGMENTS

We, the authors, express our thanks to Stephen Mitchell and other members of the SRA staff who assisted in the preparation of this text. The work of Cathy Smith, who typed the original manuscript, is greatly appreciated. Sincere thanks are due also to the following for their helpful suggestions: Lynn Hueftlein and Vince Manis, University of British Columbia; Katherine Nooning, University of Kentucky; and C. W. Gear, University of Illinois.

James L. Parker

Marilyn Bohl

INTRO

The emphasis in this book is on learning FORTRAN in order to solve problems. The structural relationship between a computer program and the real problem for which that program has been created is stressed. In many cases, programming imitates reality. As an illustration of this idea, consider the problem of computing tax deductions. If a company has both monthly and hourly employees, it probably has two different formulas for computing their pay and deductions. You should expect that a program to perform this task will also have two parts, one for each computation. In this sense then, the structure of the program follows the structure of the real problem. Deliberately identifying and following that structure may help you to avoid making errors in your programs.

To maximize its effectiveness as a problem-solving tool for both beginning and experienced programmers, the text is organized mainly into tutorial and reference sections. How the book is structured and how readers can best use it are described in the preface, which you must read in order to use the text effectively.

In the tutorial section of this chapter, we begin with a brief consideration of computers and programming. We explain what FORTRAN and WATFIV are and give a simple program as an example. The reference section describes the elements of the FORTRAN language and how to write FORTRAN statements.

By the time you have completed the tutorial section of this chapter, you will have submitted a program to the computer and seen the results.

COMPUTERS—WHAT THEY DO
TUT

Computers move information. They combine pieces of information to make new forms and change information from one form to another. When you learn to write programs for a computer, you learn how to tell the computer what steps to take for a particular information moving and combining job.

Compare this task to that of a moving company. When you use the services of the company, you must tell them what to move,

Chapter

1

COMPUTERS, PROGRAMMING, FORTRAN, AND WATFIV

where to move it, and how to place it in the rooms of the building to which it is routed. The company is ready to move anything, anywhere, any time. You must "program" the company to move particular things to a particular place in a particular way. So it is with computers. But since computers cannot understand English, you must use some other language to tell them where to move information and how to arrange it at the destination.

We know that many different languages are used by men in communicating with one another. Many different languages are also used in communicating with computers. If you know more than one, you choose the one that is most convenient for the job at hand. Since computer languages are simpler than human ones, this multiplicity of languages is not as frightening as it may seem.

WHAT COMPUTERS ALREADY KNOW

Usually, it is not realistic to speak of computers as "knowing" anything. This book emphasizes learning computer programming by studying the ways in which computers move information, and it is reasonable in this context to say that computers know how to move and combine information. But that is all. No computer "knows" how to calculate the proper path to send a man to the moon. The program directing it contains the knowledge of how to manipulate information to calculate the correct path. And that knowledge must be supplied by the programmer who writes the information-manipulating steps that calculate the path. The knowledge is always of human origin.

WHAT IS INFORMATION?

We usually speak of having information about things. We do not say, "I have the price"; rather, we say, "I have the price of the shirt." There is a set of possible prices for an item, presumably from zero cents to an arbitrarily large number of dollars. To say that we have information about a price means that, of the large set of possibilities, we know which one is correct.

HOW DO WE REPRESENT INFORMATION?

After we have acquired information, we usually want to share that information with others. To do so, we represent it by means of words uttered as sounds or written on a page. The way in which we represent or declare information (the particular price, in the example above) can be called *coding*.

In this book, we deal with coding schemes that are physical or electronic. Within this realm, there are many different ways of representing information. Different codes are used for the convenience and efficiency of different occasions. Any coding scheme is valid as long as there is a different representation for each possibility that might occur and everyone uses the code consistently.

COMPUTERS USE SPECIAL CODES

You will have to become familiar with several coding schemes as a FORTRAN programmer. The following are of initial importance:

● Characters or external coding

This is the coding scheme with which you are familiar. Numbers and words are represented by typing them as combinations of characters from some form of keyboard. Most people using FORTRAN type the characters onto cards via a keypunch. Some have access to terminals—devices permitting characters to be entered directly into the computer. The output of the computer is almost always in character form, particularly when it is to be used by people rather than by machines.

● Integers in internal form

Integers are just numbers without decimal points or fractional parts. Some examples are:

    0   1   47   23581

Inside the computer, integers are represented in a special way that usually involves the use of a *base 2 coding scheme*. This is a system that follows the binary number system and uses the binary digits 0 and 1. As a FORTRAN programmer, you need not understand in detail how this coding scheme works, but you must remember which of your numbers are treated as integers and which are not.

● Floating-point numbers in internal form

Inside the computer, numbers with decimal points and fractional parts are represented in another special way. We call these numbers floating-point numbers. Examples are:

    .05   1.   3.007   23581.

In FORTRAN, these numbers are also called real numbers. This terminology comes from the mathematical notation for numbers having fractional parts. We shall use the terms *real* and *floating-point* interchangeably in this text; you should regard them as synonymous. Here again, you need not understand in detail how the numbers are represented in computer storage. You need only recall which data values are represented as floating-point numbers.

These three coding schemes apply throughout the text; they are the primary means for representing basic items that the computer manipulates and combines. You will also see other coding schemes in this book: logical, hexadecimal, complex, and character.

THE STEPS IN A PROGRAM

The basic idea of programming is to analyze a task, or problem, so that you can group instructions to the computer in sets of steps that correspond to parts of the problem. The structure of your computer program should match the structure of the problem that you want to solve.

In some ways computers are like small children. We cannot say to a small child, "Go and buy three tomatoes." This task is too large. It must be broken into small pieces that the child can understand: "Here is some money; go to the store at the end of the block; ask the girl at the counter to help you to find three big, red tomatoes." Similarly, we must break down a task that is to be done by the computer. Since the computer only knows how to move or combine small pieces of information, we must describe a given information-manipulating task very carefully, in very small steps. In doing so, we can use only a fixed set of instructions. We cannot make up our own.

This book explains one language for instructing computers: FORTRAN. The language is made up of fixed statements. Each statement tells the machine to move, compare, or combine information in a certain way. The variety of statement forms available in FORTRAN is much smaller than the possible sentence variations in English. The text describes the statement forms and how the statements manipulate information. Examples demonstrate how to use the statement by itself or together with other statements in directing the computer to perform a certain task.

WHAT TO LOOK FOR WHEN PROGRAMMING

Several elements are common to all programming languages and to writing programs for any machine. Following is a list of things to look for as you study FORTRAN programming.

1   Information
    a)   What is the proper movement of information through a program?
    b)   How is information coded in a program? Where in the program is the information changed from one coding scheme to another?

2   Algorithm
    The algorithm for a program is a description of the steps that must be taken to produce the desired result. You must understand the algorithm before you begin to write the program.

3   Program structure
    When you look at an algorithm, you will usually see that certain steps have to be done several times. This pattern determines the structure of your FORTRAN program. Some statements are executed several times although they are written only once. This repetitive execution of instructions is called *looping*.

4   The particular machine
    As you become familiar with the FORTRAN language, you will find that some statements differ slightly from machine to machine. If you move from one machine to another, you must ask about these differences.

5   FORTRAN statements
    You must study each FORTRAN statement and learn its functions, preferably by writing and executing FORTRAN programs. No one learns programming by reading a book.

6   Principles of program design
    There are advisable ways of approaching a problem-solving task that are not dependent on a given language. Some of them are discussed in this book. Many are described in detail in C. W. Gear, *Introduction to Computer Science* (Palo Alto: Science Research Associates, 1973).

WHAT FOLLOWS PROGRAMMING?

The programmer's job is to write a program consisting of statements grouped to form a structure similar to that of the problem. Actually, the FORTRAN statements are translated by another program to an even simpler, or lower-level, language before they are used to direct the computer. This lower-level language is called *machine language*.

We can write a simple FORTRAN statement such as SUM = 49 + 95 to specify that the values 49 and 95 are to be added, and their sum is to be stored in the computer in a location referred to as SUM. The translator program, or *compiler*, converts this statement into a number of more basic steps that the computer must actually perform to calculate the sum. For example, the computer may be directed to:

- load the value 49 into a particular location in computer storage
- add the value 95 to the value 49 at that location
- store the result in the location known as SUM for further use

When, at a later time, the computer performs these steps, we say that it *executes* our statement.*

Thus, two actions are required when a FORTRAN-language program is submitted to the computer. First, the program must be translated, or compiled, into machine language. Then, the machine-language version of the program must be executed to obtain the solution to the original problem. This two-step procedure, as carried out in one type of processing environment, is shown in figure 1.1.

In this environment, the programmer's coding is punched into cards to create a source-program deck. But these cards are treated as data rather than as a program. They serve as input to a compilation run in which the FORTRAN compiler translates the programmer's coding into machine language. Two outputs are produced from this run: (1) an object-program deck that contains the machine-language version of the program, and (2) a source-program listing that contains, among other things, a printed listing of the programmer's FORTRAN statements as he submitted them and error messages describing any errors detected by the compiler during the compilation process. After an error-free compilation run is achieved, the machine-language version of the program is loaded into the computer, and input related to the original problem (such as hours worked, parts ordered, or cost per item) is read by the machine-language program. The computer executes the steps in the program and provides results (such as payroll checks or shipping orders) as output.

There are, of course, minor variations in the way in which the steps shown in figure 1.1 are carried out. For example, the programmer may enter his program into the computer from a keyboard; there may be no need for an intermediate step transferring his program to cards. As another example, the machine-language version of the program may be written to magnetic tape or magnetic disk, rather than punched into cards. Some compilers are *load and go compilers*; that is,

*Refer to C. W. Gear, *Introduction to Computer Science,* for an extended discussion of program translation and machine language if desired.

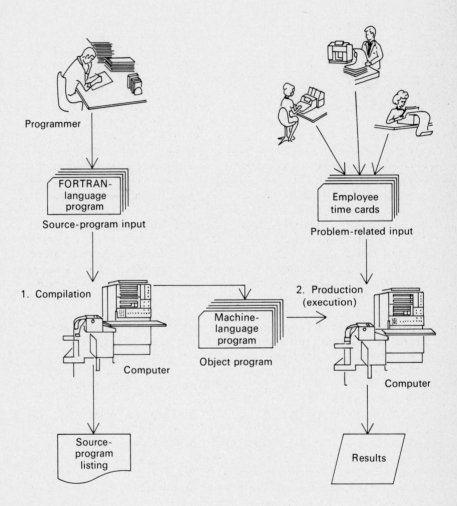

Programmer

FORTRAN-language program

Source-program input

1. Compilation

Computer

Machine-language program

Object program

Employee time cards

Problem-related input

2. Production (execution)

Computer

Source-program listing

Results

FIGURE 1.1

they translate FORTRAN programs into machine-language code that resides in storage locations and then supervise the execution of that code immediately. The distinction between compilation and execution is not as obvious as it otherwise is. In fact, the programmer may be largely unaware that two steps are involved.

WHAT ARE FORTRAN, WATFOR, AND WATFIV?

FORTRAN is probably the most widely used programming language. The name FORTRAN is derived from *for*mula *tran*slator. It was designed primarily for problems involving numerical computation, but it can be used to solve many, diverse types of problems. The language is not totally standard. That is, FORTRAN statements are not exactly the same from machine to machine. On almost any computer that you use, a FORTRAN compiler will be available to translate your FORTRAN statements (with few or no changes on your part) into the machine language of that computer. IBM's FORTRAN G and H include some features described in this text that are not included in the American National Standard (ANS) recommendations for FORTRAN IV. The features available in FORTRAN G and H but not included in ANS recommendations are listed in appendix E.

A few years ago, it was recognized that the FORTRAN language was not oriented toward teaching students of programming. Some slight changes were made to the language, and the FORTRAN compiler was rewritten, creating new versions of both the language and the compiler. The changed language was called WATFOR, an acronym for WATERLOO FORTRAN selected because the language and compiler were developed at the University of Waterloo in Ontario, Canada.

The WATFOR compiler is much faster than most FORTRAN compilers at translating FORTRAN statements into machine language. Since students usually have to change their statements many times when learning a new language, they frequently require new translations of their programs from FORTRAN to machine language. Therefore, speed of compilation is a significant factor from both student-need and computer-usage points of view.

Programming students also need clear explanations when errors are detected in their programs. Therefore, in WATFOR, emphasis was placed on complete error messages. Many programming errors that students make are of types that prevent the computer from finishing a problem-solving task as intended. WATFOR is designed to help the student find what is wrong when an abnormal termination occurs. As you will soon realize, programmers, even experienced ones, make mistakes. The program that executes correctly the first time is as rare as a hole-in-one.

WATFIV is an improvement over WATFOR. Its name comes from the fact that almost everything in computer science has a number, and that a new one of something is always given a number one greater than the previous one. Since FOR from WATFOR sounds like four, the natural next choice is WATFIV. Differences between WATFOR and WATFIV stem mainly from the fact that more statements, and capabilities associated with statements, are available in WATFIV.

In this book, an attempt is made to identify any described features that are unique to FORTRAN, WATFOR, or WATFIV. Since the three are intended to be compatible as far as possible, many statements are available in all of them. Some specific differences are identified in appendix B. When studying this text, you should assume that the capabilities described are available in both IBM 360/370 FORTRAN and WATFIV unless specifically stated otherwise.

Before using any of these systems on a particular computer, you should find out what language variations, if any, exist at the installation. Most installations maintain a list of these differences. They are usually minor and have to do with the input of information to the computer and the output of information from it.

A SAMPLE PROGRAM

One of the simplest information-manipulating tasks that a computer is called upon to perform is the transfer of information from one data medium to another. Often that transfer is from punched cards to a printed listing. When using the computer, two steps are involved. First, the information is moved from outside the computer into its storage locations, or *memory*. Second, the information is moved from memory onto paper outside the computer. As you may already know, the former is called *reading*, and the latter is called *printing*. A program that moves two integer values in this manner is shown as an example in figure 1.2. The READ statement controls movement of the values into the storage locations referred to by the names I and J. The PRINT statement controls movement of the values from those locations as output.

The STOP statement is used in this program to terminate program execution. When the computer encounters this statement, its processing task is complete. A program whose execution is terminated by a STOP statement is said to have terminated normally.

The READ, PRINT, and STOP statements are *executable statements*. Each of them is translated by the FORTRAN compiler into one or more machine-language instructions, and those instructions direct the computer in performing specific steps at program execution-time. (When we say, in this book, that a FORTRAN statement is executed, we really mean that the machine-language equivalent of that statement is acted upon by the computer.)

In contrast, the END statement that appears in figure 1.2 is a *nonexecutable statement*. No machine-language equivalent is set up for this statement. It is important at program compilation-time rather than at program execution-time. An END statement must appear as the last statement of every FORTRAN program, because it tells the FORTRAN compiler that the end of the program has been reached and compilation can be completed.

There are several things to observe in this sample program. Note that the statements are written on a special coding form, and that each part of a statement is written in a particular portion of the coding line. What we have discussed is the body of the statement. You will learn other parts of a statement as you need them.

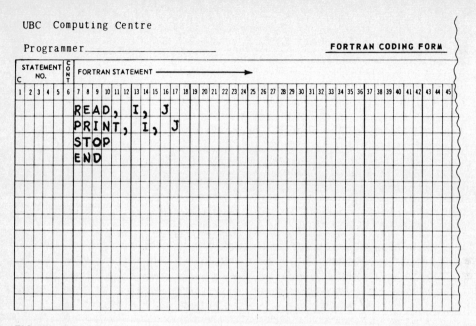

FIGURE 1.2

The FORTRAN statements in figure 1.2 are made up of recognizable English words and common English punctuation. You will see in further programs that numbers are expressed in the usual way also. However, the use of FORTRAN is more restricted than the use of English. Each statement must be written in the form specified for it. You will become familiar with these statement forms as you learn FORTRAN programming.

A BASIC APPROACH

As you prepare your first FORTRAN programs, you should follow a fundamental plan of attack. You will find that you work most effectively if you do the following:

1   Make a list of the functions that the program must perform.

2   Determine what input information is required to perform the functions.

3   Determine what output information is required by the user.

4   Make a list of basic steps to be included in the program. In doing so, you are apt to find that constructing a *program flowchart* (explained more fully below) helps you to determine the steps required.

5   Program each of the steps that you identified in 4 above.

6   Put the program together with the input data and any required control information.

7   Submit the program as a job to the computer. When it is returned, analyze the errors (assuming it didn't work correctly the first time), correct them, and resubmit the job. This is called *program debugging*.

8   When you have achieved an error-free compilation, and your program has executed to normal termination, verify that the output produced by it is the output required.

Items 1 through 4 above are essential to good programming; they are a basic part of one major prerequisite: careful, complete program design. This topic is dealt with in detail in chapter 9 of this text. You will find it worthwhile to refer to the tutorial section of that chapter as you begin to write FORTRAN programs.

A program flowchart, as mentioned in 4 above, is a visual outline of the sequence and interrelationships of processing steps required within a program. Since drawing a flowchart often helps the programmer to analyze a problem more clearly, a knowledge of flowcharting symbols and techniques is extremely valuable. A tutorial presentation of flowcharting is not within the scope of this book. For general guidelines, you can refer to chapters 3 and 5 of Gear, *Introduction to Computer Science*, or to Bohl, *Flowcharting Techniques* (Palo Alto: Science Research Associates, 1971).

The required control information mentioned in 6 above is the additional information, other than program and data, that the computer must have before it processes your job. Often this information is submitted on one or more special cards, called *control cards*, that can be recognized as such because of special identification (say, the characters // in columns 1 and 2 of the cards). If your program is submitted to the computer from a terminal, you may simply type this information into the system. For those of you who are using WATFIV systems, the general format and content of WATFIV control cards is summarized in appendix C.

Since the format and content of control information is somewhat unique to each computer installation, you must become familiar with the job-control requirements of the computer system available to you. Your instructor will tell you of control information required for the programs that you write, compile, and execute as a part of your work in this course.

Note again the mention of program debugging in item 7 above. The importance of comprehensive test and correction procedures cannot be overstated. Chapter 9 of this text deals with general debugging techniques and special features of FORTRAN and WATFIV designed primarily as debugging aids. You will find it helpful to refer to this chapter throughout your study of FORTRAN programming.

SUBMITTING A JOB

At this time, you should submit the sample program given in figure 1.2 as a job to be processed by the computer available to you. In some environments, this may involve keypunching the statements onto cards to create a source-program deck. In others, the statements may be typed directly into the computer from a terminal. In either case, you will become familiar with general operational procedures such as terminal sign-on, job submittal area, control card requirements, and authorization. Of course, you should also prepare input data to be operated on by the program after it has been compiled successfully. By referring to the program in figure 1.2 and rereading the brief description of it, you will note that two integer values are required.

RECEIVING OUTPUT

As shown in figure 1.1, when your FORTRAN program is compiled and executed in distinct steps, you normally receive two sets of output. After compilation, you should expect to receive a source-program listing that you can examine to determine whether any errors were detected during the compilation process. After execution, you can expect to receive output related to the actual problem—the results that the program is supposed to provide.

The WATFIV compiler is a load and go compiler. If your FORTRAN program is compiled and executed by such a compiler, you receive a listing of your program together with any output printed by it. Figure 1.3 shows a sample of actual output as provided by the WATFIV compiler at the University of British Columbia.

You need not be concerned with understanding all portions of this output. You can easily see that the program compiled and executed was our sample program of figure 1.2. $COMPILE and $DATA are system commands used at the particular installation. (See appendix C.) What integer values were printed as output? The statistics shown in figure 1.3 are printed automatically at job termination. They will become meaningful to you as you continue your study of programming.

```
        $COMPILE
1          READ, I, J
2          PRINT, I, J
3          STOP
4          END

        $DATA
OUTPUT IS:              1              2

CORE USAGE      OBJECT CODE=     280 BYTES,ARRAY AREA=        0 BYTES,TOTA

DIAGNOSTICS     NUMBER OF ERRORS=      0, NUMBER OF WARNINGS=        0,

COMPILE TIME=    0.04 SEC,EXECUTION TIME=      0.01 SEC.  WATFIV - VERSION
```

FIGURE 1.3

STATEMENTS

A FORTRAN program is made up of statements. Most of the time, we write one statement per input line. Our sample program is shown on a typical FORTRAN coding form in figure 1.2. Each line on the coding form has the following parts:

Columns	Use	Explanation
1–5	Statement number field	This may contain an unsigned, nonzero, integer constant that serves as a statement number (also called a statement label). It is used for program control as explained in chapter 7.
6	Continuation field	This is used in the rare situations when a statement is too long to fit on one line.
7–72	Statement body	This contains the main portion of the statement.
73–80	Identification/sequence field	This is used either to identify a particular program or to sequence lines within the program so that if cards are dropped, the deck can be reordered correctly. The contents of this field are printed on the source-program listing but the field is otherwise ignored by the FORTRAN compiler.

The following set of characters is used in statements of the FORTRAN language:

A B C D E F G H I J K L M N O P Q R S T U V W X Y Z
The letters (upper case only).

1 2 3 4 5 6 7 8 9 0
The numbers (lower case L is not the same as 1).

( ) , . * + = / blank
The special characters (blank is a character).

KEYWORDS

Each FORTRAN statement contains one or more words or symbols that identify it to the FORTRAN system. The identifying words are called *keywords*. For example, the words READ, PRINT, STOP, and END in figure 1.2 are keywords.

CONSTANTS

Not all information for a program needs to be read into the computer from outside the program. There are cases where the programmer knows the value

REF

needed at a given point. For example, he may decide to use 3.1416 as the value of π (pi). He can write 3.1416 directly in a FORTRAN statement, and that numeral is called a *constant*. For each type of internal coding scheme used to represent information, there is a way of writing a constant in a program. Some constants are written and identified by type below. All types of constants available in FORTRAN and WATFIV are discussed in chapter 4.

1	Integer constants
2	
370	
3.1416	Floating-point constants
2.1	(also called real constants)
.001	
'PAGE'	Character-string constants
'13 CHARACTERS'	(also called literal constants)
.TRUE.	Logical constants
.FALSE.	

VARIABLES

When an item of information is read into the computer from outside or is created as combinations of information already in the machine, there must be some place to put it. To tell FORTRAN where to put the information, there must be a name for that place, or location. These names are called *variable names* or, in brief, *variables*. For example, in figure 1.2, I and J are variable names. They indicate locations in computer memory where information values are stored. The FORTRAN programmer can choose variable names that help him to remember what information values are used for. Sample names are COST, INCOME, OUTFLW, and SUM1. Specific rules for writing variable names are given in the tutorial section of chapter 2.

BLANKS

Except in constants, blanks have no significance in FORTRAN statements. Generally, blanks can be inserted at will to improve the readability of a program. Wherever one blank is permitted, any number of blanks can be used. The following lines of code are equivalent in function:

```
PRINT,I,J

PRINT,      I , J

PRINT, I, J
```

Even though these statements are equivalent, most of us regard the final statement as easier to read. Since complete understandable program documentation is vital, readability is an important programming consideration.

Blanks are permitted in literal constants but there, the number of blanks is significant. Each blank is retained in storage and counts as one character.

REF

Blanks should not be used within a variable name or within any constant other than a literal constant in FORTRAN statements.

Blanks are also significant in input data. When using format-free input/output (described in chapter 3), one or more blanks can be used to separate input items. Blanks cannot be embedded within numbers, because the compiler does not interpret them that way. When using formatted input/output (discussed in chapter 10), any blanks in numeric field positions are interpreted as zeros. Thus, for example, a blank at the end of a field being read as I-format data effectively multiplies the input value by ten. In general, numeric values should not contain embedded blanks and should be right-justified (i.e., positioned as far to the right as possible) in the input fields described for them.

THE CONTINUATION COLUMN ON THE FORTRAN CODING FORM

On rare occasions, a FORTRAN statement may need to extend beyond column 72 of an input line. The identification/sequence field cannot be used for part of the statement body, but the FORTRAN statement can be continued onto the next line. The next line has to have a character other than blank or zero in column 6, the continuation field of the coding form. Because the character in column 6 signals the computer that a statement is continued, such a statement need not extend through column 72 of a continued line. The programmer may find it convenient to break the statement at another point (say, before the beginning of an expression enclosed in parentheses). The following code is recognized as one statement by the FORTRAN compiler:

```
col. 6
    ↓ IF (ANS1.EQ.ANS2)
    1 RESULT = (2.0*A + 55.9) / (B - C**2)
```

The maximum number of continuation lines for one statement is system-dependent, but usually at least ten are allowed. Any FORTRAN statement may be continued, but comment lines (see below) are not allowed within a continued statement in IBM 360/370 FORTRAN. Note also that a statement that is not continued, or the first line of a continued statement, should not have any character other than a blank or zero in column 6. If it does, it will be interpreted as a continuation of the preceding line.

COMMENTS

Frequently, FORTRAN statements alone are not enough to remind a programmer of what is happening at a given point in his program. Nor is it easy for one programmer to understand the program of another without some additional explanation. To provide such explanation at key points in a program, the FORTRAN programmer can include comment statements. The letter C must appear in column 1 of any coding line used for comments. The comment may appear anywhere between columns 2 and 80 of the line. The comment is printed on the source-program listing, but the line is otherwise ignored by the compiler.

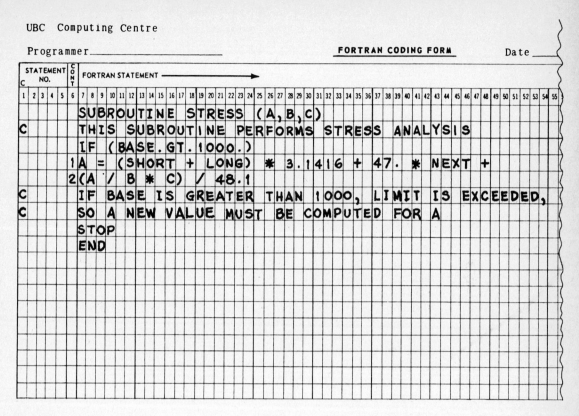

FIGURE 1.4

We can insert comments following a continued statement as shown in figure 1.4. Note, however, that we do not include comments within a continued statement. In IBM 360/370 FORTRAN, a comment line cannot immediately precede a continued line. In WATFIV, such positioning is permitted. Many programmers number continuation lines sequentially as in figure 1.4; this is an advisable programming practice, but not a requirement.

Comments are extremely valuable in debugging a program. Use lots of them. Time devoted to preparing meaningful comments is well spent; it helps to avoid hours of needless frustration and painstaking examination of every program step and declaration at a later time. Some installations require that the first line of a program be a comment line indicating program name, programmer name, and date. If the program is modified, a comment line giving the reason for change, programmer name, and date is required.

REF

EXERCISES

QUEST

1.   (REF) Explain the parts of a FORTRAN coding line, giving positions, use, and valid entries for each part.

2. (REF) What is wrong with the following code?
   a)   1PRINT, I,K,J,
          2H,G,F
   b)   PRINT, I,L,
       C   THIS WILL PRINT THE OUTPUT VALUES
          1K,L
   c)   PRINT,   I,L,K
          1L,N,B

3. (REF) Examine the following FORTRAN programs. Then prepare one or more comment statements for each, telling what it does.
   a) READ,I,J
       SUM=I+J
       PRINT,SUM
       STOP
       END

   b) READ, I
       IF (I.EQ.1) PRINT, 'DOG'
       IF (I.EQ.2) PRINT, 'CAT'
       STOP
       END

PROGRAMMING PROBLEMS

1. (TUT) Try a simple experiment with a friend. Make up a list of commands that the friend can execute. For each command, define an exact set of actions that the friend takes. Assume he has four locations in which he can write numbers, but that you cannot see the numbers. Then give him a sequence of commands to solve some problem.

   The following sample set of commands should allow your friend to solve any arithmetic problem:

   INPUT   value   location-name
   OUTPUT   location-name
   ADD location-name TO location-name
   SUBTRACT location-name FROM location-name
   MULTIPLY location-name BY location-name
   DIVIDE location-name BY location-name

   Use L1, L2, L3, and L4 as location names. INPUT should place the value in the command in the location specified. OUTPUT should cause your friend to show you the contents of the specified location. ADD should increase the value in the second location by the value in the first location. SUBTRACT should decrease the value in the second location by the value in the first location. MULTIPLY should place the product of the values in two locations into the second location. DIVIDE should place the quotient of the values in two locations into the second location. If you want to be fancy, you can also say that the remainder is to be put in the first location.

a) Now "program" your friend to do the following arithmetic:

47 + 89

47 * 89 (Call the result A.)

A / 56

b) Did you have to write more than one INPUT command for the value 47?

c) Answer (b) above, but for the value 89.

Think about any difficulties that you encountered in setting up this sequence of commands. Doing so may help you to avoid similar difficulties in FORTRAN programming. It is important that your friend do only what the commands say. He must not try to help you by guessing your intent. (Computers do not help you by guessing.)

2. (TUT) Now program your friend to provide the results of his computations for the problem above as output.

3. (TUT) Now include three new commands in your friend's instruction set:

IF   location-name   program-name
READ PROGRAM   program-name
END

These new commands should permit you to give your friend a whole list of commands at once. You must give the list of commands a name. He should keep the list of commands as a program and remember the name that you assign. IF causes your friend to execute the commands in the named program if the specified location is zero. (You must be sure, of course, that you have given him the named program before you give him the IF command.) READ PROGRAM gives your friend the list of commands identified by the specified name; it does not cause him to execute them. END marks the end of a list of commands that you give to your friend.

If you put an INPUT command in a list of commands for your friend, you may not want to indicate a value at the time you give him the commands. If you do not, he must be able to request the value when he executes the program.

Now assume that you have the balances on twenty different loans for which you must compute monthly interest. Each loan may have a different interest rate and a different balance. Program your friend to compute all twenty values but give him a program that includes only one computation sequence. Use the IF statement and the fact that the INPUT statement can read a different set of numbers each time to set up this program so that all twenty values are computed.

4. (TUT) Now write a more complex program for your friend in which you first indicate the total number of loans for which you must compute interest. Insert an IF statement into the program so that he will compute that number of values without you having to tell him explicitly to compute each one.

If you have succeeded with these exercises, you have a preview of the FORTRAN SUBROUTINE, IF, and DO statements, and their use.

5. (TUT) Suppose that we have two positive integers, A and B. We are allowed to perform the operations of increasing or decreasing either by one, and we can test either number to see whether it is zero. Draw a flow-chart for a program to change the number A into a number which is the sum of the initial values of A and B and to provide that number as output. (We really should call A and B variables, because we change them as we solve the problem.)

6. (REF) Write a FORTRAN program to perform the processing steps identified by the flowchart that you drew in response to the preceding exercise. Obtain the original values for A and B from an external data source. Test your program on the computer to verify that it performs as intended. (When you have finished, you may find that you need to modify your flowchart to ensure that it reflects accurately the steps in your program.)

7. (TUT) The flowchart that you drew in response to 5 above shows how addition can be implemented as a series of increasing and decreasing operations. Draw a flowchart to show how these operations, plus the operation of changing one number to give it the value of another, can be used to multiply two positive numbers A and B and store the result in C, which is then written as output.

8. (REF) Write a FORTRAN program corresponding to the flowchart that you constructed for the preceding problem. The program should obtain input values from an external data source. Test your program to verify that it performs correctly.

INTRO As mentioned in chapter 1, the computer uses different coding schemes for numbers with fractional parts and for numbers without fractional parts. The numbers that may have fractional parts are called real, or floating-point, numbers. Those without fractions are called integers. The tutorial section of this chapter explains how to tell the FORTRAN compiler which of these types of coding to use for the values placed in locations represented by variable names in your programs. The reference section of this chapter explains how to declare other types of coding to use for values in FORTRAN and WATFIV: LOGICAL, COMPLEX, and CHARACTER.

Data of these types may take up different amounts of storage in the computer. This chapter explains the meaning of the size variations and suggests how you can choose the sizes appropriate for values in your programs. The DOUBLE PRECISION statement is explained. The IMPLICIT statement, which allows you to specify type and size by setting up rules based on the first letters of variable names, is also covered in the reference section. Some comments on computer addressing of data of different types and sizes are included at the end of the chapter.

Always try to be aware of which coding scheme you have declared for your variables. Mismatching variable types or forgetting to take into account the types of variables are common errors in FORTRAN programming.

TUT VARIABLES A FORTRAN variable is a programmer-selected symbolic representation of a quantity that occupies a particular area of computer storage. The value represented by that name is the current value stored in the area. For example, consider the statement

I = 34 + J

Both I and J are variables. The value of J is determined by some preceding statement and may change many times before execution of this statement. The value of I is dependent on

Chapter

2

TYPE STATEMENTS

the value of J and is calculated whenever this statement is executed. In this book, when we are considering these characters, we speak of the variable name. In more general cases, we call them variables.

In most FORTRAN implementations, a variable name may be up to six characters in length. It may contain any of the alphabetic characters A through Z, the alphabetic character $, and the numeric characters 0 through 9. The first character must be alphabetic. Examples of valid variable names are given below.

    A
    BR23
    $VAR1
    AMT

But the following names are invalid, for the reasons indicated.

    2RATE   First character must be alphabetic.
    DOLLARS   Name cannot exceed six characters in length.
    L1.RET   Name cannot contain special characters.

WHY HAVE DIFFERENT TYPES?

The type of a variable corresponds to the type of data that the variable represents. The main reason for having different types is to allow variables to represent maximum ranges of appropriate numerical values but use only minimum amounts of computer storage in doing so. For example, to store the following numbers as written would take a lot of space, particularly if a single variable had to represent the first at one time, the second at another, and so on.

    .00000000000000000047
    −470000000000000000000000.0
    345.7891
    1
    5014
    −234560

Some alternatives that make the storage of values feasible are to restrict the range of values that can be represented by a particular variable, or to use a special coding scheme for values that a variable represents.

TYPES AND SIZES

Historically, FORTRAN recognized only two types of data: REAL and INTEGER. The same amount of storage was reserved for each variable name representing a REAL data item. Similarly, a uniform amount of storage was reserved for each variable name representing an INTEGER data item. The way of telling the FORTRAN compiler which type of data to use was to select particular letters as the first characters of variable names. The established convention was:

Any variable name beginning with one of the letters I, J, K, L, M, or

N is considered as INTEGER. All others (those beginning with one of the letters from A through H, or O through Z, or $) are assumed to be REAL.

As enhancements were made to the original FORTRAN language, new types and alternative sizes for data of specific types were introduced. New ways of telling data types had to be devised. The original first-letter convention was retained and is referred to as the *default*. If, for example, you use I, INVAL, and NOUT as variable names, and you do not specify otherwise, each is assumed to represent data of INTEGER type.

Since alternative sizes as well as alternative types were introduced, it was decided that defaults for size should be established. There are now two sizes for INTEGER and two sizes for REAL. The unit of size measurement is dependent on the computer on which the FORTRAN program is to be run. For IBM 360/370 computers, the unit of measurement is the *byte*. And for both INTEGER and REAL data, the default size is four bytes. The effects of size variations are explained in detail in the reference section of this chapter.

TYPE DECLARATION

Although you can allow data types and sizes to be assumed by default, it is a wiser programming practice to declare each variable that you use in a program. To declare the type and size of a variable, you use a *type statement*. Examples are

```
INTEGER*4 OUTGO, INCOME
REAL*4 SUBTOT, TOTAL
```

These statements declare that OUTGO and INCOME are integer variables of size 4 and that SUBTOT and TOTAL are real (floating-point) variables of size 4. An explicit declaration of type and size overrides the default (also called *predefined convention*) otherwise assumed on the basis of the established first-letter rule.

You may declare the type of a variable without declaring its size, permitting the latter to be assumed by default for the particular machine on which your program is executed. Examples of this simple form of declaration are

```
REAL A, S, OUTPUT, INPUT
INTEGER, I, K, ABSOL, PRICE, SCALE
```

Of course, if the default types and sizes otherwise assumed for variables do not meet your programming needs, you must make explicit declarations of the variables. But, even if the defaults apply, getting into the habit of making explicit declarations is advisable because it is a protection against forgetting to declare something and permitting the FORTRAN compiler to make assumptions that are really false. Such errors are hard to find when debugging a program.

The sample program in chapter 1 becomes the program in figure 2.1 when a type statement is included. Notice that in chapter 1 the first-letter rule was allowed to apply by default to determine the type of the variables.

```
INTEGER I, J
READ, I, J
PRINT, I, J
STOP
END
```

FIGURE 2.1

Alternative (usually called optional) sizes for INTEGER and REAL data are two and eight bytes, respectively, on IBM 360/370 computers. We might declare three variables to represent two-byte integers and one to represent a four-byte integer as follows:

```
INTEGER*2 VAL1, VAL2, VAL3
INTEGER*4 BIGVAL
```

Since four is the default (also called standard) size for data of INTEGER type on IBM 360/370, we can let the size of BIGVAL be assumed by default. That is, the following declaration is equivalent to the second statement above.

```
INTEGER BIGVAL
```

Figure 2.2 shows a program to read values for the variables described above, then to print six numbers—BIGVAL followed by VAL1, BIGVAL followed by VAL2, and BIGVAL followed by VAL3.

```
INTEGER*2 VAL1, VAL2, VAL3
INTEGER*4 BIGVAL
READ, VAL1, VAL2, VAL3, BIGVAL
PRINT, BIGVAL, VAL1
PRINT, BIGVAL, VAL2
PRINT, BIGVAL, VAL3
STOP
END
```

FIGURE 2.2

REF

OTHER DATA TYPES

A knowledge of INTEGER and REAL types is sufficient for many programming applications. There are situations, however, where it is convenient to use data of other types. The type statements below are declarations for variables of LOGICAL and COMPLEX types.

```
LOGICAL ANSWER, QUEST, LOGIC1, LOGIC2
COMPLEX A, IMAG, B
LOGICAL LOGIC3(60), F, J(9)
COMPLEX MAP(4,4), T, IMAG2
```

REF

The last two of these statements remind us that dimensions as well as types of arrays can be specified in type statements. (The tutorial section of chapter 6 explains arrays.) The statements also show that both simple variables and array variables can be declared in a single type statement. If dimensions for an array are specified in a type statement, they cannot be specified in a DIMENSION or COMMON statement in the program. (To review both DIMENSION and COMMON statements, see chapter 6.)

In WATFIV, data can be declared to be of CHARACTER type. The size for a variable of this type is expressed as a number of characters. When all character variables declared in one type statement are of the same size, it is possible to write one size indicator that applies to all, just as we did for INTEGER and REAL types of variables above. Examples are

```
CHARACTER*5 A, B, C
CHARACTER*10 D, E(4,8)
```

Alternatively, the size may be stated separately for each variable. In this case, an asterisk and the size indicator follow the variable name as shown below. If no size is specified for a variable, a size of 1 is assumed.

```
CHARACTER A*8, B(5), C*7(9,9)
```

Here A is declared to be a simple variable comprising eight characters, B is a simple variable for which a default size of 1 is assumed, and C is a two-dimensional array consisting of 81 seven-character elements.

A size declaration that applies to all variables in a type statement can be overridden for a specific variable by writing a size declaration that applies only to that variable.

```
CHARACTER*7 A, B*4, C
```

Here A and C are seven characters in size, but the size of B is four characters.

Both logical and character variables are explained in chapter 11 of this text. To learn about complex variables, see the reference section of chapter 5.

SIZE ALTERNATIVES

Character variables in WATFIV may be from 1 to 255 characters in length. In IBM 360/370 computers, each character requires 1 byte of storage, so a character-string variable may require from 1 to 255 bytes. For data of other types, only certain lengths are permissible. The data types available in FORTRAN, WATFOR, and WATFIV are listed in the left-hand column in figure 2.3. The permissible lengths for each are given in the center column. The default length assumed for each when no explicit size declaration is made is shown at the right.

Explicit sizes can be given for selected variables of any of these types in the same manner as for character variables. Some examples are

```
REAL*8 A, G, I, L*4
INTEGER*2 A(5), B*4(5)
LOGICAL*1 ANS(50), MYSW*4
```

Data Type	Permissible lengths (in bytes)	Default lengths (in bytes)
INTEGER	2 or 4	4
REAL	4 or 8	4
COMPLEX	8 or 16 (for both variables of the ordered pair)	8
LOGICAL	1 or 4	4
CHARACTER (WATFIV only)	1 — 255	1

FIGURE 2.3

THE GENERAL TYPE STATEMENT

The type statement, generally, offers many capabilities. These include not only data typing and sizing, and dimensioning of arrays, but also establishing initial values for variables.

The statement

    REAL VALUE

indicates that VALUE is a floating-point variable for which default sizing is to be applied. By writing

    REAL*8 VALUE

we indicate that VALUE is a floating-point variable of size 8. Or, we can write

    REAL*8 VALUE(3,4)

to indicate that VALUE is a two-dimensional array comprising twelve floating-point variables of size 8. And, if desired, we can write

    REAL*8 VALUE(3,4)/12*0.0/

to specify the same information as the statement above and further declare that each element of the array VALUE is to be set to an initial value of 0.0.

We summarize these capabilities by considering the general form of the type statement. It is

$$type[*s] \ a[*s_1][(d_1)][/x_1/][[, b[*s_2][(d_2)][/x_2/]] \ldots]$$

where:

> $type$ is INTEGER, REAL, COMPLEX, or LOGICAL; in WATFIV, CHARACTER may also be specified.

> s is optional and represents one of the permissible size specifications for data of the type specified.

> $a, b, \ldots$ are simple variable names, array variable names, or function names. (See "Typing of functions" in this chapter.)

REF

d is optional and gives dimension information for an array. It comprises unsigned integer constants, separated by commas, that are maximum values for corresponding subscripts of the array. Entries for *d* may also be integer variables of size 4 if corresponding *a*, *b*, . . . entries are dummy arguments of a subprogram in which the type statement appears. (See chapter 8.)

x is optional and is a list of one or more initial data values to be assigned to a simple variable or an array element, or to multiple elements of an array variable, respectively, before program execution begins.

A size specification following the keyword indicating type applies to all names appearing in the type statement unless overridden by a size specification appended to a particular variable name. If no size specification is given, the standard length for the indicated type is assumed. As noted earlier, dimension information may be specified for an array variable in a type statement but, if so, dimensions must not be specified for the array in another statement in the program.

When a simple variable is being declared, a constant of the declared data type may be given as an initial data value for the variable. When an array variable is being declared, a list of constants separated by commas may be provided. Successive occurrences of the same initial value can be represented by the form *r∗constant* where *r* is the number of occurrences of the specified *constant*. If initial data values for array elements are given in a type statement, dimension information for the array must appear in the type statement or in a preceding DIMENSION statement. Initial data values cannot be specified for function names or for variables in a common storage area. (See chapter 6.)

EXAMPLES

The statement

    INTEGER∗2 ITEM/41/, PARTS(3)

declares that ITEM is an integer variable initialized to a value of 41 and PARTS is a three-element array containing integer data. Two storage locations are reserved for ITEM and for each element of PARTS.

The statement

    REAL A(4,4)/16∗3.0/, SIM∗8/22.3/

declares that A is a two-dimensional array containing floating-point data. A standard length of 4 is assumed for each element of A, and initial values of 3.0 are established for all array elements. In addition, eight storage locations are reserved for the real variable SIM, and an initial data value of 22.3 is placed in those locations.

The statement

    COMPLEX R/(44.1,2.7)/, S, T

declares that the variables R, S, and T are of COMPLEX type. The standard length is assumed for each. The real and imaginary parts of the complex variable R are initialized to 44.1 and 2.7, respectively.

REF

Initial data values can be specified for variables of any type. The permissible forms for constants specified as initialization values are summarized in figure 4.3, which appears in the reference section of chapter 4.

DOUBLE PRECISION

The following statements are equivalent:

    REAL*8 A, B(8,6), I
    DOUBLE PRECISION A, B(8,6), I

Both of these statements declare A, B, and I to be floating-point variables. They indicate that eight storage locations—double the standard amount—are to be reserved for each variable. The first statement is, of course, a type statement. The second is a *DOUBLE PRECISION statement*. A, B, and I are called *double-precision variables*, a term distinguishing them from REAL*4, or *single-precision, variables*.

The DOUBLE PRECISION statement cannot be used for complex variables although they can have a similar degree of precision. The DOUBLE PRECISION statement also differs from type statements in another important way: It cannot be used to establish initial data values for variables. If you want to initialize double-precision variables, use REAL*8 type statements. Since the DOUBLE PRECISION statement is a nonexecutable statement, it should be positioned with the type statements of a program.

For more about the double-precision features of FORTRAN, see "Double precision arithmetic" in chapter 5.

THE MEANING OF SIZES

A certain amount of space in computer storage is reserved for each variable in a FORTRAN program. Since there is room for only so many digits in that space, only values within a certain numerical range, or up to a certain length, can be stored. The programmer must choose a size that does not waste space but allows for the full range of values expected for a given variable. As noted above, there are usually only two sizes to choose from for each variable type.

The range of numerical values that can be represented within a space is most accurately expressed using digits of the number base that the machine itself uses to represent values. Alternatively, a corresponding decimal approximation can be given. For example, IBM 360/370 computers store integer data as binary numbers. The amount of space reserved for a standard-size integer variable is four bytes, or 32 *binary* dig*it* (*bit*) positions. One of these bit positions is used to indicate whether the value is positive or negative. This leaves 31 bits for the numeral. The range of integers that can be stored is from -2^{31} to $2^{31}-1$. Using familiar decimal numerals, we describe this range as from $-2,147,483,648$ to $2,147,483,647$. In general, you should remember that integers up to nine decimal digits in length (and some having ten digits) can be stored in IBM 360/370 computers.

A variable of INTEGER type always contains room for more digits than a variable of the same size but of REAL type. Since the latter is stored in floating-point, or exponential, form, two positions are required for the characteristic, and there is less space for the fraction (i.e., the digits of the number itself). However, the variable of REAL type can always hold a larger (or smaller) numerical value than the same-sized variable of INTEGER type because of this use of exponential form. The range of values that can be stored in floating-point form in IBM 360/370 computers is from approximately 5.4×10^{-78} to 7×10^{75}. (To review exponential form, see "Floating-point constants" in the tutorial section of chapter 4.)

For floating-point variables, the rule is: Use the larger size if you are in doubt. Because of the use of exponential form, the larger size does not increase the range of values that can be represented, but it increases the number of digits that can be represented, the possible degree of precision for stored values. In IBM 360/370, floating-point values that we write as decimals are converted to a hexadecimal number system (coding scheme) before they are stored in the computer. So floating-point numbers are really just approximations to their actual values, even before they are used in arithmetic operations. The approximation, truncation, and rounding problems discussed in this text are always threatening.* A wise programming practice is to use DOUBLE PRECISION (REAL*8) variables for intermediate results of computations even if you use the usual default size (REAL*4) for final values.

In using floating-point values, you must realize that two values which should be equal but have been computed by different means may not be the same. Any test for the equality of such values always fails, and subsequent actions are fixed accordingly. The safest approach is to ensure that the flow of program control does not depend on whether or not floating-point values are equal. If you must test for the equality of floating-point values, use the absolute value function (ABS) to see whether the difference between the values is acceptably small, relative to their possible values.

```
      IF (ABS(A−B).LT..00000099) GO TO 100
C     BRANCHES ON (ALMOST) EQUAL
```

This statement causes a branch to statement 100 if the difference between A and B is less than .00000099. The test implies that we know, in general, the precision and range of the values involved. It would not work, for example, if the possible values of A and B were in the range from zero to .000000999.

Sometimes the size of one variable is chosen to correspond to the size of another, even though the size may be larger than necessary for one of them. This is done, for example, when equivalencing arrays to match data of several types. (See "The EQUIVALENCE statement" in chapter 6.) In any case, the size declared for a variable should provide for a range of values at least as inclusive as that expected for the variable. If you fail to ensure sufficient space and the range of permissible values is exceeded, an error occurs.

With logical values, the primary considerations are whether you want one logical variable to be the same size as another and how much space you

---

*The way floating-point numbers are stored in the computer varies somewhat from one computer to another, but a good indication of the approach that is used is given in section 2.5 of C. W. Gear, *Introduction to Computer Science*.

REF

can afford to use. The default size is 4. A size of 1 requires less space but logical values of size 1 may take longer to process. If you have large arrays of logical values, it is probably wise to use a size of 1.

Only WATFIV provides for CHARACTER type declarations, but characters can be placed into variables of other types with DATA or FORMAT statements in FORTRAN, WATFOR, and WATFIV. Clearly, the size that should be declared for a variable of CHARACTER type is the maximum number of characters that you may want to place in the variable. As noted above, the limit is 255. However, longer strings of characters may be placed in consecutive storage locations reserved for arrays. Since the arrays can be of other types, this approach works in FORTRAN, WATFOR, or WATFIV. Remember that one character requires one byte of storage in IBM 360/370 computers. One INTEGER*4 variable or array element can hold four characters; one REAL*8 variable can hold eight characters; and so on.

The ranges for variables of different types and sizes are summarized in figure 2.4.

Type	Size	Range of values
INTEGER	2	$\pm 32{,}767$
	4	$\pm 2{,}147{,}483{,}648$
REAL	4	5.4×10^{-78} to 7×10^{75}
	8	Same range as REAL*4 (but greater precision)
COMPLEX	8	Same as REAL*4
	16	Same as REAL*8
LOGICAL	4	.TRUE. or .FALSE.
	1	Same as LOGICAL*4
CHARACTER (WATFIV only)	1 – 255	Any character

FIGURE 2.4

TYPING OF FUNCTIONS

When a user-defined function subprogram or FORTRAN-supplied function subprogram (mathematical subprogram or built-in function) is called, it always returns one value to the calling program. Effectively, the function name takes on that value. Therefore, the function name must have a type and size, just as any other variable in the program. If these are not explicitly declared, the function name has default characteristics. If the type and size of the value returned by a function do not agree with the defaults, the function name must be declared explicitly in the calling program and, in the case of a user-defined function, in the function subprogram. (For additional information about the former, see "Functions" in chapter 5; user-defined functions are discussed in chapter 8.)

In a calling program, the function name may be placed in a type statement as is any variable name. Dimensions and initial values are not allowed.

In a user-defined function subprogram, an explicit type declaration may be given in the FUNCTION statement preceding the word FUNCTION. (See LOGICAL in figure 2.5.) The general form of the FUNCTION statement is

[*type*] FUNCTION *name* [**size*] (*argument list*)

where *type* may be LOGICAL, REAL, INTEGER, COMPLEX, or DOUBLE PRECISION and *size* may be 1, 2, 4, or 8, but must fit the possible lengths for a variable of the declared type. For example, INTEGER*8 is not valid. If DOUBLE PRECISION is specified, a size (which would be redundant or conflicting) cannot be specified. If the type is not specified, a size cannot be specified. Although WATFIV permits explicit declaration of variables of CHARACTER type, function subprograms of CHARACTER type are not allowed. The *argument list* of a FUNCTION statement must be as explained in chapter 8.

```
LOGICAL*1 ANSWER, LTEMP
LOGICAL LBACK, LFRONT
    .
    .
    .
LTEMP = ANSWER(LBACK).OR.LFRONT
END
LOGICAL FUNCTION ANSWER*1 (L1)
LOGICAL L1
ANSWER=.NOT.L1
RETURN
END
```

FIGURE 2.5

In figure 2.5, ANSWER is declared to be a function subprogram of LOGICAL type and size 1 by means of the FUNCTION statement beginning the subprogram. The function name ANSWER is also declared to be a logical variable of size 1 in a type statement in the calling program. One value is passed to ANSWER by means of the function reference ANSWER(LBACK). The negative of that value (which may be either .TRUE. or .FALSE.) is returned as the value of the function.

We can also declare the type and size of a function subprogram in a type statement in the function subprogram. If we do so, we omit the declaration from the FUNCTION statement. For example, the first two statements in the function subprogram in figure 2.5 can be replaced by

```
FUNCTION ANSWER (L1)
LOGICAL*1 ANSWER, L1*4
```

REF

IMPLICIT TYPING AND SIZING

It is possible for the FORTRAN programmer to set a first-letter rule governing sizes and types of whatever variables he chooses, beginning with whatever letters he specifies. To do so, he uses an *IMPLICIT statement*. This statement allows a broader range of defaults than the established convention whereby any undeclared variable beginning with one of the letters from I through N is INTEGER*4 and any other undeclared variable is REAL*4. Any type of variable, and any permissible size for that variable, can be specified in an IMPLICIT statement.

The IMPLICIT statement must be the first statement of a single main program or the first statement following the SUBROUTINE or FUNCTION statement of a subprogram. It can be used only once in a single main program or in a subprogram, but it must appear in each subprogram in which programmer-specified defaults are to apply. Examples are

    IMPLICIT REAL*8(A,C,E,G–I,T–S), REAL*4(B,D), LOGICAL*1(L)
    IMPLICIT INTEGER*2(A–H,W), REAL(I–K), LOGICAL(L,M,N)

As the second statement indicates, the specification of size is optional. If no size is given, the standard length for variables of the declared type is assumed.

The letters included in an IMPLICIT statement must be given as single alphabetic characters or ranges of characters from the set A, B, . . . , Z, $, in that order. A dash separates the first and last characters of a range. Single characters and ranges are separated by commas, and the complete list of letters for a type and size declaration is enclosed in parentheses. It is an error to repeat a letter within a single IMPLICIT statement. Any letters not explicitly mentioned retain their original default types and sizes.

The programmer who refers to FORTRAN built-in functions or defines functions in his program must be aware that the IMPLICIT statement applies to undeclared function names just as to other undeclared variable names. It does not affect the computations in the called function subprogram. In some cases, you may want to call a different built-in function (for example, DCOS instead of COS if you are using the IMPLICIT statement to modify a program to handle REAL*8 values rather than REAL*4). In other cases, you may need to include additional explicit declarations for function names in your program.

ALIGNMENT ON IBM 360/370

In a 360/370 computer, the set of bytes that comprise the memory looks like an array. Specific locations in memory are addressed by the machine in ways similar to those you use in indexing a one-dimensional array. The primary difference is that the first location in memory is at address zero, whereas the first position in a FORTRAN array is always identified by a subscript value of 1. To ensure hardware efficiency, the computer is designed to pick up a variable that is four bytes long as one group of four bytes, starting at a location having an address divisible by four. Similarly, it picks up eight-byte variables from an area beginning with a location having an address divisible by eight. When

REF

executing FORTRAN programs, the computer acts as if memory is made up of fixed quantities of bytes. Four-byte quantities (the defaults for INTEGER and REAL) are called *words*, or *fullwords*; eight-byte quantities are called *doublewords*; and two-byte quantities are called *halfwords*.

Data to be manipulated by the computer must be positioned correctly in memory. Generally, four-byte variables must begin at fullword boundaries (storage locations whose addresses are divisible by four); eight-byte variables must begin at doubleword boundaries; and two-byte variables must begin at half word boundaries. We say that proper boundary alignment is required.

Normally, a FORTRAN programmer need not be concerned about the alignment of variables because the compiler ensures that data values in a program are positioned as required. When using COMMON or EQUIVALENCE capabilities, however, it is possible to force incorrect positioning.

One way to ensure proper boundary alignment is to arrange variables in a fixed descending order according to length—those of size 8 first, followed by those of size 4, followed by size 2, and finally size 1. (See figure 2.6.) As a FORTRAN programmer, you need not know the actual addresses of storage locations because the compiler ensures that either a common area of storage or the first variable in an equivalence group begins at a doubleword boundary, a storage location whose address is divisible by eight.

```
REAL*8 A, B
REAL C, D, E
INTEGER*2 F
LOGICAL*1 SW1, SW2
COMMON A, B, C, D, E, F, SW1, SW2
```

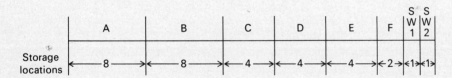

FIGURE 2.6

If the fixed descending order is not used, proper alignment can be obtained by careful planning and inclusion of dummy variables as filler to force proper alignment when necessary. For example, you can make sure that the *displacement*, or number of bytes preceding a variable in a common area, is, for size 4 variables, a number divisible by four. (See DUMVAR in figure 2.7.) You can force proper alignment of size 8 and size 2 variables by ensuring that their displacements are divisible by eight and two, respectively. Since the displacement for a size 1 variable must be one, it can be positioned at any boundary. Both COMPLEX*16 and COMPLEX*8 variables must be positioned so that their displacements are divisible by eight.

REF

```
INTEGER*2 A, B, C
INTEGER*2 DUMVAR
INTEGER*4 I, J
REAL*8 D
COMMON A, B, C, DUMVAR, I, J, D
```

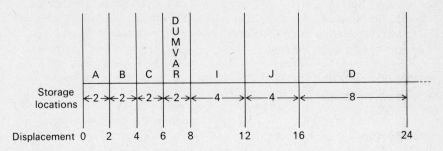

FIGURE 2.7

QUEST

EXERCISES

1. (TUT) Which of the following are valid variable names?

   a) R1   g) C
   b) 1R   h) 20
   c) $AMT   i) LLLLLL
   d) TEMP   j) DOL.CT
   e) TEMPSTOR   k) READ
   f) FUNC_1   l) MY$

2. (TUT) Refer to the preceding exercise. Give one or more reasons why each name that you did not select is invalid.

3. (TUT) Assume a FORTRAN program to be run on IBM 360/370 contains the following variable names. What are the default size and type of each?

   a) ARRAY
   b) IREAL
   c) O
   d) $ONE
   e) X
   f) RINTEG

4. (TUT) Write type statements in which you declare that FACT1 and FACT2 represent integer data and FACT3 represents a floating-point number. Permit the sizes of the storage areas reserved for these variables to be assumed by default.

5. (TUT) Suppose that the range of values to be represented by FACT3 above is very large. As a precaution, you decide that eight bytes of storage should be reserved for data items that FACT3 represents. Write a new declaration for FACT3 to provide for this.

6. (REF) Which of the following declarations are valid?
    a)   INTEGER R1, I
    b)   REAL I, R2
    c)   REAL*4 A*8, B*8, C
    d)   DOUBLE PRECISION A, B*4
    e)   REAL A*4, B*6
    f)   INTEGER*2 I, J, K*4, L*1
    g)   LOGICAL*1 L, M*4, K*2
    h)   REAL A(14,36)
    i)   REAL*(14,14) SUM
    j)   COMPLEX*16 A, B*8
    k)   CHARACTER*300 STR

7. (REF) Refer to the preceding exercise. Give one or more reasons why each statement that you did not select is invalid.

8. (REF) Refer to exercise 3. What are the types and sizes of the names if the following statement is placed at the beginning of a FORTRAN program?

    IMPLICIT LOGICAL*1(I), COMPLEX*16(M–P,X), INTEGER*2(Q–U),
    1REAL*8(A)

9. (REF) INT1 and INT2 are two-byte integers. D, E, and F are four-byte floating-point numbers. SONE and STWO are logical variables of default size. Write statements to declare these variables and place them in common storage with proper boundary alignment.

10. (REF) Write two statements, either of which causes eight storage locations to be reserved for each of the variables M, N, and P.

PROGRAMMING PROBLEMS

§ 2.3

1. (TUT) Write a program to read two integers from a card and print them in reverse order. Thus, if the card contains 105, −21, the output line should contain −21, then 105.

2. (TUT) Write a program similar to the one that you wrote for exercise 1, but print each value twice.

3. (TUT) Refer to the program that you wrote for the preceding exercise. Did you print each value twice in succession, or did you alternate the values? In this respect, the problem statement is ambiguous. Rewrite the problem statement to specify the following order: first input, second input, first input again, second input again.

4. (TUT) If your program for exercise 2 does not satisfy the problem statement that you wrote for exercise 3, rewrite it to do so. (You must beware of ambiguities and of making unrecognized assumptions throughout programming.)

INTRO The first task in learning a programming language is to write, compile, and execute several simple programs. An easy method is needed to read data and to print results in these programs. The WATFIV format-free READ and PRINT statements, explained in this chapter, meet that need. A method whereby FORTRAN users can simulate (imitate or provide capability equivalent to) these statements is given in the reference section.

The reference section also covers reading and printing arrays, and detecting when the last input card is read. It explains use of DO notation in the input/output list, alternative statement forms, and the standard formats required for input and provided for output when the PRINT statement is used.

FORMAT-FREE INPUT AND OUTPUT STATEMENTS The format-free input **TUT** and output statements, namely READ and PRINT, provide easy methods for reading data from cards and for printing. To say that they are format-free means that the programmer who uses them need not concern himself with a precise description of data to be read, or with the exact way that output is to be printed. He need only identify the values to be read or written. Since these statements are easy to set up, they are valuable for quick programming or for program debugging. (Techniques for the latter are described more fully in chapter 9.)

The format-free READ and PRINT statements are available in WATFOR and WATFIV. They are not available in the standard FORTRAN language, but they can be used in a FORTRAN program if certain other statements are included. Those of you who need this facility should refer to "Simulation of format-free I/O" in the reference section of this chapter.

The first time that you use a variable name (in a type statement, or in another statement if you permit the type and size of the variable to be assumed by default), a certain area of

Chapter

3

READ
ᴀɴᴅ PRINT
Sᴛᴀᴛᴇᴍᴇɴᴛꜱ

computer memory is set aside for that variable by the FORTRAN compiler. The variable name always represents the data in that particular area. Input data moved to the area is converted from the external coding scheme, which is character form, to the internal coding scheme established for the variable. (Look ahead to figure 3.1.) Data printed from the area as output is converted from its internal coding scheme to character form.

To execute any FORTRAN statement that moves information, two facts must be known:

- Where is the data coming from or going to?
- What type of data is it and will it change type?

For the format-free READ statement, the data is always coming from a card or an input line. (For interactive systems, the "card" may be a line typed at a terminal.) The data is always in character form. It may be stored in memory according to any of several internal coding schemes. We know that, unless the programmer has declared otherwise, names beginning with any of the letters from I through N are assumed to represent integers; all other names are assumed to represent floating-point numbers. (See REAL and INTEGER in chapter 2.)

Example 1:

    READ, I, J, R

This statement reads three values from an input card and puts them in storage locations I, J, and R. Assume default typing is applied. The values for I and J are stored as integers, and the one for R as a floating-point number. (See figure 3.1.)

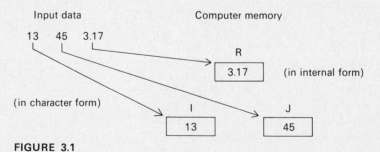

FIGURE 3.1

The READ statement always reads numbers from the next card in the input deck. If there are not as many numbers on the card as there are names in the READ statement, the next card is read. If there are more numbers on the card than names in the READ statement, the unread numbers on the card are ignored. The next execution of a READ statement causes the first number on the next card to be read, regardless of whether or not all values were read from the preceding card.

The numbers on an input card must be separated by one or more blanks or by commas. Numbers cannot be split across cards. A number to be read into a location reserved for a variable whose name denotes an integer cannot contain a decimal point. A number read into a location reserved for a floating-point number may have a decimal point. If there is no decimal point, a decimal point at the right of the rightmost digit is assumed.

Example 2:

PRINT, R, I

Assume that this PRINT statement follows the READ statement above and that the values shown in figure 3.1 were read as input. Execution of this PRINT statement provides the following output:

0.3170000E 01   13

The computer prints a floating-point number in a standard way when format-free output is used. This way of representing a number is called *scientific notation*. The letter E stands for exponent, and the number following E is the power of ten by which the digits preceding E should be multiplied to determine the equivalent, familiar form for the value. Therefore, 0.3170000E 01 means .317 multiplied by 10^1, which equals 3.17.

It is possible with FORTRAN to print numbers with decimals in familiar form, rather than in the form provided by the PRINT statement above. But doing so requires the use of a FORMAT statement. (See chapter 10 for details.) When using the quick and easy PRINT statement, we must accept the somewhat unfamiliar but standard form of output.

Example 3:

A complete program in which the statements above are used is shown in figure 3.2. The type of each variable is declared explicitly, but corresponds to the default typing that we assumed.

```
INTEGER I, J
REAL R
READ, I, J, R
PRINT, J
PRINT, R, I
STOP
END
```

FIGURE 3.2

PRINTING CONSTANTS

So far we have been talking about variables; we have said that values represented by variables may change during execution of a program. In contrast, a *constant* is a fixed, unvarying quantity. Its value does not change during program execution. Recall the statement I = 34 + J from chapter 2. I and J are variables, but 34 is a constant. Its value is always 34, no matter how many times or when the statement is executed.

Constants may appear in PRINT statements. They may be *integer constants*, say, 5 or 63, or *floating-point constants*, say, 2.55 or .0678. With WATFIV, they may also be *literal constants*, such as 'MY NAME IS '. A literal constant is written as a string of characters enclosed in single quotes.

Example 4 :

Assume that the variable X represents the value 5.38 when the statement below is executed.

PRINT, 'ANSWER IS ', X

The following output is printed :

ANSWER IS 0.5380000E 01

Example 5 :

The statement

PRINT, 2

yields

2

Example 6 :

Stock cards showing items returned to inventory contain stock number and quantity, in that order. The program in figure 3.3 displays the contents of a stock card, identifying the values as STOCK NO. and QTY.

```
INTEGER NUM, QUANT
READ, NUM, QUANT
PRINT, 'STOCK NO. = ', NUM
PRINT, 'QTY = ', QUANT
STOP
END
```

FIGURE 3.3

The capability of printing literal constants is not available in the FORTRAN simulation of READ and PRINT statements. But other capabilities can be utilized as we have discussed.

REF

EXPANDED EXAMPLES OF READ AND PRINT

Format-free input/output offers capabilities in addition to those discussed in the tutorial section of this chapter. Some of the capabilities involve use of arrays. You may want to refer to the discussion of arrays in the tutorial section of chapter 6 as you study this reference section.

The general forms of the READ and PRINT statements are

READ, *list*
PRINT, *list*

where *list* is a string of list elements separated by commas. A list element may be a simple variable, an unsubscripted or subscripted array name, or an array name with indexing. The list for a PRINT statement may also contain constants and, with WATFOR or WATFIV, may include any valid expression that does not start with a left parenthesis.

If an unsubscripted array name is specified as a list element, the array is read in by starting the subscripts for all dimensions of the array at one, increasing the leftmost until it reaches its limit, then increasing the next leftmost by one and resetting the leftmost to one. The leftmost is once again increased to its limit, the next leftmost is increased by one again, and so on. This process continues until the values of all subscripts have been increased to the maximum values for the corresponding dimensions of the array.

Example 7:

A program contains the following statements.

DIMENSION A(4,3)
READ, A
    .
    .
    .
END

Assume that the following cards are entered from the card reader. The first is a WATFIV control card; the second and third contain data items.

```
$DATA
     4    3    1    7    9    12
    13    6    4    8    2    11
```

The data items are assigned to the locations reserved for array A in computer memory. Column-by-column ordering is employed as shown below.

```
4     9     4
3    12     8
1    13     2
7     6    11
```

Use of the unsubscripted array name in the READ statement is a notational convenience. As the discussion above indicates, the READ statement in this example is equivalent to the following statement:

READ, A(1,1), A(2,1), A(3,1), A(4,1), A(1,2), A(2,2), . . . , A(4,3)

Obviously, using the unsubscripted array name requires less programming time, and coding errors are less apt to occur.

Example 8 :

Use of the array name with indexing is another notational convenience. Given the DIMENSION statement and input above, the statement

READ, ((A(I,J),I=1,4),J=1,3)

produces the same array in computer memory.

For a two-dimensional array with indexing, the general form of the array name with indexing is

((A(I,J),I=1,n),J=1,m)

where n and m are the upper limits for the dimensions of the array to be read. Each may be less than or equal to the maximum value for the corresponding dimension. We use the array name with indexing rather than either an unsubscripted array name or a list of one or more subscripted variables when we want to read or write several, but not all, elements of an array.

Example 9 :

Now consider the statement

READ, ((A(I,J),J=1,3),I=1,4)

Given the DIMENSION statement and input of example 7, this statement produces the following array in memory :

4	3	1
7	9	12
13	6	4
8	2	11

The unsubscripted array name of example 7 and the array name with indexing of example 8 cause data to be read in the standard FORTRAN order : column-by-column. The READ statement in this example is an explicit specification causing data to be read row-by-row. Note, however, that the number of elements per column, and per row, are not changed—only the established correspondence between input order and positional assignment. And, unless specified otherwise, the array is operated on column-by-column in other FORTRAN statements in the program.

Example 10 :

Arrays, and array indexing, must be used with care in FORTRAN programs. For arrays with more than two dimensions, the same notational pattern of array indexing can be followed ; each additional dimension requires an additional set of parentheses. An example is

PRINT, ((((D(I,J,K,L),I=1,4),J=1,8),K=1,8),L=1,8)

If an array has only one dimension, the list element usually has the form

(A(I),I=1,m)

REF

where m is the number of elements of the array to be read or written. We can further generalize this form to

$$(A(I), I = i, k, inc)$$

where i is the first subscript value, k is the upper limit for the subscript value, and inc is the increment. The forms for list elements of higher-dimensional arrays can be further generalized in the same manner.

Any integer variable name may be used as a subscript. As indicated by the general form above, its initial value need not be 1. Any value within the range of the corresponding dimension of the array being read or written can be specified. The list element form for reading or writing arrays is very similar to the form used in DO statements. (See chapter 7.) A list element of this form is called an *implied DO*. (See also "Implied DO" in chapter 10.)

Example 11 :

The statement

READ, I, J, (P(K),K=1,10)

reads the first two values from the next input card to be stored (as integers, if we assume default typing) in the locations reserved for I and J. The next ten values are read from the same card and as many succeeding cards as necessary into the locations reserved for the first ten elements of the one-dimensional array P. Remember that we cannot assume from this statement that array P contains only ten elements. An entire array need not be read in or written at once.

Example 12 :

As another example, assume again the DIMENSION statement and input of example 7. The statement

READ, ((A(I,J),J=2,3),I=2,4)

fills the array A as shown below. The values of the elements where asterisks appear are undefined, that is, we cannot be certain what the values are on the basis of execution of this statement. In particular, we cannot assume the elements are set to zeros.

```
*     *     *
*     4     3
*     1     7
*     9     12
```

RECOGNIZING END OF FILE

Once the computer has begun executing a program and reading data that must be processed, how does it know when to stop? In most systems, the reading of input simply continues until an attempt is made to read data that is not there.

REF

Then program execution is terminated automatically. No further processing can be performed by the program.

Sometimes, this automatic termination is acceptable. At other times, however, we need to know when all input has been read, because we want to perform some special action (say, find an average or print a total) after we have read and processed all data in the input file.

The simple form of the READ statement includes no provision for checking to determine whether or not there are more cards to be read from an input file. Since there are many programming applications in which the volume of input is unknown, such checking may be difficult. One way to get around this problem is to establish a dummy value for a certain variable, a value that never appears as a normal data item for the variable. We then test for the dummy value and recognize its occurrence as a signal that no further reading of input is necessary. (This programming technique is explained in detail under "The logical IF statement" in chapter 7.)

In WATFIV, an optional feature of format-free input/output provides a convenient alternative. To ensure that our program can detect the end of an input file, we use a READ statement such as

READ (IUNIT,∗,END=999) A

This statement looks very much like a standard READ statement for formatted input/output. (See chapter 10.) However, no FORMAT statement is referred to; the position that can be used for a FORMAT statement number contains an asterisk. When the end of the input file has been reached and this statement attempts to read another input value, control is transferred instead to the statement identified by the statement number following END= in the READ statement. In our example, IUNIT is a variable whose value is the logical unit number of the input device. The logical unit number can also be expressed as a constant. This form of the READ statement can be used with any of the logical units included in a system, rather than with only the standard (system-default, or system) card read device. The ERR option described for the formatted READ statement in chapter 10 as well as the END option described above can be utilized.

```
          INTEGER I, SUM, NUM
          SUM = 0
          NUM = 0
   10     READ, I
          IF (I.EQ.999) GO TO 20
          SUM = SUM + I
          NUM = NUM + 1
          GO TO 10
   20     PRINT, SUM, NUM
          STOP
          END
   $DATA
     4
     3
```

```
       2
       999
$STOP
```

FIGURE 3.4

```
       INTEGER I, SUM, NUM
       SUM = 0
       NUM = 0
10     READ (5,*,END=20) I
       SUM = SUM + I
       NUM = NUM + 1
       GO TO 10
20     PRINT, SUM, NUM
       STOP
       END
$DATA
    4
    3
    2
$STOP
```

FIGURE 3.5

The programs in figures 3.4 and 3.5 are similar in function. Each reads input from cards, sums that input, then prints the sum and a count of the values added after all cards have been processed. Figure 3.4 shows how to look for a certain dummy value (in this case, 999) and to transfer to an end-of-file routine when the value is detected. In figure 3.5, the READ function detects when the last card has been read. The value 999 is not entered as input to this program. If it were, it would be treated just like any other data value.

ALTERNATIVE STATEMENT FORMS

Just as we sometimes want to read data from other than the standard card read device, we sometimes want to write data to other than the standard print unit. To do so, with WATFIV, we use a statement of the form

WRITE (*unit*,*) *list*

Note that the keyword PRINT of the format-free PRINT statement is replaced by WRITE in the statement form above. The *unit* is a constant or an integer variable representing the logical unit number of an output device, the asterisk is always used, and *list* is as described for the PRINT statement earlier in this chapter. Examples are

WRITE (6,*) A, B, 'CONSTANT'
WRITE (IUNIT,*) ARR(6), Z*4, D

REF

When using WATFOR or WATFIV, it is sometimes convenient to punch output data into cards rather than print it. To do so, we use a statement of the form

PUNCH, *list*

where *list* is again as described above. The specified values are punched into 80-column cards by means of the standard punch device. Any values that will not fit on one card are punched into succeeding cards. As an example, a statement causing the first five elements of array C to be punched is

PUNCH (C(I),I=1,5)

INTEGER ±n	
58	Integer values; no decimal point allowed.
−2	Preceding sign is optional if positive.
12	
+5	

REAL ±n, ±n.m, ±n.mE±i, ±n.mD±i	
47	In general, I, F, E, or D notation. (See chapter 10.) Either sign is optional if positive. Decimal point is optional if no fractional part. E or D is needed only if a power of ten is present.
3.17	
.317E+01	
−34.1E03	

COMPLEX (real number, real number)	
(5,7)	An ordered pair of REAL quantities as described above, separated by a comma and enclosed in parentheses. The first example at the left means $5+7i$. The second means $3.4+3.4i$. In both, i is the mathematical $\sqrt{-1}$.
(3.4,.34E01)	

LOGICAL	
.TRUE.	First T or F determines whether value of .TRUE. or .FALSE. is assigned to variable.
.FALSE.	
T	
F	

CHARACTER

'THIS IS CHARACTER DATA'
       Available only in WATFIV.
       Enclosing quotes are required.

FIGURE 3.6

REF

DATA ENTRY FORMATS FOR THE READ STATEMENT

Values for variables of any of the five internal data types can be read into storage by a format-free READ statement. There are certain forms which each may take on a card. Figure 3.6 lists the types and the input forms to be punched on cards.

PRINT FORMATS FOR DATA TYPES

Output values of the various data types are printed in fixed print formats. The maximum number of values printed on a line depends on the types and sizes of the variables specified in the list of the PRINT statement and on the printer in use. (See the discussions of type and size in chapter 2.) Spacing provides clarity. If a line is filled before all values are printed, a new line is started automatically. Each execution of a PRINT statement causes printing to begin at the start of a new line.

Typical print formats for data of various types and sizes are described in figure 3.7. The descriptions are given in terms of format descriptors used for formatted input/output. (See chapter 10.) Examples of typical output of each type and size are shown in the right-hand column.

Data type and size	Description	Example
INTEGER	I12	341
REAL*4	E16.7	0.5300000E 01
REAL*8	D28.16	0.1234500016000000D 14
COMPLEX*8	'('E16.7','E16.7')'	(0.5410000E 05,0.1600000E 01)
COMPLEX*16	'('D28.16','D28.16')'	(0.1894300000000000D 02,0.4894876301010000D 10)
LOGICAL	L8	T
CHARACTER*n	An	ANYCHARS

FIGURE 3.7

SIMULATION OF FORMAT-FREE I/O*

The format-free input and output statements are available only in WATFOR and WATFIV. However, the FORTRAN programmer can use standard FORTRAN statements in a similar way. To do this, the following statement should be placed just ahead of the END statement in the FORTRAN program.

    99999 FORMAT (5G15.8)

*The basic idea for FORTRAN simulation of format-free input/output appears in *Ten Statement FORTRAN plus FORTRAN IV* by Michael Kennedy and Martin B. Solomen (Englewood Cliffs, N.J.: Prentice-Hall, Inc., 1970).

REF

The READ and PRINT statements should have the following forms:

READ 99999, *list*
PRINT 99999, *list*

The only difference between these general forms and the general forms given under "Expanded examples of READ and PRINT" in this chapter is the 99999 before the comma. The statements

READ 99999, I, J, R
PRINT 99999, R, I

are equivalent to the statements given in examples 1 and 2 in this chapter.

The only restriction imposed by FORTRAN but not by WATFOR and WATFIV is that input values must appear in certain fixed portions of an input card; they cannot be separated by commas, and leaving a random number of blanks between consecutive numbers is not adequate. The input values must be right-justified (punched as far to the right as possible) in fields of the input card, as follows:

Column
Numbers

1 – 15
16 – 30
31 – 45
46 – 60
61 – 75

There can be at most five values per card. Any unpunched column is assumed to contain zero. Figure 3.8 shows acceptable input for the READ statement above.

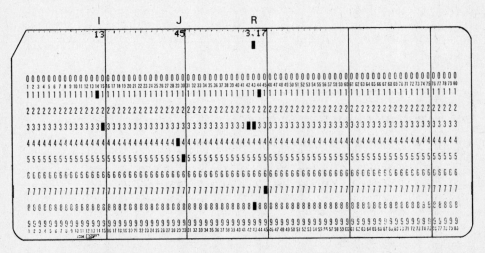

FIGURE 3.8

EXERCISES

1. (TUT) Given the following cards, write two sets of READ statements to read the data into the variables I, J, R, and P.

    Card 1 : 16.1 16.2

    Card 2 : 4 8

2. (TUT) Write PRINT statements to provide the following report, assuming that the first row contains constants and the second row displays the current values of the variables and expressions indicated by the constants.

X	Y	X*Y
0.4200000E 01	0.6100000E 01	0.2562000E 02

3. (REF) Write statements to declare two integer variables I and J and a 20 × 20 array A.

4. (REF) Given the declarations that you created for the preceding exercise and the following input cards, write statements to read the first two values on the first card into I and J and then read the next J cards as J rows of array A with I elements in each row.

    Card 1 :   4 3

    Card 2 :   1.0 .9 .8 .7

    Card 3 : 3.1 3.2 3.3 3.4

    Card 4 : 4.1 4.3 4.0 4.2

PROGRAMMING PROBLEMS

1. (TUT) Write a program to read values for one integer variable, two floating-point variables, and two more integer variables (in that order). Print out all values, displaying the integer values first.

2. (TUT) How many READ statements did you include in the program that you wrote for 1 above? If the input values are contained on three cards (one on the first, two on the second, and two on the third), will your program handle them correctly? If not, rewrite it to do so.

3. (TUT) Prepare three cards containing input values as described in 2 above to serve as input to your program.

4. (TUT) Using the cards that you prepared in 3 above as test data, compile and execute your program. Check the output to verify that your program performs correctly.

5. (REF) Write a program to print a report like the one shown below. It should read in the numerical values (including the animal numbers). The nonnumerical values should be included in the program.

		HEIGHT (FEET)	WEIGHT (LBS.)	AGE (YEARS)
COW	1	0.4800000E 01	0.3000000E 03	0.1300000E 01
	2	0.5100000E 01	0.4250000E 03	0.1800000E 01
	3	0.4200000E 01	0.2970000E 03	0.9000000E 00

6. (REF) Prepare input for the program that you wrote for 5 above. Then

run your program, using that input to verify that the program performs correctly.

7. (REF) Write a program to read numbers into an array as shown below, then print the values transposed (i.e., so that the element $A(I,J)$ prints in position $A(J,I)$). Your program should be designed to read only six numbers. Use arrays in your program.

	Input				Output	
N_1				N_1	N_2	N_4
N_2	N_3			N_3	N_5	
N_4	N_5	N_6		N_6		

Six values read from cards

8. (REF) Now write a program in which the first number read is the number of values in any triangular matrix to be processed as in 7 above. Assume that the number of elements in a row fits across one page.

9. (REF) Write a program to print out as many columns as are read in (as for 7 and 8 above) by partitioning the output into slices, ten columns per page, as suggested below.

10. (REF) Prepare input for the programs that you created to meet the processing requirements of 7, 8, and 9 above. Use that input to test your programs. Be sure that each performs correctly.

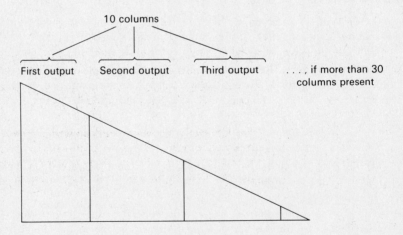

INTRO Frequently, certain values are known at the time a FORTRAN program is written. Such values can be included in the program. For example, if we are to use a certain unit of measurement (say, 5280 feet per mile), there is little reason to read 5280 as input. We can simply write the value 5280 whenever we want to use it in the program. There are many similar circumstances where constants are required. The form in which a constant is written depends on its type.

The tutorial section of this chapter explains the use of integer constants (numerals without a fractional part) and real, or floating-point, constants (which optionally include a fractional part). The reference section explains the use of logical, hexadecimal, character (also called literal), and complex constants.

In general, integer, floating-point, and complex constants can be used wherever an arithmetic expression that contains other than a single variable is permitted. They can also be specified as data initialization values. As you will learn, there are additional places where integer constants are required. The use of logical, hexadecimal, and character constants is somewhat restricted, so statements in which constants of these types can appear are noted specifically in this chapter.

A distinction must be made between constants stated explicitly in the body of a program and values for variables that are read in as data; further distinction must be made between either of these and values that are written as output. The form of a constant within the program may differ from that used for input or output. A table is given at the end of this chapter to show where various forms can be used.

TUT **INTEGER CONSTANTS** An integer constant is simply any single digit or combination of the digits from 0 through 9, optionally preceded by a + or − sign. If no sign is present, the value is assumed to be positive. Leading zeros may be present. If so, they are ignored. Valid integer constants are shown below.

Chapter

4

CONSTANTS

1

0

254

0254

+254

−254

But the following examples are invalid, for the reasons indicated.

1.	No decimal point is allowed in integer constant.
5,121	No commas are allowed.
P13	No alphabetic characters are allowed.
254CR	Credit sign is not acceptable as minus.
− 254	No blanks are allowed.
0−254	If a sign is specified, it must precede the digits of the constant.

The program in figure 4.1 reads three values, then prints those values, preceding each by a number that indicates its relative position within the group. Since the position numbers do not change, they are specified as integer constants in the PRINT statement in the program.

```
INTEGER A, B, C
READ, A, B, C
PRINT, 1, A, 2, B, 3, C
STOP
END
```

FIGURE 4.1

FLOATING-POINT CONSTANTS

Floating-point constants are used whenever a number may have either a fractional part or so many trailing zeros that it is wise to use scientific notation. The most general form of a floating-point constant includes a sign, an arithmetic value including a decimal point, the symbol E for exponent, a sign for the exponent, and a one- or two-digit exponent value. In programming, the first arithmetic value is called the *mantissa* and the second arithmetic value (the exponent) is used to form the *characteristic*. In the following example, a value is written in the most general form of a floating-point constant, in the corresponding scientific notation, and as a familiar decimal numeral.

$\pm 1.5E-01$	FORTRAN form
$\pm 1.5 \times 10^{-1}$	scientific notation
$\pm .15$	decimal numeral

The E, sign for the exponent, and exponent at the end of a floating-point constant are optional. If the sign and exponent are missing, the E must be missing also. As with integer constants, the sign at the beginning of the constant is optional. If it is missing, the value is assumed to be positive. The sign of the exponent may also be missing; if so, the exponent is assumed to be positive. This notation is a way to avoid writing many zeros. A positive exponent means that the mantissa should be multiplied by ten as many times as the exponent indicates. A negative exponent means that the mantissa should be divided by ten as many times as the exponent indicates. Thus, the following numerals represent the same value.

```
1500E−02
15.
.15E02
```

The simplest form of the floating-point constant looks like a familiar decimal numeral. It contains only the one arithmetic value with a decimal point and, optionally, a preceding sign. In floating-point constants such as we are discussing, up to seven significant digits (i.e., digits other than leading zeros) can be specified. Examples are

```
−.067
15.43
```

Examples of more complicated forms of floating-point constants are shown in the left-hand column below. Their meanings are given in the right-hand column.

0.	0
−0.E00	0
9E1	9
9.E+10	9×10^{10}
−9E−1	−.9
−.1973E4	−1973
.1973E−1	.01973
+1973E−04	.1973
1.973E+3	1973
1973E+4	19730000

Of course, certain errors must be avoided. The following examples are invalid for the reasons indicated.

78	Decimal point or exponent must be specified.
1,973.E4	No commas are allowed.
1.9E113	Exponent cannot exceed two digits.
1.9E	If E is specified, exponent is required.
1.4E.16	Decimal point in exponent is not allowed.

Sometimes a value can be expressed as either an integer constant or a floating-point constant. For example, the value equivalent to four can be represented by 4 or 4.0. If you are using the constant together with floating-point variables in an arithmetic operation, you should choose 4.0, the floating-point form. This approach is more efficient than using 4, because when 4 is used, the value is stored as an integer, then converted to floating-point before the arithmetic operation is performed.

REF

DOUBLE-PRECISION CONSTANTS

Double precision constants are similar to the floating-point constants described above except that each double-precision constant occupies twice as much space in computer memory as one of the floating-point constants above. In consequence, values having a degree of exactness, or *precision*, equivalent to more than sixteen decimal digits can be represented (as compared with slightly more than seven for the standard, or single-precision, floating-point constants).

A double-precision constant is recognized as such because it has either of two features, or both: (1) It contains more than seven decimal digits; (2) The letter D is used instead of E to denote exponentiation. Examples are

    218.45678
    −.486D4
    21.39876D−11
    9.1234569801

The letter D used as an exponent is interpreted in the same way as the letter E used as an exponent. Hence, the second and third constants above represent values that can be written as follows:

    −4860
    .0000000002139876

The letter D differs from E in that it causes double the amount of storage to be used for the internal floating-point representation of the value. (To learn more about how double-precision data is used, see "Double-precision arithmetic" in chapter 5.)

LOGICAL CONSTANTS

There are only two logical constants. They are

    .TRUE.
    .FALSE.

These logical constants can be used in logical expressions in IF statements and assignment statements. In WATFOR and WATFIV, they can also be used in logical expressions in format-free PRINT and PUNCH statements.

HEXADECIMAL CONSTANTS

It is frequently useful to specify an exact pattern of binary digits (*bit pattern*) to be set up in computer storage. To do this, we want to express a value in binary, or base 2, notation instead of the decimal, or base 10, notation that we are accustomed to using. Since it takes a lot of zeros and ones to represent a value in binary, FORTRAN permits us to use a shorthand notation called hexadecimal, or base 16. In doing so, we group binary digits into sets of four and represent each set by one hexadecimal digit. Equivalent base 2 and base 16 representations are shown in figure 4.2.

Hexadecimal constants can be specified as initial values in type statements

REF

Base 2	Base 16
0000	0
0001	1
0010	2
0011	3
0100	4
0101	5
0110	6
0111	7
1000	8
1001	9
1010	A
1011	B
1100	C
1101	D
1110	E
1111	F

FIGURE 4.2

or DATA statements referring to variables of one or more FORTRAN data types. There is no way of declaring a hexadecimal variable; a hexadecimal constant is simply a means of setting an integer, floating-point, or other type of variable to a particular bit pattern. The form of the hexadecimal constant is Z followed by one or more hexadecimal digits. If fewer hexadecimal digits are given than are required to fill the storage locations reserved for a specified variable, zeros are added at the left. If more hexadecimal digits are given than can be stored, only the rightmost hexadecimal digits are used. Some examples are

        REAL A/Z14B3/
        DATA B/Z12AC/

Hexadecimal constants cannot be used in arithmetic expressions. However, they can be read into or written from storage locations in hexadecimal form (but without the preceding Z) by using the Z format code. (See chapter 10.) Use of these constants is generally machine-dependent because their use is closely related to the structure of computer storage. In IBM 360/370, storage is structured as eight-bit bytes, and each byte can hold two hexadecimal digits.

CHARACTER CONSTANTS

A character, or literal, constant is a string of alphabetic, numeric, and/or special characters, identified as such by enclosing single quotes or by an immediately preceding nH where n is the number of characters in the string. A string of the latter type is usually known as *Hollerith data*. Examples are

REF

'THIS IS A STRING'
14HREPORT HEADING

Character constants can be specified as data initialization values for integer, real, complex, or logical variables. A WATFIV programmer has an additional facility: He can declare variables of CHARACTER type and specify character constants for those variables. (See chapter 11.) Character constants can also be used in FORMAT statements, for example, to create an output report heading as shown below.

```
      WRITE (6,99)
99    FORMAT ('1STUDENT SCHOLARSHIP FUNDS')
```

Character constants may appear in CALL statement or function reference argument lists. A character string enclosed in single quotes may be specified in a PAUSE statement. When single quotes are used to delineate a string, a single quote within the string must be represented by two single quotes. If the *n*H format is used, a single quote is sufficient. Usually, a single quote in a character constant is an apostrophe. The following constants are equivalent.

'THIS IS AN APOSTROPHE '''
23THIS IS AN APOSTROPHE '

COMPLEX CONSTANTS

A complex constant is written as an ordered pair of signed or unsigned floating-point constants, separated by a comma and enclosed in parentheses. The first floating-point constant represents the real part of a complex number; the second represents the imaginary part of the complex number. For example, (1.5,2.) represents the complex number $1.5 + 2.i$ where i is equal to $\sqrt{-1}$.

The rules for writing floating-point constants in a complex constant are the same as those for writing any floating-point constant. Both parts of a complex constant must be the same size (that is, occupy the same number of storage locations—generally either four or eight bytes). They must be in the range for floating-point constants and may be positive, zero, or negative. If unsigned, they are assumed to be positive.

Valid complex constants and their meanings are shown below.

(1.9,2.0)	$1.9 + 2.0i$
(1.,−2.)	$1. − 2.i$
(1.E+1,2.)	$10. + 2.i$
(57054D+2,38D+3)	$5705400. + 38000.i$

where $i = \sqrt{-1}$

Errors to be avoided are demonstrated below.

(1,2.5)	Floating-point constants must be used.
(1.E1,2.D1)	The constants must be the same size.
(4.)	Two constants are required.
(3.0,A)	Variables are not allowed.

DATA FORMS

Data operated on by a FORTRAN program may be included in the program as constants, read in as values for variables, or determined by the program itself using constants and/or values for variables supplied previously. For some data types, a value to be read as input must have the same form as a constant of that type within the program. But this is not always the case. The form of an output value may also differ from the constant form.

Type and Form	Executable program	DATA statement	Input	Output	Valid format codes Input	Valid format codes Output
Integer	Yes	Yes	Yes	Yes	I,G	I,G
Real with exponent	Yes	Yes	Yes	Yes	D,E* F,G	D,E* G
Real without exponent	Yes	Yes	Yes	Yes	F,D,E* G	F,G
Character with quotes or nH	Yes	Yes	See 1	Yes See 2	None	None
Character without quotes or nH	No	No	Yes	Yes	A	A
Logical .TRUE./.FALSE.	Yes	Yes	Yes	No	L,G	None
Logical T/F	No	No	Yes	Yes	L,G	L,G
Complex with parentheses	Yes	Yes	See 3	See 3	None	None
Complex without parentheses	No	No	Yes	Yes	F,D,E* G	F,D,E* G
Hexadecimal with Z	No	Yes	No	No	None	None
Hexadecimal without Z	No	No	Yes	Yes	Z	Z

Notes:
1. Character with quotes in WATFIV. No otherwise.
2. Yes—explicitly in PRINT in WATFOR and WATFIV; explicitly in FORMAT in FORTRAN, WATFOR, and WATFIV.
3. Yes in format-free I/O of WATFOR and WATFIV. No otherwise.
4. * means that the appropriate format code (from among those listed) depends on the size of the value being read or written.

FIGURE 4.3

REF

The data types and their forms are noted in the left-hand column of figure 4.3. The ways in which these forms may be used are listed across the top. When a form may be used for input or output, any appropriate format codes are indicated. (The latter are explained in detail in chapter 10.)

In FORTRAN, only literal constants can be specified in a FORMAT statement, that is, expressed as a constant to be written directly as output. We cannot specify constants as entries in the I/O list of a WRITE statement. Nor is it appropriate to use constants as entries in the I/O list of a READ statement. The list that we specify in a READ statement is a list of variables identifying storage locations into which data is to be read. Obviously, we do not want to read data into a constant.

Those of you who are writing programs to be executed on WATFIV systems can specify constants in format-free PRINT statements. These may be literal constants or constants of other data types. (For details, see chapter 3.)

Note again that figure 4.3 does not deal only with data values expressed as constants in a program. It summarizes the use of both constants and variables in FORTRAN, WATFOR, and WATFIV.

QUEST

EXERCISES

1. (TUT) Which of the following are valid integer constants; which are valid floating-point constants? Which are invalid?
   a) −123
   b) 27.4
   c) 18.5−E3
   d) 127+5
   e) 28
   f) −85.321E+4

2. (TUT) Refer to the preceding exercise. Give reasons why the items you identified as invalid cannot be used in a FORTRAN program.

3. (REF) Identify each valid constant in the list below and indicate its type.
   a) 47
   b) 47E0
   c) 47.47E+02
   d) −47.47E−47
   e) E47
   f) T
   g) .TRUE.
   h) TRUE
   i) .FALSE.
   j) 4.0+3I
   k) ZABCD
   l) 'ABCDEFGH'
   m) ZABCDEFG
   n) 47HABCDE

4. (REF) Refer to the preceding exercise. Identify the invalid items and explain why each is invalid.

5. (REF) Assume the following values are to be read as data. Identify each acceptable value and indicate its type.
    a) 47
    b) 47,48
    c) 47.
    d) 47.E
    e) .193E−04
    f) 47 48
    g) (47.0,48.0)
    h) 47.0 48.0
    i) ZABC
    j) 'ABC'
    k) ABC
    l) 2HNO

6. (REF) Refer to the preceding exercise. Identify the invalid data items and explain why each is invalid.

7. (REF) Where can data of the following types and forms be used as constants?
    a) integer
    b) floating-point (or real)
    c) complex with comma and parentheses
    d) complex as pair of reals with no parentheses or comma
    e) hexadecimal with preceding Z
    f) hexadecimal without preceding Z
    g) character with quotes
    h) character without quotes
    i) T and F
    j) .TRUE. and .FALSE.

8. Repeat the preceding exercise, but consider use of the data for input or when printed as output.

PROGRAMMING PROBLEMS

1. (TUT) Write a program that reads and prints the numbers of tickets sold by each of groups 1 through 6 working for a school benefit. Identify the group for which each number is printed by means of constants included in the program.

2. (TUT) Prepare test data for the program that you wrote in response to 1 above. Use the data as input for one or more debugging runs. Be sure that your program meets the requirements of the problem statement.

3. (TUT) Write programs to perform the following functions:
    a) Read and print two integer values.
    b) Read and print two floating-point numbers.
    c) Perform both a and b above; compute and print the sum of the integers and the sum of the floating-point numbers.

4. (TUT) Prepare test data for each program that you wrote in response to 3

above. Compile and execute the programs to verify that the required output is provided.

5. (REF) Three problem statements are given below. Write a program for each one.
    a)   Read and print two logical values.
    b)   Print your name, expressed as a character constant within the program.
    c)   Read two complex data items, then print them and their sum.

6. (REF) Prepare test data for each program that you wrote in response to 5 above. Run the programs to verify that each performs as required.

INTRO Although computers have a variety of ways of combining the data that they handle, the most common is simple arithmetic. In this chapter we explain how to direct the computer to combine numeric values already in storage locations and how to store the resulting value in another location. Conversion of data from integer to real and from real to integer is discussed. Programming situations that may lead to errors are pointed out.

FORTRAN built-in functions and their types and uses are presented in the reference section. The double-precision features of FORTRAN are explained. Complex arithmetic and associated built-in functions are described.

ARITHMETIC ASSIGNMENT STATEMENT **TUT** The FORTRAN statement associated with combining two or more values to form a new value is the *arithmetic assignment statement*. A simple example is

$$A = B + C$$

The statement above looks like a mathematical equation. If it were an equation, it would mean that the value of A equals the value of B plus C. Since the equation form is symmetric in mathematics, we could just as well have written $B + C = A$. But the assignment statement is not a mathematical equation. The assignment statement really means "take the value on the right-hand side of the symbol $=$ and place that value in the location specified by the left-hand side." You will never see a valid FORTRAN assignment statement of the form $B + C = A$.

The statement

$$B = B + 2.0$$

makes no sense at all in the realm of mathematics. We know that a value (B, in this case) is not equal to that value plus two. On the other hand, this statement is reasonable in FORTRAN because the symbol $=$ does not mean "equals." Instead, it means "is replaced by." Hence, the statement above means that

---

Chapter

5

ARITHMETIC

the value currently stored in the location named B is to be replaced by the value in that location plus two.

The assignment statement always has the meaning:

location←value

When a statement of this form is used to manipulate numeric values, *location* identifies a storage area in memory and *value* is any valid arithmetic expression. Generally, the expression is a combination of FORTRAN variables, constants, and operators describing arithmetic operations to be performed. The standard arithmetic operations are available. The operator for each is shown in figure 5.1.

Arithmetic operator	Operation
+	Addition
−	Subtraction
*	Multiplication
/	Division
**	Exponentiation

FIGURE 5.1

Some, but not all, of these operators are the same as operators commonly used in mathematics. In mathematics, we usually write an × or a dot for multiplication. Neither is used in FORTRAN because they might be confused with the letter x or the period. Exponentiation is usually written in mathematical form as a base value and a superscript (e.g., A^4). In FORTRAN programs, two asterisks are used to indicate exponentiation because characters cannot be written above lines or split across lines.

Example 1:

A program that reads values for two floating-point variables as input, then prints both their sum and the difference between them is shown in figure 5.2.

```
REAL A, B, C, D
READ, A, B
C = A + B
D = A − B
PRINT, C, D
STOP
END
```

FIGURE 5.2

Example 2:

By making slight changes to the program in figure 5.2, we can use the same storage area for the difference as for the sum. (See figure 5.3.)

```
REAL A, B, C
READ, A, B
C = A + B
PRINT, C
C = A - B
PRINT, C
STOP
END
```

FIGURE 5.3

Compare the programs in figures 5.2 and 5.3. Which program requires the lesser amount of storage for data? Can we say, therefore, that it requires a lesser amount of storage? A program that performs the same functions as another program, but requires less storage in doing so, is generally said to use storage more efficiently.

Which program probably requires the lesser amount of time for compilation and execution? Why? A program that gets the same amount of work done as another program, but does it in less time, is generally said to perform more efficiently from the viewpoint of computer (central processing unit, or CPU) time.

As a programmer, you must be aware of both storage and time considerations. The importance of either depends on the amount of computer storage available for your program and data, the number of times that your program is apt to be executed, and so on. Sometimes, you must make a tradeoff—say, use more storage for your program than is absolutely necessary in order to improve its processing efficiency, or performance.

ARITHMETIC EXPRESSIONS

Arithmetic expressions can be considered separately from assignment statements because they are used in other kinds of statements as well. Examples of valid arithmetic expressions are

```
I + 4 * J
A * B * 4.
J + I + K * 47
A ** 5 / ( - DIV)
```

Note that some of these expressions are ambiguous if we attempt to interpret them using only what we have stated thus far. $I + 4 * J$ may mean either $(I + 4) * J$ or $I + (4 * J)$. (Find values for I and J such that these expressions have different values.)

OPERATOR HIERARCHY

To eliminate ambiguity, conventions have been established as to the order in which arithmetic operations are performed. Arithmetic operators are grouped as in figure 5.4, with the highest ones in the hierarchy evaluated first.

(Highest)

↑	**	Exponentiation
	*, /	Multiplication and division
	+, −	Addition and subtraction

(Lowest)

FIGURE 5.4

Applying these conventions to the expression above, we can determine that the multiplication is done first; that is, the expression is interpreted as I + (4 * J).

USE OF PARENTHESES

Even with these conventions, it is sometimes difficult to express formulas without some further indication of which operation is to be performed first. In the same way we used parentheses above, parentheses can be used in arithmetic expressions in FORTRAN. The rule is that any operations enclosed within parentheses are computed before those outside the parentheses.

Examples of valid arithmetic expressions are

```
4. + (8.*G)
(4. + G) * 8
I**2 + J**2
A**2 + B**2
HEIGHT * LENGTH
.12 * (SALARY − DEDUCT)
(A − B) * .17E−20
(17.E+20 * (A + B)) + 2.0
```

But the following expressions are invalid, for the reasons indicated.

((A + B) * 2.0	Unmatched left parenthesis
(A + B) * 2.0)	Unmatched right parenthesis
A**5 / −5	Two operators appearing together

LEFT-TO-RIGHT RULE

If two operators at the same level of hierarchy are encountered in an expression, still another rule is applied. Generally, the specified operations are computed from left to right. Thus, the arithmetic expression A * B / C means that A is to be multiplied by B, and the result is to be divided by C. The only exception to this left-to-right rule occurs when two exponentiations are specified consecutively, as in A**B**C. Here, the computation proceeds from right to left. The value of B**C is computed first, and the result of that computation is used as the exponent for A. That is, A**B**C is interpreted as A**(B**C). Assume the values of A, B, and C are 2, 3, and 2, respectively. Then 2**(3**2) equals 2**(9), which is 512.

EXPONENTS

Both integers and floating-point values may be used as exponents. The expressions R**5.0 and R**5 have the same meaning. Because of the method of evaluation, however, the integer exponent is more efficient and more precise. In general, integer exponents should be used whenever possible.

THE UNARY MINUS

The symbol —, which is the subtraction or minus sign, may appear with a single operand. That is, an expression such as —R or —4 is allowed. It is more convenient to express the opposite of a value in this way than to write (0.—R) or (0—4). When the minus sign is used with a single operand, it is called the *unary minus*.

Even when the unary minus is used, two operators cannot appear together. Hence, the expressions A*—B is invalid. But we can easily write the valid expression A*(—B).

One must be careful in another respect when using the unary minus. For example, the expressions below represent the same value.

```
—5**2
0 — 5**2
```

They both say "square the quantity 5 and subtract the result from 0." The result is, of course, a negative value of 25 (i.e., *minus* 25, or —25).

Example 3:

The program in figure 5.5 reads values for three integer variables. It prints their sum plus twenty, and that result multiplied by four.

```
INTEGER A, B, C, SUM
READ, A, B, C
SUM = A + B + C + 20
PRINT, SUM
SUM = SUM * 4
PRINT, SUM
STOP
END
```

FIGURE 5.5

Example 4 :

A program analogous to that of figure 5.5, but handling floating-point variables, is shown in figure 5.6.

```
REAL A, B, C, SUM
READ, A, B, C
SUM = A + B + C + 20.0
PRINT, SUM
SUM = SUM * 4.0
PRINT, SUM
STOP
END
```

FIGURE 5.6

What differences do you note between the programs in figures 5.5 and 5.6? Remember that when we use floating-point variables, we should use floating-point constants. Conversely, integer variables suggest use of integer constants.

Example 5 :

Suppose that we are to print the square of the sum of the three floating-point variables of example 4, then the difference between the first two of them divided by four. To cause the computer to perform these computations correctly, we must use parentheses as shown in figure 5.7.

```
REAL A, B, C, SUMSQ, DIFF
READ, A, B, C
SUMSQ = (A + B + C)**2
DIFF = (A − B) / 4.0
PRINT, SUMSQ, DIFF
STOP
END
```

FIGURE 5.7

Note that in the first assignment statement above, we encounter an exception to our general guideline of using values of like type. As stated earlier, integer exponents should be used whenever possible.*

FORMING CORRECT ARITHMETIC EXPRESSIONS

A noteworthy programming guideline is: Know what you want to do before

*For additional insight into expression evaluation, see "Assignment Statements" and "Data Types" in chapter 3 of C. W. Gear, *Introduction to Computer Science*.

writing your first line of code. In applying this guideline to the use of arithmetic expressions, it is wise to begin with an expression form that is familiar to you.

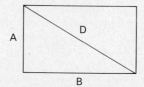

FIGURE 5.8

Assume that you want to compute the length of the diagonal of the rectangle in figure 5.8. The familiar form of the expression required to compute this value is $D = \sqrt{A^2 + B^2}$. If you were computing D by hand for fixed values of A and B, you would make the computations in a certain order. The first step in writing a FORTRAN expression is to determine that order. Most likely, you would:

1 Square A and save it.

2 Square B and save it.

3 Add the saved results and save the sum.

4 Take the square root of the sum.

To express this in FORTRAN, we write each operation and enclose it in parentheses.

1 (A**2)

2 (B**2)

3 ((A**2) + (B**2))

4 ((A**2) + (B**2))**.5

Remember that, by definition, $\sqrt{x} = {}^{.5}$.

Since we are determining a value for D, we write

5 D = ((A**2) + (B**2))**.5

It is better to use too many parentheses than too few. We cannot remove the outer set of parentheses in this assignment statement because the operation of exponentiation (in this case, finding the square root) would be done before the operation of addition. However, we can remove the two inner sets of parentheses, leaving

D = (A**2 + B**2)**.5

We want the exponentiation operations on A and B to be done before the addition operation. In this case, operations will take place as desired whether parentheses are used or not.

A common error is failing to use enough parentheses to ensure that all operations are done in the intended order. This is a difficult error to find. An expression may be a valid FORTRAN expression, even though it is not interpreted in the way that the programmer thinks it is.

Example 6 :

Assume that, in January, you take out a loan of $1450 on which you agree to pay 14% interest per year, compounded monthly. You pay $70.00 per month at the end of the month. For each month from January through March, you want to know the following information.

Month name	Interest for month	Principal for month	New balance	Total interest	Total paid

For each month, the interest that you owe is computed using the formula

Interest = Balance × (14/12 × .01)

After you have computed the interest, you can determine the portion of your $70.00 payment that is applied to the principal, the new balance, the total amount of interest that you have paid thus far, and the total amount of money (both interest and repayment of principal) that you have paid against the loan.

```
C      SPRIN     ORIGINAL PRINCIPAL
C      BALANC    CURRENT BALANCE OWED
C      TOTINT    TOTAL INTEREST PAID
C      INTRST    CURRENT MONTH'S INTEREST
C      MOPRIN    PRINCIPAL THIS MONTH
C      TOTPD     TOTAL PAYMENT VALUE
C      SET UP  STARTING CONDITIONS
       SPRIN = 1450.
       BALANC = 1450.
       TOTINT = 0.
C      COMPUTE INTEREST FOR MONTH.
       INTRST = BALANC * ((14./12.) * .01)
C      THIS STATEMENT CAUSES CONVERSION TO INTEGER AFTER
C      COMPUTATION BUT BEFORE ASSIGNMENT.  IT ENSURES
C      THAT ALL SUCCEEDING STEPS DEAL WITH WHOLE
C      DOLLAR VALUES.
       MOPRIN = 70 - INTRST
       BALANC = BALANC - MOPRIN
       TOTINT = TOTINT + INTRST
       TOTPD = 1450. - SPRIN + TOTINT
C      THEN PRINT.
       PRINT, 'JANUARY ', INTRST, MOPRIN, BALANC, TOTINT,
      1TOTPD
       STOP
       END
```

FIGURE 5.9

Since so many values must be computed for each month, you might decide to write a computer program. A program for January is shown in figure 5.9. The lines beginning with the letter C are comment statements. Such comments are printed on the source-program listing as documentation, but they do not become part of the machine-language version of the program. The last PRINT statement is a continued statement, identified by the numeral 1 in the sixth position of the continuation line. Since your program is to model reality, you can decide in advance what variables you will need. Listing the variable names and their usage as comments is advisable.

MIXED MODE

The types and sizes of all variables in the program in figure 5.9 are determined by default. You should also notice that in some expressions and assignment statements both integer and floating-point variables are used. In such cases, certain conversion rules are applied:

- If one variable in an arithmetic expression is integer and the other is real (floating-point), the integer is converted to real before the computation is made. The result is a real number.

- If the variable on the left-hand side of an assignment statement is integer and the value of the expression on the right (say, the result we noted above) is a real number, the expression value is truncated so that it has no fractional part and converted to an integer before it is assigned to the integer variable.

The second of these rules means that the fractional part of a real number is ignored during conversion. This sometimes causes surprising results. For example, assume R is of REAL type and I is of INTEGER type. After the following statements are executed, the value of I is zero.

```
R = .99999
I = R
```

One way to avoid difficulties is to avoid using mixed mode. Another way is to round any real results that you plan to assign to integer variables. After execution of the following statements, for example, the variable I has the (probably intended) value 1.

```
R = .99999
I = R + .5
```

Rounding is also valuable for retaining accuracy in a long series of arithmetic operations. (See "Errors" in the reference section of this chapter.)

A common error is to use integers when writing fractional values. The result of integer division is an integer. Hence, the following sequence leaves zero as the value of R since 3/4 (which yields zero) is computed first, then multiplied by 1.

```
S = 1.
R = 3/4*S
```

×

REF

MULTIPLE ASSIGNMENT IN WATFIV

In WATFOR and WATFIV, several variables may be assigned values in one assignment statement. For example, the following statement is permissible:

$$B = A(I) = G(I,J,K) = 4.0 + K$$

It has the same effect as the sequence of statements

$$G(I,J,K) = 4.0 + K$$
$$A(I) = G(I,J,K)$$
$$B = A(I)$$

The general form of the multiple assignment statement is

$$v_1 = v_2 = \ldots = v_n = expression$$

where each v_i is a simple variable or subscripted array variable and *expression* is any valid arithmetic or logical expression. That is, this form can be used for both arithmetic assignment statements (discussed in this chapter) and logical assignment statements (discussed in chapter 11).

The general interpretation of the multiple assignment statement is

$$v_n \quad = expression$$
$$v_{n-1} = v_n$$
$$\cdot$$
$$\cdot$$
$$\cdot$$
$$v_1 \quad = v_2$$

The order of assignment is particularly important when not all variables are of the same type and size. For example, if I and J are INTEGER, and B is REAL, then

$$I = J = B = 14.3$$

does not have the same effect as

$$I = B = J = 14.3$$

Notational convenience does not imply processing efficiency. Specifying several assignments in one assignment statement does not make the assignments easier or faster to perform at program execution-time. It may help to camouflage unanticipated conversions or results. Multiple assignment statements cannot be used in IBM 360/370 FORTRAN G and H and are not included in ANS recommendations for FORTRAN.

ERROR

Error in the evaluation of FORTRAN arithmetic expressions comes primarily from the fact that a floating-point representation is just an approximation of a decimal value. This approximation becomes apparent in two ways. First, whether single-precision or double-precision floating-point representation is specified, a fixed number of decimal digits are used to represent a number. Few input values contain long strings of decimal digits, but values that are the

REF

results of internal computations frequently do. When these values are computed, they must be either truncated or rounded to eight or seventeen digits (for single-precision or double-precision, respectively) before they can be stored in the locations reserved for them. In FORTRAN, truncation generally occurs.

The second source of approximation error is the fact that decimal numbers are not represented in the machine in base 10; instead, they are converted to base 2. There is not a one-for-one correspondence between base 10 representations and base 2 representations. Some base 10 numerals cannot be represented exactly in base 2. Because of the physical limitations of memory components and organization, two different representations in base 10 may have the same representation in base 2, or vice versa. Of course, no two numbers that differ widely in one base have the same representation in the other base. However, a number read in as 1. may be printed as .99999999. Or, if floating-point expressions are used to compute the parameters of a DO loop, the loop may not be executed the intended number of times. You should be very careful when using the results of floating-point expressions. (For further discussion of potential errors, see chapter 9.)

When using long series of arithmetic computations, you must beware of errors due to truncation. When results are always truncated, the final value is always closer to zero than the true value is. Unless the sign of the result changes, the direction of error is always the same. If an extended sequence of arithmetic computations repetitively involves the same numbers, an error can propagate, giving a highly inaccurate result. The study of error propagation is a complete discipline, but an example may indicate how extreme the danger is. Assume, for ease of example, that a machine stores floating-point values as three-digit decimal numerals. Let us evaluate $(A * B) - X$ for $A = .425$, $B = .625$, and $X = .264$.

$$
\begin{array}{r}
.425 \\
\times\ .625 \\
\hline
2125 \\
850 \\
2550 \\
\hline
\end{array}
$$

.265625	truncates to	.265
−.264		−.264

.001625 or   .001 or
$.1625 \times 10^{-2}$ $.100 \times 10^{-2}$
Actual   Machine
result   result

Percentage of error = 62.5%

More than a sixty per cent error is generated after only two simple arithmetic computations.

Propagation of errors frequently occurs in numerical programming such as matrix inversion or the solution of partial differential equations. Since most FORTRAN and WATFIV compilers do not round when significant digits cannot be stored, it is often wise to declare double-precision variables for holding intermediate results. It is always wise to step through calculations and explicitly estimate the effect of accumulated error.*

INTEGER ARITHMETIC

When only whole numbers must be manipulated, arithmetic operations can be performed more rapidly if integer operations rather than floating-point are used. Furthermore, they tend to be more accurate. In general, then, integer arithmetic should be used when dealing with whole numbers.

An exceptional case may arise, however, when one integer is divided by another. This is the case where the dividend is not an even multiple of the divisor. In common terminology, we say that "the result doesn't come out even." In such a case, the fractional portion of the result is ignored. The result is always an integer, and no rounding occurs. For example, if I and J are integers having the values of 13 and 5 respectively, then I/J is 2.

USING MODULAR RELATIONSHIPS

While we must be aware that integer division yields an integer result, we need not regard this fact as always unfavorable. It can be used, for example, in computing one integer modulo another. I modulo J is simply the remainder after dividing I by J; hence, in our example above, I modulo J is 3. Of course, we know this because we know what values were operated on, but if we did not, we could direct the computer to find it for us. We need only write

$$K = I - (I/J*J)$$

By substituting 13 for I and 5 for J and doing the indicated arithmetic, you can verify that K has a value of 3 after execution of this assignment statement.

Example 7:

To appreciate how modular values are used, assume that the following statement reserves storage locations for a one-dimensional array A. These locations are to contain statistics of corn yield—the number of bushels of corn produced by each plot within a 100-plot area of land.

DIMENSION A(100)

Further assume that the actual plots of land are along a river and have been assigned the numbers from 1 to 100 as shown in figure 5.10.

A current hypothesis is that the distance a plot is from the river affects the productivity of the land in that plot. Can we estimate the distance between a plot and the river if we know only the plot number?

Clearly the plots in figure 5.10 are arranged in a specific order. Let us describe that order as being 5 rows 20 columns. We don't particularly care which row a plot is in, but knowing the column number of a plot would certainly

*For further discussion of numerical errors, see chapter 6 of C. W. Gear, *Introduction to Computer Science*.

REF

be helpful. We number the columns from 1 through 20 and say that each column is a unit of distance. The column next to the river is at distance 1. To compute the column number (unit of distance) for a particular plot, given the plot number, we use the fact that

column number = plot number modulo 20

We express this formula in FORTRAN by the assignment statement

C = P − (P/20*20)

where C and P are declared to be integer variables and represent the column number and plot number, respectively. Trying our method for plot 65, we find that

$$\begin{aligned} C &= 65 - (65/20*20) \\ &= 65 - (3 * 20) \\ &= 65 - 60 \\ &= 5 \end{aligned}$$

We verify by looking at figure 5.10 that plot 65 is in column 5—at the fifth unit of distance from the river.

ISLAND

Col.												Col.	
1	2											20	
81 ...							...	97	98	99	100		Row 1
61 ...								...	...	79	80		2
41	42	43	44	...	...				...	59	60		3
21	22	23	24	...	...				...	39	40		4
1	2	3	4	5	6	7	8	9	10 ...	19	20		5

RIVER

Units of distance

FIGURE 5.10

This technique is frequently useful in computing subscripts for arrays, which must be integer values. The FORTRAN built-in function MOD can also be used to obtain this kind of a result. (See the discussion below and the list of built-in functions in appendix F.)

FUNCTIONS

Frequently there is a need to compute a value by means that cannot be represented easily as a combination of standard arithmetic operations (i.e., using

REF

+, −, *, /, and **). Even in cases where the computations can be so expressed, the expression may be complicated and may have to appear many times in a program. To permit the programmer to refer to standard mathematical functions and to allow complicated expressions to be referenced by name instead of written in full whenever they are needed, FORTRAN provides certain predefined computations and allows the programmer to define his own as well. As in mathematics, these defined computations that can be referenced by name are called *functions*.

The FORTRAN notation for functions is similar to mathematical notation. In mathematics we write

A = Sin (X)

to set A equal to the sine of the value X. The X is called an argument and Sin is the name of the mathematical function that finds the sine of a specified argument value. In FORTRAN, we write SIN(X) to refer to the sine of a REAL*4 variable X. Again, X is an argument. SIN is a *built-in function* provided as part of the FORTRAN language. The argument passed to the SIN function need not be a simple variable; it can be any arithmetic expression of REAL*4 type and size. For example, if X and Y are REAL*4 variables, then SIN(X**2+Y**2) is acceptable. On the other hand, if X and Y are explicitly declared to be REAL*8 variables, we cannot use the SIN function. Instead we write DSIN(X**2+Y**2) to refer to DSIN, the FORTRAN built-in function to find the sine of a REAL*8 value. The built-in functions to find the sine of COMPLEX*8 and COMPLEX*16 expressions are CSIN and CDSIN respectively.

In like manner, built-in functions (also called *FORTRAN-supplied mathematical subprograms*) that compute other trigonometric values, logarithms, exponentials, maximums, minimums, and numerous other commonly required mathematical values are available for various FORTRAN data types. A complete list of them is given in appendix F. When there is no built-in function available to perform a computation required repeatedly, the FORTRAN programmer can define his own by writing a function subprogram. Guidelines for doing so are given in chapter 8.

Functions may be used in arithmetic expressions. Examples are

W = SIN(X**2+Y**2) + T
Y = SIN(X)**2 + COS(X)**2

Here SIN is the built-in function discussed above and COS is another built-in function—a defined computation analogous to the mathematical function that finds the cosine of a number. The result of the function evaluation, performed on the specified argument, effectively replaces the reference to the function.

One common error made by FORTRAN programmers is to provide an argument of the wrong type for a function, whether user-defined or built-in. For example, if I is an integer variable, the expression COS(I) is invalid, because the COS function is defined to operate on real numbers. The compiler might not detect this error, in which case the user would be alerted only by strange numerical results.

A function name is like any variable name selected by the programmer. A type and size must be declared for it, or they are assumed. The type and size

REF

of the function name must coincide with the type and size of the returned value that the function is designed to provide. An explicit declaration of the function name may be necessary to ensure that its type and size are established correctly. (To review how this is done, see "Typing of functions" in chapter 2.)

DOUBLE-PRECISION ARITHMETIC

Sometimes it is desirable, or even mandatory because of requirements imposed by a problem statement, to do computations using floating-point arithmetic but with more significant digits than REAL*4 (standard, or single precision) allows. For such cases, the double-precision features of FORTRAN can be used.

Because both single-precision and double-precision values are stored with a two-digit exponent, the range of values that can be represented by either is about the same—between 10^{-78} and 10^{75}, approximately. But the degree of exactness can be much greater when double precision is used. Single-precision variables can represent values equivalent to slightly more than seven significant decimal digits. With double-precision, values having a precision equivalent to more than sixteen significant decimal digits can be represented. Since the possible degree of precision is actually more than doubled, double precision is sometimes called *extended precision*.

Double-precision constants can be expressed in the form of familiar decimal numerals having more than eight digits or in exponential form with the letter D used to denote exponentiation. (See chapter 4.) Double-precision variables must be declared as such in type statements identifying them as REAL*8 variables or in DOUBLE PRECISION statements. (See chapter 2.) A double-precision expression contains either a double-precision constant or a double-precision variable or both.

The arithmetic operators and rules of hierarchy apply with double-precision values just as with single-precision values. Whenever an integer appears in an expression containing a double-precision value, the integer is converted exactly to double-precision form. Whenever a single-precision value appears with a double-precision value, zeros are added to the single-precision value, so that it occupies twice as much storage; it appears as a double-precision value, but the converted value does not really have more than single-precision accuracy.

Double-precision arithmetic capabilities are important when high degrees of exactness must be maintained in computation. But we must recognize that double-precision values require twice as much storage space as single-precision values and that computations usually are slower in double precision than in either integer or single-precision form.

DOUBLE-PRECISION BUILT-IN FUNCTIONS

Many common mathematical routines have been defined for single-precision values and for double-precision values and are available as FORTRAN built-in functions. Examples are ALOG10 and DLOG10, EXP and DEXP, TAN and DTAN, and so on. A complete list is given in appendix F.

REF

All double-precision function names should be declared as double precision by means of a type statement or a DOUBLE PRECISION statement. For example

    REAL*8 DEXP, DTAN
    DOUBLE PRECISION DGAMMA, DCOSH

INPUT/OUTPUT OF DOUBLE-PRECISION VALUES

Double-precision values to be read by a WATFIV format-free READ statement can be punched as familiar decimal numerals with decimal points or in exponential form with the letter D preceding the sign (if any) and exponent. A comma or at least one blank must separate values if more than one appears on a single card. A double-precision variable specified in the I/O list of a format-free PRINT statement is printed with up to sixteen significant digits and a D exponent.

Formatted input/output of both single-precision and double-precision floating-point values is explained in detail in chapter 10.

COMPLEX ARITHMETIC

Complex arithmetic can be handled just as any other form of arithmetic, using complex constants and variables defined to be COMPLEX. The same FORTRAN arithmetic operators and the usual rules of hierarchy apply. Required operations take place in their appropriate complex forms. If any constants and variables that are not complex appear in an arithmetic expression containing complex constants and/or variables, they are converted to complex form. For example, if R is a complex variable, and R + 5.6 appears as an expression, the constant 5.6 is converted to (5.6,0.0) before addition is performed. Exponentiation of complex values is permitted, but the exponent cannot be complex; it must be integer. Neither complex constants nor complex variables can be used as exponents.

Recall that complex constants and values represented by complex variables can appear only as two floating-point values of identical type and size (either 4 or 8). The name on the left-hand side of an assignment statement can be a complex variable. Given the declarations

    COMPLEX A, B, C
    REAL R1, R2

the following expressions and assignment statements are valid.

    A = B * C
    A = R1 + R2 * (1.1,.5)
    C = (R1 + B) * (2386E−4, −5.1)
    R1 = B

The last of these statements causes R1 to be set to the same value as the real part of B.

Assuming the same declarations, the following statements are invalid, for the reasons indicated.

B = C * (1,1)	A complex constant must have real terms.
C = (1.,R1)	A complex constant cannot contain variables.
B = B**4.0	A complex expression cannot contain a real exponent.
A = 4.**B	A complex expression cannot be used as an exponent.
C = 4+5i	A form in which i appears is not acceptable as a FORTRAN complex constant.

To review valid forms for complex constants, see chapter 4. Declaration of complex variables is discussed in chapter 2.

COMPLEX BUILT-IN FUNCTIONS

Many common mathematical routines have been defined for complex values and are provided as FORTRAN built-in functions. Examples are CSQRT and CLOG, which find the square root and logarithm, respectively. In general, these functions accept a complex expression as an argument and return a complex value. A complete list of them is given in appendix F.

All complex function names, whether of user-defined or built-in functions, must be declared as COMPLEX in type statements. (See chapter 2.)

One complex built-in function worthy of special mention is CMPLX, which can be used to express two REAL*4 arguments in complex form. We know that a complex constant can contain only floating-point constants. We cannot, for example, write (5.8,R) as a complex expression, even when R is a variable of correct type and size. But, using the CMPLX built-in function, we can write CMPLX(5.8,R) to cause a complex constant having 5.8 as its real part and the current value of R as its imaginary part to be created for us.

The general form of the CMPLX built-in function is

CMPLX(*r1,r2*)

where *r1* and *r2* are REAL*4 constants, variables, or other expressions involving either or both, with operators. Its return value is of COMPLEX*8 data type.

An analogous built-in function that accepts two REAL*8 arguments is DCMPLX. Its general form is

DCMPLX(*r1,r2*)

where *r1* and *r2* are REAL*8, and its return value is of COMPLEX*16 data type.

REAL-VALUED COMPLEX BUILT-IN FUNCTIONS

There is another category of complex built-in functions that accepts complex arguments but returns real values. The functions must not be declared as COMPLEX because their names do not represent complex values. However, they are often convenient to use when working with complex numbers. They are:

| AIMAG(c) | gives the imaginary part of a COMPLEX*8 expression as a REAL*4 value |
| REAL(c) | gives the real part of a COMPLEX*8 expression as a REAL*4 value |

REF

CABS(c)   gives the absolute value of a COMPLEX∗8 expression as a REAL∗4 value

CDABS(c)   gives the absolute value of a COMPLEX∗16 expression as a REAL∗8 value

INPUT/OUTPUT OF COMPLEX VALUES

Complex variables are treated as pairs of real values for input and output. Complex values to be read by a WATFIV format-free READ statement must be in the same form as complex values that appear in a program—pairs of real constants separated by commas and enclosed in parentheses. A comma or at least one blank must separate pairs if more than one pair is punched on a single card. Complex values provided as output by a WATFIV format-free PRINT statement appear as two adjacent real constants. If the values are single-precision, each has up to seven significant digits and an E exponent. If double-precision, each has up to sixteen significant digits and a D exponent.

A complex value to be read by a formatted READ statement should not contain the comma and parentheses required for complex constants in a program. It should appear as two real constants of the same precision. The FORMAT statement referred to by the READ statement must contain two field descriptors (or one, used twice) for each complex value. There is no special format code for handling a complex value. Hence, a pair of E, F, or G codes, or any combination of these is used for single-precision; a pair of D, F, or G codes or any combination of these is used for double-precision. Examples are

```
      COMPLEX A, B
      READ (5,99) A, B
99    FORMAT (2F14.4,E13.5,G14.3)
```

The FORMAT statement above is also appropriate for reference by a formatted WRITE statement controlling output of complex values. That is, the general guidelines stated in the preceding paragraphs apply to output as well as input. The format of the output is, of course, determined by the format descriptors specified.

EXERCISES

QUEST

1. (TUT) Write the following expressions in FORTRAN form.

   a) $\dfrac{a}{b+c}$

   b) $\dfrac{b}{b \times c}$

   c) $\dfrac{a}{b} \times c$

   d) $2a^4$

   e) $\dfrac{-b+4ac}{-a}$

§ 3.1

2. (TUT)
   a) Which pairs of FORTRAN arithmetic operators have the same precedence level?

b) Is there an arithmetic operator which has a higher precedence level than at least one other operator and a lower precedence level than a third?

c) Give an expression that uses both unary and binary minus operators. (*Unary* is the same as *monadic; binary* is the same as *diadic*.)

d) Mathematically it does not matter whether we evaluate A + B + C as (A + B) + C, or as A + (B + C). Is this true for every operator?

§ 3.1   3. (TUT) Rewrite the following assignment statements using sequences of single-arithmetic-operation assignment statements such as A = B * C. You can use as many storage cells T1, T2, . . . , as you need.

     a) P = Q + R * S

     b) D = (G + H)**(I / J)

     c) U = V**W * (X + Y)/(Z − U)

§ 3.2   4. (TUT) Assume the types of the variables in the expressions below are determined by default. Which of the expressions have integer values? Which are of REAL type?

     a) A + Z * I

     b) I ** J − 2

     c) X ** 2 − 3

     d) I / J + K

§ 3.2   5. (TUT) What value is assigned to the variable on the left in each of the following statements if the variables A, B, C, I, and J contain the values 3.5, 1.7, −10.5, 10, and −3, respectively?

     a) D = I * 3 − J

     b) X = C / A + 3.4

     c) E = I / J + 4.

     d) K = J ** 2 + A / B

     e) D = (I + J) * B

     f) E = A + B + I − 7

     g) L = C + (−B) * I

§ 2.2   6. (TUT) There are usually several sequences of instructions which can be used for any assignment statement. We usually want the shortest, either in number of instructions or in execution time.

     a) Give two different sequences of the same number of instructions that will perform the assignment

         A = (B * C + D) * (B * C)

     b) Which of the sequences that you gave above is faster?

   7. (REF) Assume default declarations except where variables are explicitly typed below. List all variables, giving the type, size, and dimensions (if any) of each.

     a) COMPLEX C
        C = A + 5.*I

     b) DIMENSION B(2,4), A(3,4)
        A(I,J) = B(I +2,J)

     c) DIMENSION B(2,4), A(3,4)
        A(I,J) − B(I,J−5)

     d) (A**(5+I)*R)

e) $(A**(5+I) - (R**2)$
f) $R*I$
g) $A/-B$

8. (REF) Refer to the preceding exercise. Identify the valid expressions and assignment statements.

9. (REF) For the expressions and statements that you identified in response to exercise 8, note mixed mode, conversions, and truncations.

10. (REF) Explain why each of the items listed in exercise 7 but not identified by you in response to exercise 8 is invalid.

PROGRAMMING PROBLEMS

§ 2.3   1. (TUT) Write a program that reads A, B, and C from one card, then performs the following assignments:
$$X = A * B$$
$$Y = C + A/B$$
$$Z = A - B + C$$
The program should print two lines, the first containing A, B, and C, the second containing X, Y, and Z.

2. (REF) Write a program that reads a single value X from each input line. Count the number of lines, sum the values of X, and sum the squares of the values of X. After the last input value has been processed, print the number of lines, the average value of X, and the average of the squares of X. Compute

$$\frac{N(\Sigma X^2) - (\Sigma X)^2}{N^2}$$

where N is the number of lines, ΣX is the sum of values of X, and ΣX^2 is the sum of squares. This is called the *standard deviation* of X. It measures the average distance of each value from the mean, or average value. (The reference section of chapter 3 explains how to execute part of your program only after the last input line has been read.)

3. (REF) Write a program to evaluate a polynomial of order 4. In the first statement, give an X value for the polynomial. In the second statement, read in the five coefficients for it. Print the computed value of the polynomial, which is of the form

$$a_4X^4 + a_3X^3 + a_2X^2 + a_1X + a_0$$

4. (REF) Read in the coefficients of a polynomial $aX^2 + bX + c$ where a, b, and c are complex. Print out the two complex roots using the formula

$$X = -b \pm \frac{\sqrt{b^2 - 4ac}}{2a}$$

INTRO This chapter deals with FORTRAN statements that declare to the FORTRAN system the characteristics of data items and the way they are stored in computer memory. Each data item used by a program may be represented by a variable name. There are cases, however, in which single variable names are not convenient means for referring to data items. For example, consider a program dealing with monthly salaries, in which twelve values of salary are read for each individual. It is not handy to use twelve different names in such a case. The DIMENSION statement is a way of declaring one name that can be used for all values.

It is often wise to break a single FORTRAN program into separate subprograms, each of which performs a set of related functions. Frequently, these subprograms need to refer to the same variables. The FORTRAN COMMON statement allows variables to be declared in such a way that several subprograms (called functions and subroutines, in FORTRAN terminology) can refer to them.

Sometimes storage should be used for one purpose at the beginning of a program, another purpose in the middle, and a third at the end. The EQUIVALENCE statement permits the same space to be referred to by several names and thus provides this capability.

Variables in common blocks of storage are sometimes initialized (set to original values) before beginning execution of the main program or of a subprogram. Variables in storage used by a single program unit may be also. This chapter discusses the method for explaining to the FORTRAN compiler which initial values should be given to which variables.

The statements explained in this chapter are nonexecutable statements. The programmer should place all nonexecutable statements other than END at the beginning of his program or subprogram. A good order to follow is:

SUBROUTINE or FUNCTION
(If needed, see chapter 8.)

Chapter

6

DATA DECLARATIONS

IMPLICIT
type   (If needed, see chapter 2.)
DOUBLE PRECISION

DIMENSION
COMMON   (If needed, see this chapter.)
EQUIVALENCE
DATA
statement function definitions   (If needed, see chapter 8.)

executable statements   (Assignment, READ, PRINT, DO, IF,
                                     GO TO, and so on, see chapters 3, 5,
                                     7, 10, 12.)

END

THE DIMENSION STATEMENT

Because FORTRAN is often used to express mathematical formulas, the FORTRAN programmer frequently desires to refer to a group of values by a single name, as one does a vector or matrix in mathematics. Notational features whereby one refers to elements of such a group (e.g., analogous to A_i in mathematics) are needed also. These capabilities are available in FORTRAN. We can declare a single name to represent a group of data items (called an *array*) by means of a *DIMENSION statement*. One or more array names, separated by commas, are given in the DIMENSION statement. Following each array name is an indication, enclosed in parentheses, of the maximum number of elements that can be included in the array. Each value within the parentheses is the maximum for a corresponding *dimension* of the array.

    DIMENSION A(47), B(6), C(100), D(2,100)

Arrays, A, B, and C above are *one-dimensional arrays*, or vectors, of up to 47, 6, and 100 elements, respectively. Array D is a *two-dimensional array*, or matrix, having up to 2×100, or 200, elements. We can visualize the storage space reserved for these arrays as shown in figure 6.1. Each box represents a fixed number of locations in computer memory.

A | 1 | 2 | 3 | 4 | 47

B | 1 | 2 | 3 | 4 | 5 | 6

C | 1 | 2 | 3 | 4 | 5 | 6 | 7 | 8 100

D   1   2   3   4   5 ...   100
     1
     2

FIGURE 6.1

As the DIMENSION statement above indicates, the dimensions of several arrays can be declared in one DIMENSION statement. However, a variable name may not appear more than once in DIMENSION statements. If a variable name is used as an array name, it cannot be used as the name of a single (also called simple) variable.

Except in certain usages in subprograms (about which you will learn more later), dimensions must be specified as integer constants. In most FORTRAN systems, an array can have up to seven dimensions. WATFIV does not impose this limitation.

Many DIMENSION statements may be included in a program, but they must appear at the beginning of the program after any SUBROUTINE, FUNCTION, or IMPLICIT statements. Space is allocated for the variables at the time the program is read and translated by the compiler. All dimensioning is done before execution of the program actually begins, and that is why integer constants are required. The DIMENSION statement, like all the statements in this chapter, is a nonexecutable statement. It is just a set of declarations for the compiler and is not translated into instructions for the computer. Remember, the compiler is just another program like the programs you write. It merely translates your program (its input) from FORTRAN to the language of the machine.

SUBSCRIPTING

When we want to specify a particular location in an array (that is, to refer to a particular element), it is not enough to give just the array name; such a reference is ambiguous. Given the DIMENSION statement discussed above, for example, the assignment statement below does not make sense.

A = 3.0 + R

This statement fails to identify the location in A to which the value of the expression 3.0 + R should be assigned.

To be more specific (and also use correct FORTRAN), we identify a particular location in A by appending a *subscript* to the array name. Subscripting is the correct way of referring to specific elements of arrays. A subscript indicates the relative position of an element in an array.

A(4) = 3.0 + R

Clearly, the fourth element of array A is intended. A(4) is a *subscripted variable*. You can use a subscripted variable in any statement in which you can use a simple variable. In most cases, the number of subscripts, separated by commas, that appear in a subscripted variable must be the same as the number of dimensions specified for the array.

If FORTRAN required that subscripts be expressed by constants, the array capabilities offered by the DIMENSION statement would be interesting but not of great significance; every value would still have to be referred to explicitly. Fortunately, an arithmetic expression can be used as a subscript. Assuming that appropriate values have been given to I, J, and R, the following statements are valid.

```
SALARY(I,3) = 125.00
A(I*J−4) = D(I+3,J*4+8)
B(R) = 4.0
```

The value of a subscript must be calculatable when it is used, and that value must be between one and the maximum value declared for the corresponding dimension of the array. Any real value is truncated to an integer before it is used as a subscript. The truncation can cause problems. For example, if R has a value of .999 or less when the third statement above is executed, the reference to B(R) is invalid. Truncation yields the value zero, which is always invalid as a subscript in FORTRAN. Current FORTRAN implementations for IBM 360/370 computers do not give a warning when an out-of-range subscript occurs. Generally, the program "blows up" at some later point, and the cause may be hard to find. WATFOR and WATFIV systems automatically check that array subscripts are within the dimension bounds declared for arrays and give an error message indicating the point of the error if an out-of-range subscript occurs. Those of you who are using FORTRAN systems that include the debug facility (explained in chapter 9) can cause subscript checking to be performed automatically for debugging purposes by specifying the SUBCHK option on the DEBUG statement. This makes debugging easier, particularly since attempting to use out-of-range subscripts is a common error in programming.

CHOOSING DIMENSIONED VARIABLES

Remember that in programming you are using the structure of your program and the structure you give computer memory to model external reality. This is most true of the DIMENSION statement. The information items you decide to process in your program form the structure that models the outside world.

The one-dimensional array is easy to understand. For example,

DIMENSION SALARY(12)

could well appear in a program that deals with twelve values of salary, one for each month of a year. But what real-life situation might be modeled by an array with more than one dimension? How does such a situation arise in programming?

DIMENSION SALARY(100,12)

Here we might have one hundred individuals, and for each individual we might have twelve values of salary. Figure 6.2 shows how the array can be visualized. Clearly, the number in a column identifies an individual; the number in a row is the number of a month. To refer to a single value, two integers are required: an individual number and a month number. The following assignment statement contains a valid reference; it gives to individual 47 the salary of 125.00 for month 12.

SALARY(47,12) = 125.00

There are situations that can be modeled most effectively by arrays having more than two dimensions. For example, we might use a three-dimensional array to provide three characteristics of shape: length, width, and depth. Solutions to simultaneous linear equations can be obtained through use of higher-dimensional arrays.

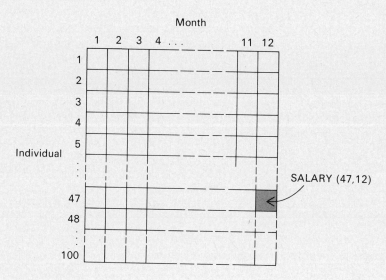

FIGURE 6.2

DATA TYPES

The type of each element in an array is the same as that of every other element in the array. That type is determined in the same way that type is determined for a simple variable. Similarly, the size of each element is the same as the size of every other element. It can be determined by default or by explicit declaration. (See chapter 2 for a review of data types.)

Dimensions, as well as type and size declarations, can be given in type statements. Hence, the following sequences are equivalent.

```
DIMENSION AI(2,4), AR(3,6), AZ(4)
REAL AR, AZ, R, Q
INTEGER AI

REAL AR(3,6), AZ(4), R, Q
INTEGER AI(2,4)
```

As the second sequence shows, simple variables and array variables can be declared in the same type statement. In most cases, dimensions in type statements must be integer constants, just as they must be when specified in DIMENSION statements.

CHOOSING MAXIMUM SIZES

It is difficult to choose the maximum sizes for arrays in most FORTRAN programs. Roughly, the larger the storage area reserved for an array the more general the program. Usually, a tradeoff between the generality of the program and the number of storage locations that can reasonably be set aside for the array is required. Obviously, if machine charges are based on the amount of memory used, it is best to use only what is needed. But one should usually avoid programming for a specific-sized problem. A wise approach for a general program is to read in a value for each array dimension, indicating the actual maximum value required for that dimension for a particular problem. The value should be read at the beginning of program execution and should be checked against the declared value for the dimension of the array. The value declared for an array dimension must be equal to or greater than the actual value read as input.

The real power of the FORTRAN language comes from combining use of arrays with the ability to loop through a sequence of steps, performing the same operations on many different array elements by changing subscript values. This is covered in chapter 7 under the DO, IF, and GO TO statements.

THE DATA STATEMENT

It is frequently desirable to assign certain constant values to simple variables or arrays before execution of a program begins. Such values might be tables of statistics used by the program or header lines to be printed on reports. Since it is not convenient to include a sequence of executable assignment statements to assign such values, FORTRAN provides the *DATA statement*, which performs this function. The DATA statement puts initial fixed values into simple variables and arrays before execution of a program begins. For example, the statements below cause every value in B to be set to zero and A(1), A(2), and A(3) to be set to 1.0, 2.0, and 3.0, respectively.

```
DIMENSION A(3), B(2,4)
DATA A/1.0,2.0,3.0/, B/8*0./
```

The general form of the DATA statement is

DATA *list-1 of variable names/list-1 of values/*[, *list-2 of variable names/list-2 of values/* . . .]

A list of variable names may include simple variable names, unsubscripted array names, and subscripted array names, in which case the subscripts must be integer constants. A list of values may contain a repetition factor followed by an asterisk before any value to be used repeatedly. The values in both types of lists are separated by commas.

Use of a list of names, together with a repetition factor in the corresponding list of values, is particularly convenient when several variables must be initialized to similar values. For example, the DATA statement below puts zero into the three locations of A, the eight locations of B, and the single location C.

```
DIMENSION A(3), B(2,4)
DATA A,B,C/12*0./
```

With FORTRAN, when array elements are to be initialized, either all elements must be referred to by the array name, or single array elements must be referred to individually by subscripted variables. For example, storage is reserved for a ten-element array, and the second through eighth elements of the array are initialized to 5.0 as shown below.

```
REAL A(10)
DATA A(2),A(3),A(4),A(5),A(6),A(7),A(8)/7*5.0/
```

The values of the array elements that are not initialized are undefined. That is, they are not known (and cannot be assumed to be blank or zero) until the program itself has caused values to be placed in the reserved locations. The same is true of the values of any other uninitialized variables.

The WATFIV compiler allows a more flexible form for specifying array elements. With WATFIV, we can write

```
REAL A(10)
DATA (A(I),I=2,8)/7*5.0/
```

If we want to initialize only the odd-numbered subscripted variables, we write

```
REAL A(10)
DATA (A(I),I=1,10,2)/5*5.0/
```

The values 1, 10, and 2 are the start, end (i.e., maximum, not to be exceeded), and increment values, respectively. Because the DATA statement is acted upon before program execution, these values must be expressed as integer constants. If the increment is omitted, as in our first example, 1 is assumed. We might consider this notation a shorthand for a FORTRAN DO statement, about which you will learn in chapter 7. If you have need of this capability, you should refer to that chapter.

Data of different types may be assigned values within a single DATA statement, or even within a single pair of lists. You need only be careful that the entries in the value list match the entries in the variable list, and that the types correspond as you want them to. The following sequence is permissible.

```
REAL A(10), B
INTEGER I(9), J, K(3,4)
DATA A/10*0./,B,K/20.,12*5/
```

A number of DATA statements may appear in a program. Each DATA statement may appear anywhere following all statements that give types or dimensions to the variables named in the statement (and after COMMON or EQUIVALENCE statements, which are explained below). But even though DATA statements may appear at various points, you should remember that they are not executable statements. They give values only at the time that the compiler translates your program. Once program execution begins, a DATA statement can neither assign values nor restore values that have been altered.

```
K = I
I = 0
DATA I/5/
J = I
I = 6
```

When the statement K = I is first executed, I has the value 5 as given by the DATA statement, and that value is assigned to K. After all assignment statements have been executed, K, I, and J have the values 5, 6, and 0, respectively. The position of the DATA statement in relation to the assignment statements is not significant. Its effect is determined prior to execution of any statements in the program.

Variables of any of the data types described in chapter 2 can be initialized by DATA statements. See chapter 4 for the forms of constants of these data types.

REF

WARNING ABOUT DATA STATEMENT

Programmers may use DATA statements to give initial values to variables that they expect to change during program execution. Although this is a common practice, in large-scale computing environments it frequently causes problems. If an executing program is stopped and then restarted from the beginning, the variables whose values were set at compile-time are not reinitialized; any values that have been changed will remain as changed. For this reason, use of a DATA statement to set values that may be changed is generally bad programming practice and should be avoided.

An alternative approach is to include a subprogram at the beginning of the main program to initialize all of the data values in question. (See chapter 8.) This approach is called making a program serially reusable. Although it may appear to be more trouble than it is worth, it makes programs easier to debug. A serially reusable program can be restarted from the top and work correctly. Another advantage of this approach is flexibility; programs originally intended to run on only a single set of data at one execution can be changed to run on multiple data sets of the same kind. The technique of subprogram reinitialization of variables ensures that beginning values are reestablished as required.

EXECUTION-TIME DIMENSIONING

If an array is passed as an argument to a subprogram, the dimensions of the array need not be known in the subprogram until the subprogram is called. Other values passed as arguments in the calling sequence can be taken by the subprogram as the dimensions of the array. Flexibility—the capability of using a subprogram to perform operations on arrays of various sizes—is provided. The dimensions must be expressed as integer constants or integer variables of length 4. If a variable is used, it may appear in a COMMON statement as well as in the calling sequence. (See "The COMMON statement" in this chapter.) Only arrays named in a calling sequence can be dimensioned during execution of a FORTRAN program.

A portion of a subroutine to perform matrix multiplication is shown in figure 6.3. Because dimension values as well as array names are passed as arguments, the subroutine can operate on two-dimensional arrays of widely varying sizes.

```
SUBROUTINE MATMUL (A,B,C,I,J,K)
DIMENSION A(I,J), B(J,K), C(I,K)
     .
     .
     .

DO ...
   DO ...
     .
     .
     .

END
```

FIGURE 6.3

LAYOUT OF ARRAYS IN STORAGE

Array elements are placed in contiguous locations in storage; they follow one after another. With a one-dimensional array, the order is obvious. The first element of an array in storage is referred to by subscript 1; the last element in the array is referred to by the largest subscript used for the array. When positioning a higher-dimensional array in storage, there are two alternatives: The array can be stored either by going across a row and then starting at the next row, or by going down a column and then starting at the next column. FORTRAN uses the column approach. In order to store the elements of an array, FORTRAN varies the leftmost subscript first. After the leftmost subscript has been varied to its maximum value, it is returned to 1, and the next leftmost subscript is increased by 1. This resetting and increasing continues until the next leftmost subscript has reached its maximum. Then the leftmost and next leftmost are returned to 1, and the third leftmost (if any) is increased by 1. This same approach holds until all subscripts of the array have been varied (i.e., until all elements have been stored).

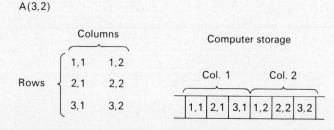

FIGURE 6.4

REF

Figure 6.4 deals with a two-dimensional array A(3,2). We can visualize the array as having three rows, two columns. Of course, each element of the array can be referred to by a subscripted variable containing two subscript values. We can say that column 1 contains A(1,1), A(2,1), and A(3,1); column 2 contains A(1,2), A(2,2), and A(3,2). As the right-hand portion of figure 6.4 indicates, the order that we just used in naming the elements (by column, or with the leftmost subscript varying most rapidly) is precisely the order in which they are laid out in storage.

A three-dimensional array B(2,2,2) contains eight elements as shown in figure 6.5. It is not convenient to visualize this array as having rows and columns, but, as before, the array elements are laid out in storage with the first element varying most rapidly, then the second, and, in this case, then the third.

B(2,2,2)

1,1,1	1,1,2
2,1,1	2,1,2
1,2,1	1,2,2
2,2,1	2,2,2

Computer storage

1,1,1	2,1,1	1,2,1	2,2,1	1,1,2	2,1,2	1,2,2	2,2,2

FIGURE 6.5

Once we understand this ordering, we realize several other things about the dimensioning of arrays. First, the number of elements in an array is just the product of its dimensions. For example, B(2,2,2) contains 2*2*2, or 8. Second, these elements are strung out in a line in computer memory. The computer accesses a particular element by means of a single number called an *address*. Therefore, when an element is referred to by multiple subscripts, the FORTRAN system must convert the reference to a single number which is the relative position of the element in the line of values.

Assume that a program contains the statement

A(I,J) = B(2,I,J)

In general, until program execution has begun and the variables I and J have been assigned values, their values are not known. Therefore, the positions of the elements of A and B referred to in this assignment statement cannot be calculated at the time the program is compiled. Instead, the compiler generates machine instructions to calculate the positions when they are needed (i.e., when the assignment statement is executed). And the positions are recalculated every time this statement is encountered during program execution.

In general, the greater the number of subscripts whose values must be calculated at program execution-time, the less efficient the program. Also, the

REF

more complex the calculation, the longer it takes. Use of higher-dimensional arrays tends to be less efficient than use of arrays having fewer dimensions. If the value of an expression is needed repeatedly as a subscript, it is often wise to calculate the value of the expression only once, then use the results of the expression evaluation as a subscript. (See figure 6.6.)

```
          .
          .
          .
       DO 25 I=1,1000
       AMT(I) = INVAL
       SUB = N * I
       STOCK(SUB) = STOCK(SUB) − OUT(SUB)
          .
          .
          .

25     CONTINUE
          .
          .
          .

       END
```

FIGURE 6.6

THE COMMON STATEMENT

The use of subroutine and function subprograms is explained in the tutorial section of chapter 8. We know that values listed as arguments in a calling sequence can be passed from one subprogram to another; in effect, they can be referred to by more than one subprogram. But this capability is somewhat limited. It is often valuable when using subprograms to store some data values where they can be referred to by any of a set of subroutines or functions.

All variables discussed up to this point except those passed as argument values have been *local variables*. A variable is said to be local when it cannot be referred to by any subprogram other than the one in which it is declared. There is a way of generating a pool of data items that can be referred to by multiple subprograms. This pool is declared by means of a *COMMON statement*. The COMMON statement contains the names of all variables in the pool. Each subprogram that includes the COMMON statement in its data declaration section can refer to the variables in the pool.

AN EXAMPLE

Assume that a main program uses three arrays: MILES, REPAIR, and COST. These represent a series of repairs made on engines, where MILES is the engine mileage, REPAIR is the repair type, and COST is to be computed by the program. Assume that there are several places in the main program at which we want to compute cost. Sometimes we want to compute a cost to be stored

REF

as the Kth element of the array COST (because K is the name of the integer we are using for a subscript at that point in the program); other times we want to compute cost for the Ith element. In either case, we use values from MILES and REPAIR in doing so.

It seems advisable to construct a subroutine to compute cost, passing the subscript value K or I as an argument. The subroutine must also have access to the arrays. However, it is not convenient (or necessary) to list the three array names as arguments in each call. Since the same arrays are used in every execution of the subroutine, a better approach is to place the arrays in a common storage area (COMMON) where they are available to both the main program and the subroutine. (See figure 6.7.) The statements to set up this sharing capability are suggested in figure 6.7 and shown as they appear in the subroutine CCOST and in the main program in figure 6.8.

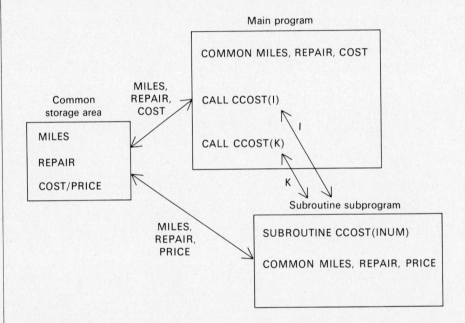

FIGURE 6.7

This example illustrates several properties of COMMON. Notice that the array referred to as COST in the main program is referred to as PRICE in the subroutine. Names referring to the same areas of common storage have to be in the same order in COMMON statements, but the names themselves may or may not be the same. The COMMON statement only allocates space. There is no reason why the space cannot be given different names in different program units, though each program unit must always use the names specified in its COMMON statement. In this case, then, the main program must always refer to the third array as COST, and the subroutine must always refer to it as PRICE.

REF

```
           ⎧ COMMON MILES, REPAIR, COST
           ⎪ DIMENSION MILES(100), REPAIR(100), COST(100)
           ⎪ .
           ⎪ .
           ⎪ .
  Main      ⎨ CALL CCOST (I)
  program   ⎪ .
           ⎪ .
           ⎪ .
           ⎪ CALL CCOST (K)
           ⎪ .
           ⎪ .
           ⎪ .
           ⎩ END
           ⎧ SUBROUTINE CCOST (INUM)
           ⎪ COMMON MILES, REPAIR, PRICE
           ⎪ DIMENSION MILES(100), REPAIR(100), PRICE(100)
  Subroutine⎨ .
  subprogram⎪ .
           ⎪ .
           ⎪ RETURN
           ⎩ END
```

FIGURE 6.8

   Why put the arrays in figures 6.7 and 6.8 in COMMON, but not INUM, the subscript pointing to the element for which cost is to be calculated? As we pointed out, the same arrays are used in every execution of the subroutine. But different variables are used by the main program to identify its value corresponding to INUM. If the subscript value were in COMMON, either it would always have to be identified by the same variable name, or the subroutine would have to know which variable to use. Neither approach would be convenient. Generally, we put into COMMON those variables that a set of routines use every time they are executed. We put in the calling sequence those variables that are appropriate for one execution of a subroutine but not for another. In the latter case, the subroutine makes the same computations, but on data represented by different variable names, and, hence, in different areas of storage. The values of variables in COMMON need not always be the same, but the same storage locations in COMMON are always referred to for a particular data item.

   In general, use of COMMON is more efficient than passing values. Since more information is known at the time a program is compiled (where the variables are, their sizes, and so on), more efficient machine-instruction sequences can be generated, and less memory is used.

   You should always draw a map of your common areas and the routines that refer to them, just as we have done in figure 6.7. This step should be part of the design process before you begin coding. In fact, COMMON can be used to isolate certain data from other parts of a program. This sometimes prevents accidental storage of data into the wrong data area or even into locations

REF

containing instructions of the program. It also conceptually keeps the data areas separate from the program, thus promoting clean design.

NAMED COMMON

Sometimes it is useful for certain subprograms to be able to communicate with one another through common areas that are not used by other subprograms. It may be desirable for a subprogram to share some data with one group of subprograms and other data with a different group of subprograms. To accomplish this, we must be able to declare more than one common area within a subprogram and to use the appropriate one for a certain interprogram communication. To declare separate common pools, the FORTRAN programmer gives a name to each pool. The name of a pool appears in the COMMON statement enclosed in slashes just preceding the list of names of variables in that pool. Each pool is a *named COMMON*.

COMMON /SUB1/A,B,C/TABLE/LIST,VAR

The statement sets up two separate common areas: SUB1 and TABLE. The former contains the variables A, B, and C; the latter, LIST and VAR.

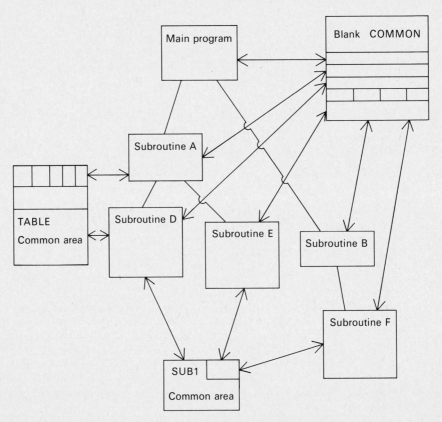

FIGURE 6.9

All program units have access to one common area. It is an unlabeled common area called *blank COMMON*. This common area was used in the program in figures 6.7 and 6.8. Figure 6.9 is a schematic showing the use of blank COMMON by all program units in a system and of two named COMMONs (SUB1 and TABLE) by groups of subroutine subprograms (three use the former, and two the latter).

Whether named COMMONs should be established depends on the information requirements of program units. Named COMMONs, or even just one unlabeled COMMON, can be used to define the data to be used by subprograms of a system. A wise programming practice is to let each subprogram refer to only the data it requires. This helps to keep modules independent of one another. (See discussions of modular program design in chapter 9.)

ADDITIONAL FEATURES AND RULES FOR COMMON

The programmer who uses common storage areas must be aware of certain programming considerations. These considerations are summarized below.

1   COMMON statements are cumulative within a subprogram. If you write two or more COMMON statements giving variables for the same common area, the variables are interpreted as a single list. Thus, the following sets of statements are equivalent.

        COMMON /TABLE/A,B,VAR
        COMMON MILES, COST

        COMMON /TABLE/A,B
        COMMON MILES, COST
        COMMON /TABLE/VAR

2   More than one common area may be referred to in one COMMON statement. Blank COMMON can be referred to at any point by leaving the name blank (i.e., by writing two consecutive slashes). The statement

        COMMON /TABLE/A,B // MILES, COST /TABLE/VAR

is equivalent to the sets of statements above. We should be aware of this capability, but we need not always use it. To maintain a modular approach, it is sometimes best not to include declarations for more than one common area in a single COMMON statement.

3   Remember that variables are placed in a common area in the order in which they are named in COMMON statements referring to the area. Variables that refer to the same space must appear in the same respective positions in COMMON statements. You cannot omit a name from within a list because all succeeding names would refer to different locations accordingly. You can omit unused names from the end of a list, but this doesn't save any storage space. The amount of space allocated for a common area is the largest amount necessary for any subprogram referring to the area. Omitting unused names at the end of a list is only a convenience for the programmer.

4   In using named COMMON, the name specified for an area must be the

REF

same in every subprogram referring to the area. The FORTRAN system uses the name to relate the declarations. Within the common area, variable names do not have to be the same, but using the same names is a good programming practice. It helps others to understand your program and may help you to understand it later. Some programmers attempt to minimize the likelihood of errors by duplicating COMMON statements in subprograms.

5 Arrays can be dimensioned in COMMON statements just as in type statements. That is, the dimensions for an array may be specified in either, but not both.

        COMMON A(100), B(34)

Dimensions specified in COMMON statements must be integer constants. Execution-time dimensioning such as can be achieved by means of arguments cannot be used in COMMON statements. Since the sizes of arrays must be known to establish not only the relative positions of arrays but also those of other variables, the dimensions of arrays must be fixed to provide this information.

6 The sizes and types of arrays and variables in common storage must match across subprograms. Otherwise the amount of space needed for values would differ, and references to variables, even if ordered properly, would not address the same storage. As noted earlier, it is wise to draw a map of each common area to be sure that you have an accurate understanding of where the values represented by your variables are.

7 On the IBM 360/370, different types of data require different amounts of storage. To ensure that variables are aligned on appropriate address boundaries, it is best to position variables requiring more storage first in a common area. Since a common area always begins on a doubleword boundary, this approach ensures that all variables are properly aligned. (See "Alignment on the IBM 360/370" in chapter 2.)

8 Variables appearing in a COMMON statement cannot be specified as dummy arguments in a subprogram. (See chapter 8.) Any attempt to do so would be giving the FORTRAN system contradictory information about the source of the data. However, a variable in a common area can be specified as an actual argument. That is, the main program or a subprogram can pass a variable listed in a COMMON statement to another subprogram. The first example below is invalid; the second is permissible.

        Invalid

        SUBROUTINE P (I,ARRAY)
        COMMON ARRAY
           .
           .
           .
        END

REF

Valid

```
SUBROUTINE V (I,ARRAY)
COMMON APAR
    .
    .
    .
CALL  W  (I,APAR)
END
```

9   It is bad practice to use common storage as a means of passing values to general subprograms. If the SQRT built-in function required that you make values available to it in a common area called SQRTC, you would have to write special instructions to do so. But SQRT isn't coded to require it. When coding your subprograms, write them as though they were to be widely used. Doing so will prove to be a convenience for you, the user.

THE EQUIVALENCE STATEMENT

It is sometimes valuable to design a FORTRAN program so that the same space in computer memory is used for several different simple variables or arrays. To do this, we must inform the FORTRAN compiler that several variables are to be mapped into the same area. We use an *EQUIVALENCE* statement such as the one shown below.

```
DIMENSION A(10,10), B(5,4), C(10), D(20,2,4)
EQUIVALENCE (A,B), (D,C)
```

The DIMENSION statement is used to declare the sizes of four arrays. The EQUIVALENCE statement causes the first twenty elements of A to occupy the same space as the twenty elements of B, and the ten elements of C to occupy the same space as the first ten elements of D. A simple storage map of the equivalencing is given in figure 6.10.

A | 1,1 | 2,1 | 3,1 | 4,1 | 5,1 | 6,1 |... ...1,2 2,2... ...100 elements

Same locations

B | 1,1 | 2,1 | 3,1 | 4,1 | 5,1 | 1,2 | 2,2... 20 elements

D | 1,1,1 | 2,1,1 | 3,1,1 | 4,1,1 ... ...160 elements

Same locations

C | 1 | 2 | 3 | 4 ... 10 elements

FIGURE 6.10

The variables in an EQUIVALENCE statement can be subscripted. This technique enables us to shift one array along another. For example, assuming

REF

again the DIMENSION statement above, the following storage sharing is permissible.

EQUIVALENCE (A(1,1), B(3,1))

This statement specifies that A(1,1) and B(3,1) are to share the same storage. It implies that A(2,1) and B(4,1) share the same storage, A(3,1) and B(5,1) share the same storage, and so on. (See figure 6.11.) The following statement achieves the same storage sharing.

EQUIVALENCE (A, B(3,1))

| A(1,1) | A(2,1) | ... A(9,1) | A(10,1) | A(1,2) | A(2,2) | ... A(8,2) | ... A(10,10) |

Same locations

| B(1,1) | B(2,1) | B(3,1) | B(4,1) | ... B(1,3) | B(2,3) | B(3,3) | B(4,3) | ... B(5,4) |

FIGURE 6.11

You can include as many names as you like in one list in an EQUIVALENCE statement. The simple variables C and D and the sixth element of array F share storage as a result of the statement below.

EQUIVALENCE (C,D,F(6))

Be sure to put parentheses around a complete list as well as around any subscripts that you specify.

Before using EQUIVALENCE statements, the programmer must understand how arrays are laid out in storage and how subscripts are varied in FORTRAN. Always draw at least a rough map of storage when you are equivalencing. It reveals obvious errors.

DIMENSION A(13,14), B(45), I(65)
REAL A, B
INTEGER I
EQUIVALENCE (A,B,I)

In this example, the total amount of space required for the arrays is the amount required for the largest array, which is A. A(1,1), B(1), and I(1) share the same storage. This is acceptable even though the arrays differ in type. The following sequence of statements is not acceptable.

I(4) = 6
A(4,1) = 7.2
J = I(4) + 8

Because of the EQUIVALENCE statement, I(4) and A(4,1) share the same storage. When the third statement is executed, that storage contains 7.2 in floating-point form. The computer tries to add 8 and this value as though it were an integer. An error occurs.

REF

As this example demonstrates, the FORTRAN programmer who uses EQUIVALENCE must be careful not to use a single area of storage for different purposes at the same time. Sometimes, resultant errors do not stop the machine but are reflected in incorrect output. This is one of the great dangers of equivalencing. You must know the flow of program execution as well as the exact manner in which information is stored in a particular machine when you use EQUIVALENCE. Notice also that you cannot make any assumptions about the relative locations of two variables declared in your program (unless they are in COMMON, as discussed below). For example, if you write

DIMENSION A(10,10), B(78)

you cannot be sure that B follows A in memory just because you have declared them that way. The location of B relative to A is compiler-dependent and computer-dependent. Elements of A are contiguous, and elements of B are contiguous, but where A is in relation to B is not determined by their order of appearance in the DIMENSION statement.

REASONS FOR EQUIVALENCING

The most common reason for equivalencing is that only a certain amount of computer storage is available for a program and the data on which it operates. When a program does not need all of its data at any one point in time, it is often wise to use storage for data required during the first part of execution, then reuse that storage for different data.

It is frequently convenient to read data into, or write data from, a block of storage under one name, even though there may be many distinct data items in the block, referred to by many variable names elsewhere in the program. Usually, we refer to the block of storage as an array, then equivalence simple variables or other arrays to selected portions of the array. We have shown several examples providing for such equivalencing in this chapter.

When equivalencing array elements, we must plan carefully. For example, assume that the matrix MONEY contains salary and taxes for 100 individuals for a single month. Further assume that we want to be able to refer to the elements representing salary as a unit under a separate name as well as to the matrix MONEY. If we use the DIMENSION statement below, there is no way to generate a single name, because the salaries are not contiguous in memory. (See figure 6.12.)

```
        DIMENSION MONEY(2,100)
C       MONEY(1,I) IS USED FOR SALARY
C       MONEY(2,I) IS USED FOR TAXES
```

In contrast, the following statements ensure that the data is positioned as required. The elements containing salary information are contiguous in storage, so we can refer to them as the array SALARY.

```
DIMENSION MONEY(100,2), SALARY(100), TAXES(100)
EQUIVALENCE (SALARY, MONEY(1,1)), (TAXES, MONEY(1,2))
```

REF

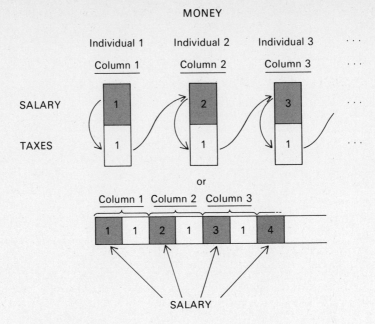

FIGURE 6.12

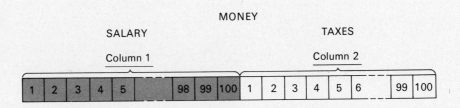

FIGURE 6.13

Sometimes a programmer likes to use (or accidentally uses) two names for the same data item. Equivalenced, they become synonyms. Such equivalencing may be misleading, however, and produce programs that are difficult to interpret at a later time.

ADDITIONAL RULES AND WARNINGS FOR EQUIVALENCE

The programmer who uses EQUIVALENCE statements must be aware of certain programming considerations. These considerations are summarized below.

1 The EQUIVALENCE statement is not executable; it must appear at the beginning of a program. You cannot cause two arrays stored in different

parts of the machine to suddenly come together at the time your program is executing just by inserting an EQUIVALENCE statement.

REF

2   Although the same name may appear in more than one list, you must not declare contradictions. For example, the following sequence is illegal.

```
DIMENSION A(10), B(10), C(10)
EQUIVALENCE (A(2),B), (B(2),C), (C(2),A)
```

A simple storage drawing will reveal that you cannot equivalence these array elements without bending straight lines.

3   The number of subscripts appearing for an array may be none (refers to the first element), the same as the number of dimensions in the DIMENSION or type statement (as is usual in array references), or one, which indicates the relative position of a selected element in its memory layout. For example, having declared an array A(5,5), we can write A and A(10) in an EQUIVALENCE statement to refer to A(1,1) and A(5,2), respectively.

4   Dummy arguments cannot appear in EQUIVALENCE statements.

5   On IBM 360/370 computers, different types of data take up different amounts of space in memory. This is also true of other machines. You must take such differences into account when you think about where one array is stored relative to another.

6   On IBM 360/370, certain types of variables must be on addresses that are divisible by 2, 4, or 8; that is, the data must be aligned properly. To avoid creating inefficient code, the variables requiring more storage should be listed first, and the shorter ones equivalenced to them. Do not equivalence a variable whose address must be divisible by 8 to a variable whose address need not be divisible by 8. While you can work around the rules in specific cases, programs containing such equivalences are more rigid, and it generally takes so long to figure out the tricky equivalences that the net advantage is questionable.

EQUIVALENCING VARIABLES IN COMMON

The EQUIVALENCE statement can be used for variables also appearing in COMMON statements. For example, the following sequence is permissible.

```
COMMON A, B, C
DIMENSION D(10)
EQUIVALENCE (A,D(1))
```

These statements cause the variables A, B, and C to be equivalenced to D(1), D(2), and D(3), respectively.

Note that one, but not both, of the variables appearing in the EQUIVALENCE statement above is in a common storage area. Two items, both of which are in a common storage area or even in different common storage areas, cannot be equivalenced. When we declare variables in COMMON, we tell the FORTRAN system something about where each variable is located. If we list the same variables in an EQUIVALENCE statement, we again tell the FORTRAN system how to position the variables. In general, such instructions conflict. Common areas are totally independent of each other, and we cannot relate them by equivalencing. The first two sequences below are not acceptable, but the third is valid.

Invalid
COMMON /TAB/A(100),B(47)
EQUIVALENCE (A,B)
.
.
.

Invalid
COMMON /TAB2/B
COMMON /TAB3/C
EQUIVALENCE (B,C)
.
.
.

Valid
COMMON /TAB/A(100),B(100)
DIMENSION C(200)
EQUIVALENCE (A,C)
.
.
.

An EQUIVALENCE statement can make a common area longer than it would be otherwise. For example, the following sequence extends the size of a common area as shown in figure 6.14. This is permissible.

COMMON A(10)
DIMENSION B(20)
EQUIVALENCE (A,B)

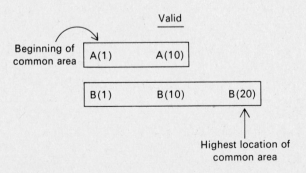

FIGURE 6.14

REF

But an EQUIVALENCE statement cannot change the starting point of a common area. We cannot extend a common area to locations preceding what would otherwise be its starting location. The following sequence, which attempts to equivalence variables as shown in figure 6.15, is invalid.

```
COMMON A(10), B(100)
DIMENSION C(40)
EQUIVALENCE (B,C(20))
```

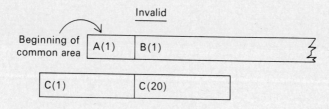

FIGURE 6.15

Different names can be given to the same space by means of COMMON statements in different subprograms, and this is, in effect, a way of equivalencing data of different sizes and types. However, this technique is machine-dependent and can lead to programming errors that are hard to find. It may be a good way of reusing space, but the first usage should be completed before the second usage is begun. You must know the sequence in which machine-language instructions of your program will be executed. This sequence is not necessarily indicated by the physical order of the statements in your program.

INITIAL DATA VALUES IN COMMON

WATFIV allows initial values to be specified for variables in common areas by means of DATA or type statements just as for variables in any other data areas (except for variables that are dummy arguments). Most FORTRAN systems do not allow this. Instead, variables in blank COMMON cannot be initialized, and a separate subprogram must be written to assign values to variables in a labeled COMMON. This subprogram, a *block data subprogram*, begins with a *BLOCK DATA statement* and ends with an END statement. It contains no executable statements and has no name because it is never called. Only the following statements are allowed:

```
BLOCK DATA
IMPLICIT
DIMENSION
REAL, INTEGER, LOGICAL, COMPLEX
COMMON
EQUIVALENCE
DATA
END
```

REF

From here on, the rules for declaration are the same as the usual rules. If the names of some variables in a common area appear in a block data subprogram, all variables in that common area must be declared so that the size of the common area can be determined correctly. However, not all variables need be initialized. If an IMPLICIT statement is specified, it must come before all other statements except the BLOCK DATA statement, as it does in the block data subprogram in figure 6.16.

```
BLOCK DATA
IMPLICIT INTEGER(B)
COMMON /C1/FILL(3)
DATA FILL/2*0.,1.5/
COMMON /C2/B(5)
DIMENSION A(30)
EQUIVALENCE (A,B)
DATA B/1,2,3,4,5/
END
```

FIGURE 6.16

QUEST

EXERCISES

1. (TUT) What is an array?

2. (TUT) What FORTRAN statements can be used to declare the characteristics of an array?

3. (TUT) What is the maximum number of elements that can be contained in each of the following arrays?
   a) DIMENSION A(30)
   b) REAL B(2,5)
   c) DIMENSION C(4,10,3)
   d) INTEGER I(1,10)

4. (TUT) Given the declarations
   DIMENSION A(5), B(4,5)
   INTEGER B, C
   REAL A, L, R
   a) Set all locations of A to zeros.
   b) Set the third element (as arranged in storage) of B to six.
   c) Set B(4,3) and C to one.
   d) Set B(4,1), B(4,2), and B(4,3) to twenty, assuming only capabilities available in FORTRAN.
   e) Repeat (d) above, but assume capabilities available with WATFIV.

5. (TUT) Write a declaration for ARR1, a two-dimensional array having six columns, two rows, to contain floating-point numbers.

6. (TUT) Write a statement to initialize the elements in the first column of ARR1 above to ones, those in the second row to twos, and so on.

7. (REF) Write DIMENSION statements to reserve space for data of ten years of corn yield, assuming 1/4-mile by 1/4-mile sections within a total

area that is 20 miles by 30 miles. Record yield (per section), rainfall (per section), fertilizer used on each section, a soil type, and topsoil thickness. Plan to refer to a section by specifying its relative mile location and its section number within the square mile. Assume that soil type and top-soil thickness do not change over time.

8. (REF) For the above problem, use additional DIMENSION and EQUIVA-LENCE statements to put all arrays over time into a one-dimensional array, those over space in another, and those over both in a third.

9. (REF) Use DATA statements to fill the above arrays. For the first year, store 4.5 for rainfall, 1.0 for all soil types, and zeros in the rest of the arrays.

10. (REF) Declare an array for the months of a calendar year and store the names of the months as initial values. You may assume WATFIV character declaration capabilities.

11. (REF) Write a formula for finding the location of a variable in a FORTRAN array, given the dimensions of the array.

§ 3.6   12. (REF) Assume that locations are counted in bytes and that each element of the array A requires four bytes. Use the formula that you derived in response to the preceding exercise to answer the following questions.
a)   If array element A(13) is in location 1451, in what location is element A(29)?
b)   If A(2,3) is in location 1756 and A(3,3) is in location 1760, where is A(4,4)?
c)   If A(1,1) is in location 245, A(3,4) is in location 262, and A(2,2) is in location 253, where is A(5,3)?
d)   If A(2,2) is in location 127, and A(7,5) is in location 144, where is A(6,6)?

13. (REF) Assume that a card is read into an array CARD, which is 20 words long (and that each word is four bytes in length, i.e., can hold four characters). Write DIMENSION and EQUIVALENCE statements to give the names L20, L21, L22, and L23 to the twentieth through twenty-third characters. Use logical variables of size 1 as names for characters.

14. (REF) Given the declarations
DIMENSION A(20,10), B(2)
REAL Z
LOGICAL L1, L2
Write DATA statements to do the following:
a)   Zero out A
b)   Set L1 to .TRUE. and L2 to .FALSE.
c)   Put the string A $\emptyset$ C $\emptyset$ D $\emptyset$ $\emptyset$ $\emptyset$ in B ($\emptyset$ means blank.)
d)   Put the hexadecimal pattern 10AF10EF in Z

PROGRAMMING PROBLEMS

§ 3.6   1. (REF) The array A(I) contains N elements, I=1, . . . , N. Write a program to find the values of the largest and smallest elements in the array.

§ 3.6   2. (REF) Modify the program that you wrote in response to 1 above to also find the indexes of the smallest and largest elements, that is, to find a J and K such that A(J) is the smallest element and A(K) is the largest element.

§ 3.6   3.   (REF) The array VALUE(I) contains M elements. Write a program to find the number of elements less than the average value of all elements and the number of elements greater than that average.

§ 5.1   4.   (REF) Write a program to read in N cards, each containing two numbers A(I) and B(I), I=1, ... , N, in that order. Then compute the means

$$AX = \frac{1}{N} \sum_{I=1}^{N} A(I) \quad \text{and} \quad BX = \frac{1}{N} \sum_{I=1}^{N} B(I)$$

Finally, compute and print the *correlation*

$$C = \frac{1}{N} \sum_{I=1}^{N} (A(I) - AX) \times (B(I) - BX)$$

INTRO One of the ways computers can out-perform people is in the repetitive execution of identical tasks. We use this ability by directing it to use the same set of instructions over and over on different sets of data. To do this, there must be methods for controlling which sets of instructions are executed, how many times they are executed, and what data is used for each execution. The process of repeating a set of instructions is called *looping*. Executing other than the next instruction in sequence is called *branching*. The GO TO, IF, and DO statements can be used to control these processes. Various forms of these statements are introduced in this chapter and applied in problem solving.

TUT **THE GO TO STATEMENT** Recall the first complete program that we discussed—the program to read two values and print them. (See chapter 1.) It is not likely that we would write a program to read and print values from only one card, but we might if we had several cards to process.

```
REAL A, B
READ, A, B
PRINT, A, B
READ, A, B
PRINT, A, B
STOP
END
```

FIGURE 7.1

If we had only two cards, we could write the program shown in figure 7.1. A pair of READ and PRINT statements is included for each card. Obviously, this approach would become very tedious and time-consuming if we had a hundred, a thousand, or several thousand cards. We need some way of giving the computer a set of statements to execute and some additional statement or statements that instruct the computer to execute those statements repeatedly.

Chapter

7

Flow of Control

Normally, in FORTRAN, statements are executed sequentially. The order in which they are placed in storage determines the order in which they are executed. The simplest deviation from this routine is to tell the computer to go to a statement other than the one immediately following the current one and to execute that statement next. To do this, we must have (1) a way of telling the computer that a change in sequence is wanted, and (2) a way of naming the statement to be executed next. For the first of these, we use the *GO TO statement*; for the second, a *statement label.*

Assume that we have many cards, each of which contains three values; we want the computer to execute READ and PRINT statements over and over until all cards have been processed. A program directing the computer to do so is shown in figure 7.2.

```
        REAL A, B, C
10      READ, A, B, C
        PRINT, A, B, C
        GO TO 10
        END
```

FIGURE 7.2

Here, the statement label 10 appears before READ in the READ statement. When the GO TO 10 statement is executed, the computer branches back to the READ statement, and execution continues from there. The READ-PRINT-GO TO loop is executed repeatedly until there are no more cards to process. Notice that the program does not include a STOP statement. At this point in our study of FORTRAN, we have no way of telling the computer when to stop reading cards. In most computer systems, a program is stopped automatically if it tries to read another card after all cards have been read. We assume that this method of termination applies in this program.

The GO TO statement in this program could have been written as GOTO 10. The compiler interprets either GO TO or GOTO correctly. A statement label must be an unsigned nonzero integer constant. It may appear anywhere in columns 1 through 5 of the coding line, with blanks on either side if necessary, but no blanks can appear within it. Leading zeros are ignored. Hence the following statements are equivalent:

```
10      READ, A
 10     READ, A
010     READ, A
```

Since labels of FORTRAN statements must be numbers, we use the terms *statement label* and *statement number* interchangeably.

Statement numbers do not have to be specified in ascending numerical order. For example, a statement identified by statement label 85 may appear before a statement identified by statement label 10 on the source-program listing and may be executed before that statement when the program is run on the computer. Nonexecutable statements such as DIMENSION and DATA cannot have labels. This is reasonable, because the computer never needs to branch to one of these statements during program execution anyway.

THE COMPUTED GO TO STATEMENT

Whenever a GO TO statement is executed, control is transferred to the statement identified in the GO TO statement. Because this transfer always occurs, we say that the GO TO statement causes an *unconditional branch*. The form of the GO TO statement discussed above is sometimes called the *unconditional GO TO*. FORTRAN provides a degree of flexibility in this unconditional branching capability by means of other forms of the GO TO statement. Either of the forms permits variation in determining the destination of the unconditional branch (i.e., the statement to be executed next).

Assume that we must write a program to compute either the sum, product, or quotient of pairs of numbers provided as card input. For each pair, we need some way of knowing which operation to perform. A likely approach is to require that each card contain a third number, indicating which of the three operations is to be performed on the two preceding numbers on the card. We establish a code value for each operation and say that the third number on a card must be one of the code values.

1   MULTIPLY
2   ADD
3   DIVIDE

Having done this, we still have the problem of interpreting the code— of deciding which part of our program should be executed for each input card. The *computed GO TO statement* does this well. Given an integer, the statement picks a label out of a list accordingly. We write our program so that statement 101 begins the multiply section of code, 201 begins the add section, and 301 begins the divide section. (See figure 7.3.) The computed GO TO statement determines whether the third number on an input card is 1, 2, or 3 and causes a branch accordingly.

```
10      READ, A, B, I
        GO TO (101,201,301), I
101     C = A * B
        GO TO 1000
201     C = A + B
        GO TO 1000
301     C = A / B
1000    PRINT, C
        GO TO 10
        END
```

FIGURE 7.3

The computed GO TO statement has the form

GO TO (s1,s2,s3, . . .), i

where s1,s2,s3, . . . are statement labels and i is an integer variable. The values assigned to i may range from 1 through the total number of statement labels included in the GO TO statement. Control goes to the statement in the *ith* position. If the value of the integer variable is 3 at the time the GO TO statement is executed, the program branches to the third statement label in GO TO.

The computed GO TO is useful when choosing a statement to execute from among a set of alternatives. Since it always causes a transfer of control (albeit, to a variable point), it is a form of unconditional branch.

THE ASSIGNED GO TO STATEMENT

The *assigned GO TO statement* is similar to the computed GO TO. In this case, however, instead of specifying an integer that points to a statement label in a list, the statement label itself is assigned to the variable by execution of a statement elsewhere in the program.

GO TO ILABEL, (30,40,1,3)

When this assigned GO TO statement is executed, it causes control to go to the statement identified by the label that was last assigned to the integer variable ILABEL. The label must be one of the labels specified in the list of the assigned GO TO: 30, 40, 1, or 3. An error occurs if one of these labels has not been assigned to the integer variable before the GO TO is executed.

The general form of the assigned GO TO statement is

GO TO i, (s1,s2,s3, . . .)

where i is an integer variable and s1,s2,s3, . . . are statement labels. The specified statement labels are the permissible values for i.

THE ASSIGN STATEMENT

To assign a statement label to an integer variable, we use the *ASSIGN statement*. Several of these statements may be included in a program. For example,

ASSIGN 40 TO ILABEL

may appear several times in the program that contains the assigned GO TO statement above. Also possible are

ASSIGN 30 TO ILABEL
ASSIGN 1 TO ILABEL
ASSIGN 3 TO ILABEL

The general form of this statement is

ASSIGN s1 TO i

where s1 is any statement label appearing in an assigned GO TO statement in which the integer variable i is specified.

The ASSIGN statement is executed independently of the assigned GO TO statement. Figure 7.4 shows how we might use our statements above in a program that branches to statement 100 from a number of points, then returns control to the statement following the branch point by means of an assigned GO TO.

```
            .
            .
            .
        ASSIGN 3 TO ILABEL
        GO TO 100
3       SUM = 0.
            .
            .
        ASSIGN 40 TO ILABEL
        GO TO 100
40          .
            .
            .
100     PRINT, A, B, C
            .
            .
        GO TO ILABEL, (30,40,1,3)
            .
            .
        END
```

FIGURE 7.4

The ASSIGN statement must be used to assign statement labels to an integer variable named in an assigned GO TO statement. You cannot use an arithmetic assignment statement such as we learned about in chapter 5.

THE ARITHMETIC IF STATEMENT

Assume that we must write a program to read two values from an input line, then divide the first by the second. If our program attempts to divide when the second value is zero, an error will occur. On most systems, the program will be stopped. To prevent this, we can take some special action or print an error message rather than attempt to divide by zero. To do so, we need a statement that causes a branch away from the statement that performs division whenever the value of the divisor is zero. We can use the *arithmetic IF statement* as shown in figure 7.5.

This program reads input values into A, which is potentially the dividend, and B, which is potentially the divisor. Then the arithmetic IF statement is executed. If B is negative, control goes to the first label; if B is zero, control goes to the second; if B is positive, control goes to the third. Thus, if B is zero, a branch is made to statement 200, avoiding the division operation.

```
1       READ, A, B
        IF (B) 100,200,100
100     C = A / B
        PRINT, C
        GO TO 1
200     PRINT, 'CANNOT DIVIDE BY ZERO'
        GO TO 1
        END
```

FIGURE 7.5

The general form of the arithmetic IF statement is

IF (*arithmetic expression*) *s1,s2,s3*

where any *arithmetic expression* can be used, and *s1*, *s2*, and *s3* are labels of statements in the program. The IF statement causes a branch to one of these statements, depending on whether the current value of the arithmetic expression is negative, zero, or positive, respectively. It is another means of setting up an unconditional branch.

THE LOGICAL IF STATEMENT

Let us suppose that we are once again reading cards, each of which contains three values. In this program, we are not only to print the values but also to add the first values recorded on the cards and print the result after all cards have been processed. To do so, we must be able to tell when we have read the last card. We can't just let the computer system detect when we try to read beyond the last card and terminate our program automatically. Although this approach is acceptable in some cases, it is not acceptable in this situation because certain processing steps within the program must be performed after end of file has been encountered.

A common approach in this kind of situation is to establish the convention that the last card will contain a certain dummy value, say, all 9s, as input for a particular variable. We must also ensure that no other card in the deck will

```
        INTEGER SUM, A, B, C
        SUM = 0
3       READ, A, B, C
        IF (A −9999) 1,2,1
1       PRINT, A, B, C
        SUM = SUM + A
        GO TO 3
2       PRINT, SUM
        STOP
        END
```

FIGURE 7.6

contain the dummy value as a normal data item for the same variable. Then
we can check for the dummy value and, when we encounter it, assume that
we have processed all cards. Let us suppose that 9999 has been established
as a dummy value for A. The program is shown in figure 7.6. The logic of our
program is shown in the flowchart in figure 7.7.

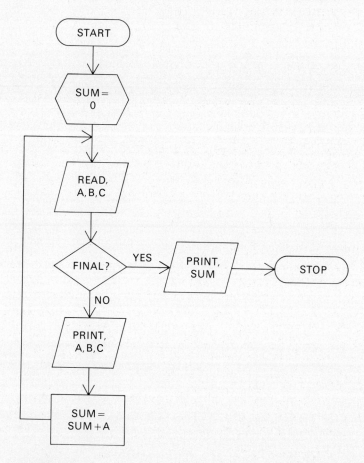

FIGURE 7.7

Notice that an arithmetic IF statement is used to find out if A has the
value 9999. Since the expression in the arithmetic IF statement must be an
arithmetic expression, we subtract 9999 from A, and branch, dependent on
whether the result is less than zero, equal to zero (the last card), or greater
than zero accordingly.

What we really want to know is whether A is equal to 9999. Another form
of IF statement, called the *logical IF statement*, permits us to express our

branch condition in a more straightforward manner. Use of the logical IF statement is shown in figure 7.8.

```
      INTEGER SUM, A, B, C
      SUM = 0
3     READ, A, B, C
      IF (A.EQ.9999) GO TO 2
      PRINT, A, B, C
      SUM = SUM + A
      GO TO 3
2     PRINT, SUM
      STOP
      END
```

FIGURE 7.8

In most cases when making a test for branching, we are really trying to select between two alternatives. For example, in figure 7.7, we probably knew that A would never be greater than 9999. We wanted to know whether A was less than 9999 or equal to it. The case A-9999 greater than zero could never occur, but, when using the arithmetic IF, we had to provide explicitly for this case anyway.

Further, in selecting from among two alternatives, it is often the case that either we want to branch or we do not. If we do want to branch, there is often only one special action (one additional statement) that must be executed. We don't need to execute a complete, different routine. Notice that two of the branch points in the arithmetic IF statement in figure 7.7 are just the next statement in sequence. To code the arithmetic IF statement correctly, we must specify three branch points. But, here, if we did not have to specify each branch, we could just let statement 1 be executed as next in sequence in these cases.

Finally, it is often easier to express a condition in terms such as "if a equals b" (rather than "if a − b is less than, equal to, or greater than zero") or "if b is less than 4" (rather than "if b − 4 is less than, equal to, or greater than zero"). The logical IF statement provides these capabilities.

The general form of the logical IF statement is

IF (*logical expression*) *single statement*

where *logical expression* is any valid logical expression, examples of which we have been discussing, and *single statement* is any valid executable statement except a DO statement (explained below) or another IF statement. If the logical expression is true, control passes to the single statement, which is then executed. If the logical expression is false, the next instruction in sequence is executed instead. Since control may or may not be transferred to the single statement, the logical IF statement is a *conditional branch*.

Other examples of logical IF statements are

```
IF  (A.GT.B)  GO  TO  200
IF  (I.NE.4)  SUM = SUM + ARR(4)
```

If the logical expression in the first IF statement is true, control passes to statement 200. If the logical expression in the second is true, the assignment statement is executed. Then normal sequential execution resumes with the statement following the logical IF.

RELATIONAL OPERATORS

The symbols .GT. and .NE. in the IF statements above are relational operators, the FORTRAN abbreviations for the English phrases "greater than" and "not equal to." FORTRAN has a set of relational operators, just as it has a set of arithmetic operators. They are listed and explained in figure 7.9.

Relational operator	Meaning	Mathematical equivalent
.GT.	greater than	$>$
.GE.	greater than or equal to	$> =$, or $\geq$
.EQ.	equal to	$=$
.NE.	not equal to	$\neg =$, or $\neq$
.LT.	less than	$<$
.LE.	less than or equal to	$< =$, or $\leq$

FIGURE 7.9

To form a simple logical expression like those above, we write an arithmetic expression, a relational operator, and another arithmetic expression. The arithmetic expression may be an integer constant or variable, or a real constant or variable. It may also be a more complicated expression involving subscripted variables, arithmetic operators, functions, or a combination thereof, that yields an integer or real result. Examples are

```
A*4.GT.B
I.NE.J
R.LE.SQRT(V)
```

At any time, each of these logical expressions has either of two values: .TRUE. or .FALSE. The first asserts that the current value of A multiplied by four is greater than the current value of B. Either this assertion is true, or it is not. As noted previously, when such an expression appears in a logical IF statement, the computer branches or fails to branch accordingly.

Further discussion of logical expressions and of their use in logical IF and logical assignment statements is given in the tutorial section of chapter 11.

SUBSCRIPTING AND LOOPING

Assume that we have read in twelve values for monthly rainfall and we want to calculate an average rainfall amount for the year. We could write an arithmetic expression summing all the values and then divide, but that would be very tiresome. A question that presents itself is "Can we use the IF statement to simplify our programming task?"

Assume that the rainfall values are in array RAINF, declared by the statement

DIMENSION RAINF(12)

Remember that we can use either variables or constants as subscript values. If we can control the execution sequence, we can set a subscript, say, I of RAINF(I) to 1, add the corresponding value from RAINF to a variable called SUM, increase the subscript by 1, add the next value from RAINF, and so on. We can repeat this process until all values in RAINF have been summed. Each time a different value from RAINF is added because the value of the subscript I is different. Clearly we want to stop after twelve times. One way to set up the program logic is shown in figure 7.10.

After reading the input into array RAINF, we set I to 1 and SUM to 0. Then we add RAINF(1) to SUM, increase I to 2, and test the value of I. Since we want to go completely through the loop 12 times, and we increase the value of I before we test it, we must check for I equal to 13.

This kind of thinking occurs constantly in programming. You must count the number of times you want to do something and make sure that you test for the correct value. The easiest way to determine the correct value is to say to yourself "What if I only wanted to go through the loop once? What would the value of I be at the point where I make the test?" Then you must consider how that value of I compares with the number of times you want to go through.

Here I had an initial value of 1 and we added 1 to it before testing. Therefore, after one execution of the loop, I had the value 2. If we had only wanted to go through the loop once, that would have been one greater than the number of times we wanted to go through. Since we wanted to go through twelve times, we checked for 13, which is one greater than 12. If we had tested I before adding 1 to it, we would have had to check to see whether I had the value 12.

There are several ways that we can use IF statements for loop control. We must learn to choose the way that is appropriate for a particular programming situation. Sometimes we want to test before we add, sometimes after. Sometimes we use the arithmetic IF to determine whether a difference is negative, zero, or positive. Sometimes we use the logical IF to check for equal, sometimes for less than, and sometimes for greater than. The programs shown in figures 7.11 through 7.13 are equivalent. The first corresponds to the flowchart given in figure 7.10. You should understand all of them and why they all do the same thing. They are worth extensive study because loop control is a fundamental process of programming.

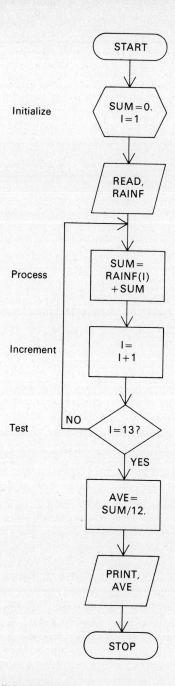

FIGURE 7.10

THE SIMPLE DO STATEMENT

A need for the logic shown in figures 7.11 through 7.13, where we execute a loop a certain number of times and vary the value of an integer used as a loop control, occurs throughout FORTRAN programming. It is so common that a special statement has been included in the language to combine the processes of setting an integer to a starting value (1 or 0 in the above examples), adding a value to it each time through a loop (1 in the above examples), and testing the integer to see whether the loop has been executed the required number of times. When this statement, called the *DO statement*, is used, the FORTRAN

```
          DIMENSION RAINF(12)
          SUM = 0.
          I = 1
          READ, RAINF
1         SUM = RAINF(I) + SUM
          I = I + 1
          IF (I−13) 1,2,2
C         I−13 WILL NEVER BE GREATER THAN 0, BECAUSE WE
C         BRANCH OUT OF THE LOOP WHEN I=13.  THEREFORE,
C         THE POSITIVE RESULT IS IMPOSSIBLE.  WE IGNORE IT.
2         AVE = SUM / 12.
          PRINT, AVE
          STOP
          END
```

FIGURE 7.11

```
          DIMENSION RAINF(12)
          SUM = 0.
          I = 1
          READ, RAINF
C         NOW WE TEST BEFORE ADDING 1 TO I.
1         SUM = RAINF(I) + SUM
          IF (I−12) 2,3,3
C         AGAIN THE POSITIVE RESULT IS IMPOSSIBLE.
2         I = I + 1
          GO TO 1
3         AVE = SUM / 12.
          PRINT, AVE
          STOP
          END
```

FIGURE 7.12

```
          DIMENSION RAINF(12)
          SUM = 0.
          I = 0
          READ, RAINF
     C    NOW WE ADD 1 TO I BEFORE READING OR TESTING.
     1    I = I + 1
          SUM = RAINF(I) + SUM
          IF (12−I) 2,2,1
     C    HERE THE NEGATIVE RESULT IS IMPOSSIBLE.
     2    AVE = SUM / 12.
          PRINT, AVE
          STOP
          END
```

FIGURE 7.13

compiler sets up the program to do the initialize, increment, and test steps automatically, just as you would if you used assignment and IF statements.

To use the DO statement, you must give the compiler several pieces of information. You must identify the integer (index variable) that is to be used as a loop control and specify its start and end values. You may also specify an increment value. If you do not, 1 is assumed. You must identify the last statement in the loop by assigning a label to the statement and writing that label immediately following the keyword DO in the DO statement as well. We consider the most common case where the start value of the index variable is 1, the increment is 1 (and, hence, need not be stated), and the end value is an integer constant. The form of the DO statement providing for this case is

DO *statement-label index-variable* = 1,*integer-constant*

We rewrite the program shown in figure 7.11 so that it appears as shown in figure 7.14. Three statements are effectively replaced by one. Use of the DO statement is infinitely simpler than doing the initializing, adding, and testing ourselves. We need only specify the first and last values of the index variable. The FORTRAN compiler sets up the correct steps in our program.

```
          DIMENSION RAINF(12)
          SUM = 0.
          READ, RAINF
          DO 100 I=1,12
    100   SUM = RAINF(I) + SUM
          AVE = SUM / 12.
          PRINT, AVE
          STOP
          END
```

FIGURE 7.14

You should be aware that the FORTRAN compiler always sets up the initializing, adding, and testing steps in that order. That is, the steps corresponding to a DO statement are always as shown in figure 7.11. The DO statement in its more general form is considered in the reference section of this chapter. Some of the pitfalls to avoid when using DO statements are pointed out. Also explained is the use of nested DOs.

THE CONTINUE STATEMENT

Sometimes it is handy to have a way of marking a place in a program without actually including a regular FORTRAN statement there. This is the function of the *CONTINUE statement*. The following DO loops are equivalent. The CONTINUE statement merely marks the end of the DO loop.

```
        DO 100 I=1,30
        NUM = NUM + 5
100     SUM = SUM + ARR(I)

        DO 100 I=1,30
        NUM = NUM + 5
        SUM = SUM + ARR(I)
100     CONTINUE
```

Although not particularly significant in this example, except perhaps for documentational purposes, there are cases where CONTINUE is required. An example is shown in figure 7.15.

```
        .
        .
        DO 100 I=1,30
        .
        .
50      NUM = NUM + 5
        IF (SUM−LIMIT) 20,100,100
20      SUM = SUM + ARR(I)
        .
        .
        GO TO 50
100     CONTINUE
        .
        END
```

FIGURE 7.15

The CONTINUE statement in figure 7.15 is used as the last statement in the DO loop to avoid ending the loop with a GO TO statement. When using

FORTRAN as implemented for IBM 360/370, the last statement in a DO loop cannot be a DO, RETURN, STOP, PAUSE, GO TO, arithmetic IF statement, or logical IF statement containing any of these forms. (RETURN is explained in the tutorial section of chapter 8. The other statements mentioned here are explained in this chapter.) Certain WATFIV implementations differ slightly in that they allow a logical IF containing any statement other than DO to be specified. As in figure 7.15, these restrictions sometimes force use of a CONTINUE statement as a placeholder, or branch destination. A CONTINUE statement may be branched to or referenced by any IF, GO TO, or DO statement.

THE GENERAL DO

REF

In creating loops in a program, it is frequently desirable that the limiting value for the index variable be an integer variable rather than a constant, or that its starting value be other than 1. Sometimes the value added to the index variable should be expressed as an integer variable or as an integer constant other than 1. The general form of the DO statement allows these variations.

DO *statement-label index-variable* = *start,end,increment*

Here *start*, *end*, and *increment* can be integer variables or constants. They are 4, 98, and the current value of the integer variable L, respectively, in figure 7.16.

```
      DIMENSION SKIP(100)
      INTEGER I, K, L, SUM
      SUM = 0
      L = 1
      READ K, SKIP
      IF (K.GT.4) L = 2
      DO 200 I=4,98,L
      SUM = SUM + SKIP(I)
  200 CONTINUE
      PRINT, SUM
      STOP
      END
```

FIGURE 7.16

The DO loop in figure 7.16 causes every value, or every other value, from the fourth through the ninety-eighth values of the array SKIP, to be added to SUM, depending on whether the input value for K is less than or equal to 4, or greater than 4, respectively. The statements that physically follow the DO statement, up to and including the statement whose number is specified in the DO statement (200, in figure 7.16) are called the *range of the DO*.

Sometimes the value computed for the DO-loop index variable never equals the end value specified for the variable. In this case, the loop is executed as long as the value of the index variable is less than the end value. When the

REF

value of the index variable exceeds the end value, the loop is exited. For example, the DO loop in figure 7.17 is executed four times, with the index variable I having values of 2, 5, 8, and 11.

```
            .
            .
            .
      DO  78  I=2,12,3
            .
            .
            .
 78    CONTINUE
            .
            .
      END
```

FIGURE 7.17

A DO loop is always executed at least once, even if the start value of the index variable exceeds its specified end value. The FORTRAN compiler sets up the test of the value of the index variable at the bottom of the loop, so the statements between the DO and the test are executed once before the test is made. Executing a DO loop once when the loop should have been skipped is a common source of error in FORTRAN programming. It leads to problems such as referring to variables that have not been assigned values, dividing by zero, and the like. You must learn to anticipate these potential error situations and include statements to prevent them from occurring during execution of your programs.

SOME PROGRAMMING GUIDELINES

Important points to remember when using DO statements are given below.

1 The increment and end values specified in a DO statement must be un-signed integer constants or integer variables whose current values are positive. You cannot specify values to cause the index variable to be decreased rather than increased.

2 You must not change the values of any of the variables specified in a DO statement within the range of the DO. For example, statement 300 and the two succeeding statements in figure 7.18 are invalid.

```
      DIMENSION  MEAS(100)
            .
            .
            .
      DO  100  I=1,K,INC
      IF  (I−3)  200,300,200
 300   I = I + 1
```

REF

```
        K = K + 1
        INC = INC − 1
200     SUM = SUM + MEAS(I)
100     CONTINUE
            .
            .
            .
        END
```

FIGURE 7.18

3   The final statement of the DO loop must physically follow the DO statement. You cannot DO backward to an earlier statement.

4   In most FORTRAN systems, the value of the index variable is not known outside the DO loop. After the loop is executed the required number of times, you cannot assume that the index variable has the final loop value, or the final value plus the increment. The actual value varies from system to system. Because this is a compiler implementation feature, it is not safe to use the index variable in this situation if the program is expected to produce the same results on different computer systems.

5   You can branch to a statement outside the range of a DO before the DO loop has been executed the number of times determined by the start, end, and increment values in the DO statement. In this case, the value of the index variable is the value it had just before the branch.

6   You cannot branch into the range of a DO. The DO statement itself initializes the index variable, so if you branch into the loop, the beginning value of the variable is not set as required.

NESTED DO

It is possible, and permissible, that one DO statement appears within the range of another. When using DO statements in this manner, you need follow only one additional programming guideline: All statements within the range of the inner DO must be in the range of an outer DO. DO loops satisfying this rule are called *nested DOs*.

```
        DO  100  I=1,4                                        ⎫
        A(I) = B(I) * B(I)                                    ⎬ Range of
        DO  100  J=1,5            ⎫ Range of                  ⎭ outer DO
100     C(J+1) = A(I) * 5         ⎭ inner DO
```

FIGURE 7.19

An example of valid usage of nested DOs is given in figure 7.19. The outer DO loop is executed four times, causing the squared values of B(1), B(2), B(3), and B(4) to be stored in A(1), A(2), A(3), and A(4). The inner DO loop is

REF

executed five times for each execution of the outer loop. Its first set of executions is equivalent to the following sequence of statements:

$$C(1+1) = A(1) * 5$$
$$C(2+1) = A(1) * 5$$
$$C(3+1) = A(1) * 5$$
$$C(4+1) = A(1) * 5$$
$$C(5+1) = A(1) * 5$$

Similar assignments of $A(2) * 5$, $A(3) * 5$, and $A(4) * 5$ are made during the second, third, and fourth executions of the outer loop (executions 6–10, 11–15, and 16–20 of the inner loop). When the nested DOs are completed, four assignments will have been made to elements of A, and 4×5, or 20, will have been made to elements of C.

As figure 7.19 indicates, nested DOs may end with the same statement. Since the last statement in a DO loop is within the range of any DO statement in which it is named, a nested DO that ends with the same statement as an outer DO is within the range of that outer DO.

The depth to which DO loops may be nested is system-dependent. In most FORTRAN systems, from a practical viewpoint if not in actuality, they may be nested to any level. There is sometimes a limit on smaller machines, but this limit usually far exceeds normal programming requirements.

It is wise to use a separate CONTINUE statement as the final statement for each DO loop in a complex nest of DOs, even when one would suffice. The logic of the program is easier to follow and easier to change. Programming errors are less apt to occur. When a single CONTINUE statement is used, it is within the range of every DO, including the innermost DO. Any branch to that statement from outside the innermost DO loop is a branch into the inner DO from outside its range. The branch to statement 100 in figure 7.20 is not acceptable because the CONTINUE statement is in the range of the inner DO, but the arithmetic IF statement is not.

```
          .
          .
          .

       DO  100  I=1,6
       IF  (TOT−3000.)  300,300,100
       DO  100  J=1,10
          .
          .
          .

100    CONTINUE
          .
          .
          .

       END
```

FIGURE 7.20

REF

Valid branches are shown at the left in figure 7.21, but those at the right are invalid.

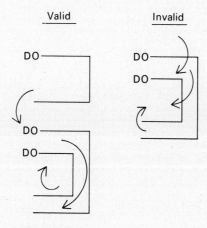

FIGURE 7.21

The need for nested DOs is perhaps most apt to occur when using higher-dimensional arrays. For example, to set each element of a 20 × 35 array X to zero, we can write the statements below.

```
        DIMENSION  X(20,35)
        DO  100  I=1,20
        DO  100  J=1,35
  100   X(I,J) = 0.
```

For each row of X (i.e., for each value of I), the computer performs 35 instructions, zeroing out the elements in that row.

As another example, assume that we declare a two-dimensional array RAINF to hold rainfall amounts for 12 months for each of 23 regions. (See

```
        DIMENSION  RAINF(12,23)
        READ,  RAINF
        SUM = 0.
        DO  100  I=1,12
        DO  100  J=1,23
  100   SUM = SUM + RAINF(I,J)
        AVE = SUM / (12.*23.)
        PRINT, AVE
        STOP
        END
```

FIGURE 7.22

REF

figure 7.22.) We want to calculate an average amount. We declare an array in which each row represents one month and has 23 entries, one for each region. We set SUM to an initial value of zero. Then we sum the values in the first row and add their total to SUM, sum the values in the second row and add their total to SUM, and so on, until the values in all rows have been added to SUM. Then we divide SUM by the number of values added to determine the average, print that average, and stop.

THE PAUSE STATEMENT

Look again (in the discussion above) at the list of statements that cannot be used as the last statement in the range of a DO. All of these statements can be classified as control statements; they govern the flow of program execution.

The control function of the *PAUSE statement* is to cause execution of a program to be halted temporarily. PAUSE 00000, PAUSE n where n is a string of up to five digits, or PAUSE '*message*' where '*message*' is a literal constant is printed on the computer system console, depending on which of the following forms of the PAUSE statement is encountered.

        PAUSE
        PAUSE n
        PAUSE '*message*'

A typical use of the PAUSE statement is to suspend processing for positioning or changing of paper prior to printing of output, or for mounting magnetic tape reels during a run. Although such usage is convenient, the PAUSE statement is not implemented in some systems because of its potential nuisance value. A sequence of important jobs cannot be interrupted at will; generally, time is too valuable, for there is much work to be done.

Examples of PAUSE statements of the forms above are

        PAUSE
        PAUSE 140
        PAUSE 'CHANGE PRINTER FORMS'

THE STOP STATEMENT

The STOP statement appears in numerous programs in this text. It causes program execution to be terminated, thus freeing the computer to work on subsequent jobs. In some installations, two forms of STOP are available:

        STOP
        STOP n

In the second form, n is an integer of up to five digits in length, printed on the computer system console just prior to program termination. Since any number of STOP statements can be included in a program, this integer serves as an indication of which STOP statement terminated execution. As noted for PAUSE, this form of the STOP statement is not implemented in some systems. WATFOR and WATFIV treat either form as STOP. Usually, STOP is a means of returning control from an application program to the operating system controlling overall system operation.

REF

EXERCISES

§ 2.4   1.   (TUT) Convert the following flowcharts into sequences of instructions.

QUEST

a)   c)

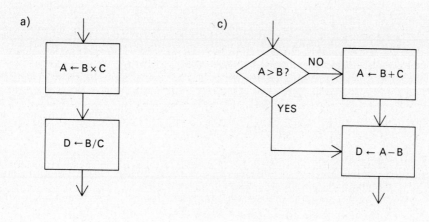

b)

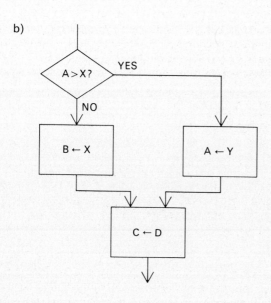

§ 2.4   2.   (TUT) Write a sequence of instructions to transfer to location X if $A + B \geq C + D$. Use as few instructions as possible.

§ 2.4   3.   (TUT) Write as short a sequence of instructions as possible to represent the logic shown below.

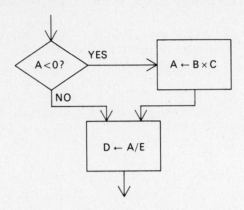

§ 2.2   4.   (TUT) Write a sequence of instructions to exchange the contents of cells A, B, and C; that is, after execution of the program,
A should contain the original contents of B;
B should contain the original contents of C; and
C should contain the original contents of A.

§ 3.5   5.   (TUT) What are the three important parts of a program loop?

§ 3.5   6.   (TUT) When a counter is used to control the termination of a loop, what are the three numbers which determine its action?

7.   (REF) Which of the following nested DO patterns are valid?

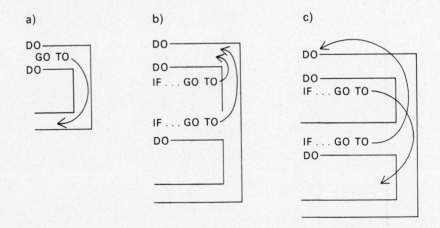

8.   (REF) Write DO and IF statements to control summing of the values in a three-dimensional array that touch the diagonal elements of the array.

PROGRAMMING PROBLEMS

§ 2.4   1.   (TUT) Write a program to read a number N, transfer to a statement that prints PRIME if N is prime and greater than 1, but prints NOT PRIME otherwise.

2.   (TUT) A deck of cards, each containing a negative number, is to be processed. Write a program to read these cards and print out the number of cards, the value of the smallest number on any of them, and the value of the largest.

§ 3.5   3.   (TUT) A deck of cards, each containing a pair of numbers A and B, is to be read. Write a program to do this and to find the sum S1 of those numbers B for which A < B, the sum S2 of those numbers B for which A = B, and the sum S3 of those numbers for which A > B. Print S1, S2, and S3. You may assume that the numbers A and B are positive.

§ 5.1   4.   (REF) The array A(I), I=1, . . . , N contains N numbers. Write a program to find the difference between the smallest and the largest.

§ 5.1   5.   (REF) Using only one loop, write a program to find the second largest number in the array A(I), I=1, . . . , N. Assume that N ≥ 2.

6.   (REF) Write a program to read values for two matrices and compute their product. For a given element of the output matrix, the computation is

$$C(I,J) = \sum_{K=1}^{M} A(I,K) * B(K,J)$$

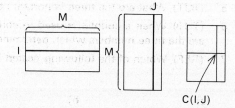

7.   (REF) Write a program to zero the upper half of the matrix R(20,20), which is shown below.

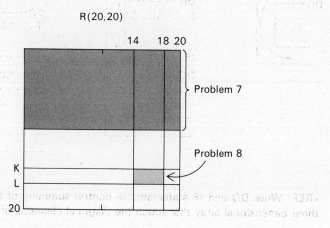

8. (REF) Write a program to zero the portion of R bounded by A(K,14), A(K,18), A(L,14), and A(L,18).

9. (REF) In terms of integer arithmetic, write a FORTRAN program to compute the number of times the loop established by the following DO statement will be executed.

   DO 100 I=INIT,IFINAL,INC

10. (REF) (Requires some thought.) Write a program to play tic-tac-toe. Represent the game by an array in memory. If you have access to an interactive system, code your program to print out a representation of the game and the first move. Then read in the opponent's move. If you don't have an interactive system, write the program to play itself. To avoid playing the same game over and over, the program should call a function to obtain a random starting value. Most FORTRAN systems provide such a function (a random number generator) that you can use. Divide its range of values into nine parts, one for each possible first move. In deciding which move to make from a given set of possibilities, notice that some decisions are really the same as others. For example, once the situation below has been established, a move from any corner is essentially the same decision as a move from any other corner (fill the middle square). Consider picturing the status of the game with similar computer output.

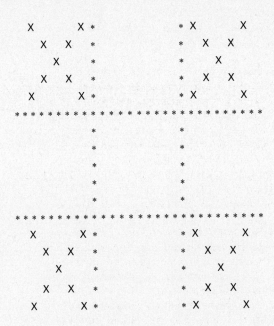

INTRO Suppose that you were asked to write a FORTRAN program to compute some of the standard statistical functions on arrays of observed data. Persons familiar with statistics would probably agree that your program should include analysis of variance, correlations, regression analysis, and frequency counting. You might set it up to accept as its first input an integer indicating the function required. One does not need to know much about statistics to realize that this program would be very large. It would probably include from 6,000 to 10,000 lines of coding.

What would happen if a mistake were discovered in your program? Or if a modification to one of the functions were required? You would have to submit the whole program (most likely, in source-deck form) to the computer each time you wanted to make a change. Even if you could store the program on disk or tape, you would have to recompile the entire program to modify it.

Perhaps, as an alternative, you would create a separate program for each statistical function. This approach would be less convenient for users of the functions, but it would somewhat lessen the handling problems.

Now consider that most statistical techniques require matrix multiplication in some parts of their computations. If you broke the program into several programs, you would have to make copies of the routine for matrix multiplication and insert one copy into each program requiring it. Later, if you wanted to change the routine, you would have to change each copy. Errors would be likely. Clearly, what is needed is a way of writing a program in sections, so that each section can be checked separately and perhaps even be used by other programs. These are important characteristics of FORTRAN subprograms.

Until now we have written programs as single units of coding. But it is often convenient to break a program into several subprograms. The subprograms can be compiled separately and debugged separately. They can be used by many people for many purposes.

Chapter

8

PROGRAM STRUCTURE

There are two types of subprograms in FORTRAN: (1) function subprograms, each of which returns a single value, and (2) subroutine subprograms, each of which may operate on many data items and change many values. This chapter discusses the coding of subroutines and functions (the FUNCTION, SUBROUTINE, and RETURN statements) and their use (the CALL statement and the function reference). It also explains how the EXTERNAL statement can be used to permit the name of one subprogram to be passed to another. Techniques for establishing variable return points (RETURN i) and multiple entry points (the ENTRY statement) are described. Finally, statement functions are discussed. Although the latter portion of the chapter is identified as reference material, you should read it as soon as you have written and executed your first small subroutine or function.

SUBROUTINES

Frequently, one particular operation involving several statements must be performed in several different places in a program. It is somewhat annoying to consider writing this part of the program several times. Furthermore, if we do, each part takes up space in computer memory whenever the program is run. As suggested in the introduction to this chapter, an example of such a program is one that performs analyses, each of which requires numerous matrix multiplications. Another example is a program in which printing of the values of array elements is required at several points. This is a standard operation and it would be convenient to call upon a standard sequence of instructions to perform the printing for us.

With only the tools explained so far, there is no easy way to avoid writing the code for each particular matrix multiplication or for each print operation. But certain FORTRAN statements allow exactly this kind of reuse of pieces of code. A separate program can be written to do the desired processing and can be called or referred to whenever it must be used. Such a program is identified as a *subprogram*, and the first kind of subprogram that we shall consider is known as a *subroutine subprogram*, or *subroutine*.

A subroutine subprogram begins with a *SUBROUTINE statement* such as

    SUBROUTINE PRSUB (I,J,MAT)

Here, PRSUB is the name of the subroutine, and I, J, and MAT are *dummy arguments*—simple variable names and/or array variable names to be replaced wherever they appear by the names of values specified for a particular execution of the subroutine. Details of subroutine usage are given below.

THE CALL STATEMENT

Assume that PRSUB is an instruction sequence that prints two-dimensional arrays. The programmer writes this sequence once, as a subroutine subprogram. The SUBROUTINE statement above is the first statement of that subprogram. Then, whenever two-dimensional arrays must be printed, he refers to the subroutine by its name, PRSUB. Specifically, he writes a *CALL statement* to transfer control from a calling program to PRSUB. A call to PRSUB might look like this:

CALL PRSUB (40,50,A)

Figure 8.1 shows a FORTRAN main program containing CALL statements at several points. It also shows the subroutine subprogram PRSUB. Each CALL statement causes a transfer of control from the main program to PRSUB to print the current values of elements in a two-dimensional array.

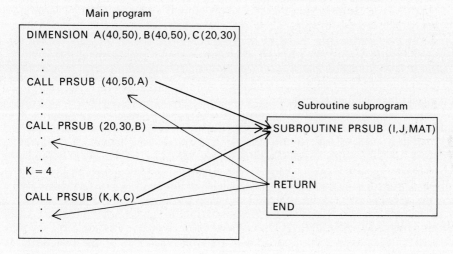

Main program

Subroutine subprogram

FIGURE 8.1

ARGUMENT LISTS

In the above example, it is necessary for the main program and the subprogram not only to communicate but also to refer to some of the same data. The main program has to tell PRSUB which array to print and the dimensions of the array. Both the main program and the subprogram must have access to the array data. For these reasons, each CALL statement in figure 8.1 contains a list of constants and variables, separated by commas and enclosed in parentheses. This is called an *argument list*. The variables and constants in the list are called *actual arguments.* The subroutine PRSUB is set up as a general program; it prints any two-dimensional array whose name and dimensions are passed to it as arguments. The actual arguments in the CALL statement tell the number of elements in each dimension of a particular array and the name of the array. The name of the array is a definite indication of where in storage the array data can be found.

For each execution of a CALL PRSUB statement, there is one complete execution of the subroutine. The dummy arguments specified in the SUB-ROUTINE statement are replaced throughout the subroutine by the actual arguments specified in the CALL statement. When called by the first CALL statement in figure 8.1, for example, any reference to MAT in the subroutine PRSUB is effectively a reference to A. Since this is true, actual arguments must correspond in number, order of appearance, type, and size to dummy arguments.

For example, if an actual argument is an integer constant, the corresponding dummy argument must be an integer variable. If a dummy argument is an array, the corresponding actual argument must be an array or an array element. Errors may result if the dimensions specified for an array passed as an actual argument are not the same as dimensions declared for the corresponding dummy argument in the called subprogram. (To avoid this problem, see "Execution-time dimensioning" in chapter 6.)

In most cases, when control is returned from a subroutine, the values of the actual arguments specified in the subroutine call are those values most recently established for the corresponding dummy arguments. Of course, some of the values may not be changed by the subroutine (in our particular example, all of the arguments are in this category). But a subroutine may change the values of several or all of its arguments, any number of times. In general, any change to a data item represented by a dummy argument is a change to a data item represented by the corresponding actual argument, because both arguments represent the same data.

One of the significant advantages of a subroutine is that it uses a set of names that are totally independent of the set of names used in any program by which it is called. A name used in a subroutine bears no necessary relation to a name used in a main program. Looking again at figure 8.1, we could include the statement

    CALL PRSUB (K,K,I)

in the main program. The third argument, I, would be taken as the name of the array to be printed and would, in effect, be substituted for MAT in the subroutine. There would be no confusion between this I and the first dummy argument I; the fact that the names are alike has no significance.

In the same way, statement numbers appearing in a subroutine subprogram have no relation to statement numbers appearing in a program by which the subroutine is called. This ensures, for example, that a GO TO statement in a main program can never be used to transfer control to a statement within the subroutine. Unanticipated conflicts over duplicate names cannot arise.

THE RETURN STATEMENT

When a subroutine is completed, it executes a *RETURN statement*. There must be at least one RETURN statement in a subroutine. There may be several, but only one is executed each time the subroutine is called. RETURN causes control to be transferred from the subroutine to the statement immediately following the CALL statement by which the subroutine was called. Execution of the calling program resumes at that point.

SUBPROGRAM CALLS

A FORTRAN subroutine may call another subprogram, but it may not call itself or any other subprogram that leads back to itself. That is, there may be no complete loop of calls. The calling sequence shown schematically at the left in figure 8.2 is acceptable, but those suggested by the drawings on the right are invalid.*

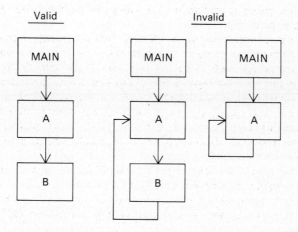

FIGURE 8.2

AN EXAMPLE

Except for the programming considerations mentioned in this chapter, a sub-routine subprogram is written in much the same way that you have written any of the programs suggested in this text. A subroutine to print two-dimensional arrays as proposed earlier in this chapter is shown as an example in figure 8.3. You need not examine all of the details of this subroutine at present, but you should understand its general flow. You will learn to use the statements that are new to you as you continue to study FORTRAN programming.

Note that the last statement in a subroutine is an END statement just as the last statement in a main program is. The subroutine is a separate unit for purposes of compilation, so the END statement is required at compilation time to tell the compiler that compilation of the unit can be completed. In many respects, the distinction between a main program and a subroutine is an artificial one. A main program is actually called by an operating-system program when it is to be executed. In most computer systems, the only distinction made between a main program and a subroutine is that the main program is the first one that begins execution when a set of programs is run.

---

*A call that leads back to a calling program or subprogram is known as a *recursive call*. There are some languages in which this is permitted. Those of you who are studying C. W. Gear, *Introduction to Computer Science*, will find a discussion of recursive calls in chapter 5 of that text.

```
        SUBROUTINE PRSUB (I,J,MAT)
        DIMENSION MAT(I,J), INTEG(10)
99      FORMAT (1H1,10X,10I12)
98      FORMAT (1H ,' LINE ',I3,4X,10I10)
        NSTRIP = (J+9) / 10
C       STUDY THE ABOVE AS AN EXAMPLE OF INTEGER
C       ARITHMETIC.  HOW DOES IT WORK? THERE WILL BE
C       UP TO 10 COLUMNS PER PAGE; EACH REPRESENTS
C       ONE STRIP DOWN THE MATRIX.
        NFIRST = 1
        NLAST = 10
        IF (NLAST.GT.J) NLAST = J
C       NFIRST AND NLAST ARE INTEGERS FOR PAGE HEADERS.
C       NLINES COUNTS THE LINES ON A PAGE. NSTRIP COUNTS
C       STRIPS.
        DO 100 ISTRIP=1,NSTRIP
        NLINES = 1
        NCOL = NLAST - NFIRST + 1
        M = NFIRST
        DO 1 K=1,NCOL
        INTEG(K) = M
1       M = M + 1
        DO 200 ILINE=1,I
        IF (NLINES.LT.51) GO TO 300
        WRITE (6,99) (INTEG(M),M=1,NCOL)
        NLINES = 1
300     WRITE (6,98) (ILINE, (MAT(ILINE,M),M=NFIRST,NLAST))
200     NLINES = NLINES + 1
        NFIRST = NFIRST + 10
        NLAST = NLAST + 10
        IF (NLAST.GT.J) NLAST = J
100     CONTINUE
        WRITE (6,99)
C       OPTIONAL FINAL PAGE SKIP.
        RETURN
        END
```

FIGURE 8.3

FUNCTIONS

Because FORTRAN is often used to solve mathematical problems, a section of
code often calculates a single numerical result that is needed in several different
parts of a program, or in several programs. This programming problem is similar
to that solved by subroutines except that we always know beforehand that a

single numerical value need be changed, that is, provided as a result by the section of code. For this purpose, we write a *function subprogram.*

The form of the *FUNCTION statement* that begins a function subprogram is similar to the form of a SUBROUTINE statement. For example:

FUNCTION POLY (N,C,X)

This is the FUNCTION statement for a subprogram identified as POLY. N, C, and X are dummy arguments of the subprogram. When POLY is executed, actual arguments replace these dummy arguments in much the same way that actual arguments replace dummy arguments in a subroutine subprogram. But a function differs significantly from a subroutine in the way that it returns results. Instead of assigning values to arguments that can be referred to when control is passed back to a calling program, the function itself takes on a value. Any reference to the name of the function in the main program causes control to be transferred to the function subprogram. The function subprogram is executed, determining a single numerical result. When control is returned to the main program, the name of the function represents that value.

THE FUNCTION REFERENCE

Instead of a CALL statement, we use a *function reference* to activate a function subprogram. The function reference consists of the function name followed by its arguments, enclosed in parentheses. There must be at least one actual argument in a function reference. Whether there must be more than one depends on whether the FUNCTION statement of the function being activated contains more than one dummy argument. The number of actual arguments in a function reference must be the same as the number of dummy arguments specified for the function. Having written the function subprogram POLY, for example, we might refer to it in arithmetic assignment statements such as shown in figure 8.4. Use of a function reference in an expression as though it were any variable name is a programming convenience. Control is returned from a function subprogram to the point at which the activating function reference appears.

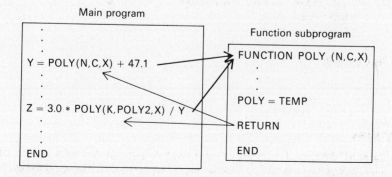

FIGURE 8.4

TYPES AND SIZES OF FUNCTIONS

Since a function subprogram actually takes on a value, a data type and size must be established for the function name, just as for any variable name in a FORTRAN program. The type and size of the function may be declared explicitly in a type statement or are established by default. (See "Typing of functions" in chapter 2.) Its type and size must be known in the function subprogram and in any program that refers to the function. Also, the type and size established must be the same in each. A function name for which type and size are established correctly can appear anywhere that a variable name of that type and size may be used.

AN EXAMPLE

As was noted for subroutine subprograms, a function subprogram must contain at least one RETURN statement and may contain several. Execution of a RETURN statement returns the current value of the function name and control to the calling program. For purposes of compilation, the last statement in a function subprogram must be an END statement. Since the function is a separate subprogram, the variables and statement numbers within it do not relate to those in any other program. Because the function must have a value upon return to the calling program, the name of the function must be assigned a value at least once in the subprogram—either as the variable name to the left of the equal sign in an assignment statement, as an argument of a CALL statement, or in an input list of a READ statement within the subprogram. A function cannot refer to itself or to any subprogram that leads back to itself.

```
      FUNCTION POLY (N,A,X)
      DIMENSION A(N)
C     NOTE THE EXECUTION-TIME DIMENSIONING (EXPLAINED
C     IN THE REFERENCE SECTION OF CHAPTER 6).
C     M IN THE MATHEMATICAL FUNCTION ABOVE IS ONE
C     LESS THAN N IN THE ARGUMENT LIST.  THIS ALLOWS
C     FOR THE COEFFICIENT A(0).
      TEMP = 0.
      DO 100 I=1,N
      K = N - I + 1
C     COEFFICIENTS ARE IN ORDER A(0), A(1), ETC.
C     EVALUATION IS DONE BY 0*X + A(M); THEN A(M)*X +
C     A(M-1); THEN (A(M)*X + A(M-1))*X + A(M-2);
C     ...+A(0).  SINCE A(0) CANNOT BE USED IN FORTRAN,
C     1 IS ADDED TO EACH SUBSCRIPT.
100   TEMP = TEMP*X + A(K)
      POLY = TEMP
      RETURN
      END
```

FIGURE 8.5

Within these guidelines, writing a function subprogram is much the same as writing any other FORTRAN program. To emphasize this fact, a complete function subprogram, POLY, is shown in figure 8.5. POLY computes the value of a polynomial. Its arguments are the number of coefficients in the polynomial, the array of coefficients, and the x value to which it is to be evaluated. The mathematical function to which POLY corresponds is

$$f(x) = \sum_{i=0}^{m} a_i x^i$$

ADVANTAGES OF SUBROUTINES AND FUNCTIONS

REF

Some of the advantages of subprograms have to do with the actual design and coding of a system, some have to do with the execution of programs and machine efficiency, and others have to do with standardization and the maintenance of programs.

One of the advantages having to do with both program coding and efficient use of storage was mentioned at the beginning of this chapter: Subprograms help to avoid the necessity to repeat sections of code. Another advantage insofar as program design and coding is concerned is that of program modularity. As emphasized in the discussion of program design in chapter 9, it is wise to organize a program as independent modules, each of which performs a particular function. Subprograms provide the basis for such design. Information boundaries are easier to establish. A subprogram can operate on information items that are local to it and cannot be referred to by other subprograms.

Also noted earlier, subprograms allow use of separate groups of names. Since names used within a subprogram are local to it, they bear no relation to names in other parts of the program. Using the same name for different purposes in different subprograms causes no problems.

Under FORTRAN compilers such as IBM's FORTRAN G and FORTRAN H, which produce object modules, subprograms allow separate compilation and the production of separate object modules. Each object module is a copy of the machine-language version of a program unit. The unit may be either a main program or a subprogram. This means that an entire program does not have to be recompiled every time a change is made to part of the program.

As independent units having well-defined information boundaries and capabilities for separate compilation, subroutines are replaceable units. Assume that an operation is performed by a subroutine and that it becomes necessary or advisable to modify that operation or replace it by another. A program calling for the operation may not have to be modified, even though the subroutine (i.e., the operation itself) is modified or replaced.

Because of subprogram capabilities, a FORTRAN programmer does not usually have to code every sequence of statements required in his program. A standard library of functions and subroutines for use in a wide variety of applications can be built up by an installation. The programmer need only write CALL statements or function references at appropriate points in his program to cause the required operations to be performed. You should consult the library documentation at your installation to learn what subprograms are available for use in your programs.

In fact, subroutines can serve as standardized procedures within a system of programming or even within an installation. This feature is particularly important in the input/output areas where standard interfaces are vital. It is always a good design practice to separate input/output operations from internal processing operations of a program.

SHARING DATA AMONG SUBPROGRAMS

Sometimes information should be known to a whole set of subroutines. Passing this information in each calling sequence may be possible but not particularly convenient for the programmer, especially if numerous data items are involved. An alternative is to declare a common block of storage for the information and mention the common block in each subroutine. The information can be accessed by all subroutines that refer to the common block. This approach differs from the passing of values as arguments in a calling sequence in that, when using variables in common storage, the same variables (and, therefore, the same storage locations) are referred to in every execution of the subroutine. In contrast, different variables, representing different storage locations, may be operated on by a subroutine when the names of the variables are specified as arguments and, hence, may change from one call to another.

When preparing a subprogram, you should analyze the data-sharing requirements of that subprogram. Determine which values must be shared with other subprograms. Then determine, for each value, whether it should be passed as an argument or referred to via a common storage area. To learn more about the use of common blocks of storage, see the discussion of the COMMON statement in chapter 6.

THE EXTERNAL STATEMENT

Sometimes we want to write a general subroutine to perform some operation on the results of a function and to call that subroutine in any number of programs. As an example, we might want to call a subroutine to compute the area under a curve and that subroutine could well operate on values provided by a function that computes the curve. It is possible to refer to the function that computes the values, place the values in an array, and call the subroutine, passing the array as an argument. This means work for the calling program, and it implies that the calling program knows the function arguments for which the subroutine needs the function values.

A more convenient approach is to tell the subroutine which function to call and allow the subroutine to obtain values computed by the function as it needs them by direct references to the function. To permit such references, FORTRAN allows a function or subroutine name to be passed as an argument to another function or subroutine. If we use this approach, we must tell the compiler that the name being passed is a subprogram name rather than simply

REF

a variable name for which default characteristics apply. To do so, we specify the subprogram name in an *EXTERNAL statement* in the calling program.

```
EXTERNAL MYSIN, MYCOS
   .
   .
   .
CALL INTEG (RESULT,X1,X2,MYSIN)
   .
   .
   .
CALL INTEG (RESULT,X3,X4,MYCOS)
   .
   .
   .
END
SUBROUTINE INTEG (R,XMAX,XMIN,FUNC)
   .
   .
   .
R = R + ((XMIN − XMAX) * (FUNC(XMIN + XMAX))) / 2.0
RETURN
END
```

FIGURE 8.6

Figure 8.6 shows a main program that makes two calls to INTEG, a sub-routine subprogram. Four arguments are listed in the calling sequence, and the last of these is the name of a function subprogram. MYSIN is the function name passed in the first call; MYCOS is the function name passed in the second call. So that these variables are recognized by the compiler as subprogram names, they are listed in an EXTERNAL statement in the calling program.

Care must be taken when using subprogram names as arguments. All sub-programs whose names are passed as arguments must have calling sequences identical to that of the corresponding dummy argument. Both MYSIN and MYCOS effectively replace the dummy argument FUNC in the subroutine subprogram INTEG in figure 8.6. Since FUNC accepts one real argument, MYSIN and MYCOS must be subprograms that accept one real argument. Any other subprogram whose name is passed to INTEG must also accept one real argument.

The EXTERNAL statement is a nonexecutable statement and must precede the executable statements of a program in which it is used. The general form of the statement is

EXTERNAL *a, b, c,* . . .

where *a, b, c,* . . . are the names of subprograms that are passed as arguments to subprograms. The names may identify user-defined function or subroutine

REF

subprograms or FORTRAN-supplied subprograms, known as built-in functions. (See "Functions" in chapter 5.)

FURTHER COMMENTS ON SUBPROGRAM ARGUMENTS

FORTRAN offers quite a bit of flexibility as far as the form of the arguments in a calling sequence is concerned.

1 Arithmetic expressions as well as variable names can be passed as actual arguments in a calling sequence. This implies that subscripted variables can be passed, since a subscripted variable is a form of arithmetic expression.

    CALL QPOLY (X,X*Y−5.,A(45,I))

An arithmetic expression should not be used as an actual argument if the corresponding dummy argument might be changed during execution of the called subprogram. Since there is no way for the calling program to look at the changed value (i.e., no storage location containing the new data that it can access), this is an error in design on the part of the programmer. Another point to remember is that the type and size of the result obtained by evaluation of the expression must be the same as the type and size of the dummy argument to which the expression corresponds.

2 Literals and other constants may be passed as actual arguments in a calling sequence.

    CALL PLABEL (21,'MATRIX LABEL')
    CALL PLABEL (21,12HMATRIX LABEL)

The statements above are equivalent. Neither the single quotes nor the 12H is passed as part of the character string. As noted above for arithmetic expressions, constants should not be passed as actual arguments if the called subprogram may change the values of the corresponding dummy arguments.

3 Actual arguments specified in a calling sequence may also appear in COMMON or EQUIVALENCE statements in the calling program. Within a subprogram, however, names appearing as dummy arguments in a SUBROUTINE, FUNCTION, or ENTRY statement cannot appear in COMMON or EQUIVALENCE statements. If an array to be passed to a subprogram is of two types somehow intermixed (say, because two unlike arrays have been equivalenced to one in the calling program), about the only way to pass both parts of the array is to pass an argument pointing to each part.

4 If a subscripted variable appears in a calling sequence, the called subprogram can interpret that variable as a simple variable or as an array of reduced size. If the array is one-dimensional, the reduced size is the element number minus 1. If it is two-dimensional, the number of rows in the matrix remains the same, but the number of columns is reduced. For arrays of higher order, the rightmost dimension is always the one affected.

    Two calls to the function subprogram QPOLY are shown in figure 8.7. Here the two-dimensional array A in the calling program is made to look like a one-dimensional array C in the function subprogram, and the one-dimensional array N in the calling program is made to look like the simple variable M.

```
DIMENSION  A(21,30), N(30)
     .
     .
     .
B = QPOLY  (A(1,3),N(3))
     .
     .
K = 25
D = QPOLY  (A(1,K),N(K))
     .
     .
END
FUNCTION QPOLY  (C,M)
DIMENSION  C(20)
     .
     .
     .
RETURN
END
```

FIGURE 8.7

The storage usage set up by these calls is shown schematically in figure 8.8.

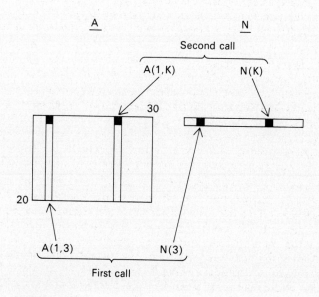

FIGURE 8.8

REF

TYPES OF CALLS

Many FORTRAN compilers copy the value of each simple variable passed in a calling sequence into local working storage. If the corresponding dummy argument is changed during execution of the called subprogram, the new value is copied back into the locations reserved for the variable in the calling program. This copying is done when the RETURN statement is executed. The technique is known as *call by value* because the subprogram operates on the value of the argument that was passed rather than on the argument itself in its original memory locations. At first thought, this copying may seem inefficient, but on many machines, it is more efficient to work on a copy that is local to the subprogram than on the actual argument. Otherwise, the process of manipulating the address for each reference is expensive in terms of both time and memory.

The programmer can construct a subprogram to use an actual argument rather than make a local copy of it by enclosing the corresponding dummy argument in slashes. Suppose the following SUBROUTINE statement is used.

SUBROUTINE BYLOC (/X/,/Y/,47)

The memory addresses of the first two actual arguments specified in any CALL statement for subroutine BYLOC are considered to be the names of the arguments, and the locations of the actual arguments are referred to throughout execution of the subroutine. The compiler reserves no storage locations in the subroutine for any values to be represented by X and Y. This technique is known as *call by location*. If you refer to a variable only once in a subprogram, it may be wise to force a call by location to avoid wasteful duplication of space and copying and recopying when only one address manipulation is required.

Copies are not made of array arguments. That is, there is no call by value for arrays. The compiler treats an array argument as though call by location is specified explicitly for it. As noted above, this avoids duplication of excessive amounts of space in storage and prevents time-consuming copying of values when a call is made.*

VARIABLE RETURN POINTS

It is not always desirable to return from a subroutine to the statement following the activating CALL statement in the calling program. The most common case arises when an error condition is encountered during execution of the subroutine, and the calling program must be notified that an error has occurred. A subroutine subprogram can be designed so that control can be returned to any of several alternate points.

A first step in designing such a subroutine is to set up dummy arguments to correspond to actual arguments that are statement labels of desired return points in the calling program. Since there is no way of naming statement labels

---

*For additional discussion of types of subprogram calls, see chapter 5 of C. W. Gear, *Introduction to Computer Science*.

in FORTRAN, an asterisk (*) is placed as the dummy argument corresponding to each statement label. (See figure 8.9.)

```
        SUBROUTINE INPUT (A,M,*,*)
          .
          .
        RETURN
          .
          .
10      RETURN 1
          .
20      RETURN 2
        END
```

FIGURE 8.9

The second step in providing this variable return capability is to include one or more RETURN statements of the general form shown below in the subroutine subprogram.

    RETURN *i*

The unsigned integer constant *i* is a position number. The actual argument (statement label) in the activating CALL statement that corresponds to the *ith* asterisk in the SUBROUTINE statement is taken as the return point if this RETURN statement is encountered during a particular execution of the subroutine.

As figure 8.9 shows, RETURN statements of the standard form RETURN and of the form RETURN *i* can be included in one subroutine. RETURN causes a return to the statement following the activating CALL statement; RETURN 1 causes a return to the statement identified by the label corresponding to the first asterisk in the SUBROUTINE statement; and RETURN 2 causes a return to the statement identified by the label corresponding to the second asterisk. One, and only one, of these RETURN statements (the first one encountered) is executed during one activation of the subroutine subprogram.

A CALL statement for the subroutine subprogram INPUT of figure 8.9 might appear as

    CALL INPUT (AREA,N,&90,&98)

Each actual argument that corresponds to an * in the SUBROUTINE statement is of the general form &*n* where & is a required identifier for a statement label appearing as an actual argument and *n* is the statement label (i.e., the number of a statement in the calling program). If the RETURN 1 statement in INPUT is executed as a result, control returns to statement 90 in the calling program. If the RETURN 2 statement is executed, control returns to statement 98. In all other cases, control returns to the statement following this CALL statement.

REF

MULTIPLE ENTRY POINTS

Sometimes a subroutine or function subprogram is responsible for more than one process. Either type of subprogram can be designed to accept an integer argument indicating the process to be performed for a particular call. The subprogram can then execute a computed GO TO statement to branch to the proper section of code in the subprogram. (See chapter 7.)

An easier approach is to establish several entry points in a single subprogram. Normally, a function or subroutine is executed from its beginning— the first executable statement after the FUNCTION or SUBROUTINE statement. But *ENTRY statements* can be used to define additional entry point names and their locations in the subprogram.

The subroutine subprogram in figure 8.10 has two entry points: INIT, which is established by the SUBROUTINE statement, and DOIT, which is established by an ENTRY statement. It may be called by either name, and the point at which execution of the subroutine begins is determined accordingly.

```
      .
      .
      .
      CALL INIT (A,B,47,20.0,21.0)
      .
      .
      .
      CALL DOIT (A,B(I))
      .
      .
      .
      END
      SUBROUTINE INIT (AR1,AR2,I,X,Y)
      DIMENSION AR1(40), AR2(50)
      J = I * 2
      .
      .
      RETURN
      ENTRY DOIT (AR1,AR2)
      .
      .
      RETURN
      END
```

FIGURE 8.10

Any number of ENTRY statements can be used in a subprogram. Each must contain a different entry point name, and they may differ from each other in number, types, and sizes of arguments. As the example in figure 8.10 suggests, the number, types, and sizes of dummy arguments specified in an ENTRY statement may also differ from those specified in a SUBROUTINE or FUNCTION statement. However, the actual arguments in a CALL statement or function reference must correspond in number, type, and size to the dummy arguments of a selected entry point. It would be an error, for example, to specify only two actual arguments in a call to INIT or to specify other than two actual arguments in a call to DOIT in figure 8.10.

The general form of the ENTRY statement is

ENTRY *name* (*a1,a2, . . .*)

where *name* is a unique entry point name and *a1*, *a2*, . . . are dummy arguments used as placeholders in succeeding statements. A dummy argument cannot be specified in an executable statement of a subprogram until after it appears in either a SUBROUTINE or FUNCTION statement or in an ENTRY statement of the subprogram. If an array is defined with execution-time dimensioning (as shown in chapter 6), all variables used for the dimensions must be included in the calling sequence at any entry point at which the array is passed unless the dimension variables appear in common storage.

An ENTRY statement is not executable. Therefore, it may appear within coding that may be executed because of an entry at some other point. If encountered in such cases, it is ignored. An ENTRY statement cannot appear in the range of a DO, because (as explained in chapter 7) control cannot be transferred into the range of a DO. Mention was made earlier that a subprogram cannot refer to itself. This holds for all entry point names. A subprogram cannot refer to any of its entry points.

A requirement for multiple entry points often arises when there is initialization to be done. In this case, the initializing entry point is given one name and calling sequence, and the main entry point is given another name and calling sequence. If you design a subprogram that initializes variables on one call and uses them on another, you must be certain that the defining is always done before the use. Remember that the order of use is not necessarily determined by the physical order of statements in the subprogram. The initializing entry point may appear near the end of the subprogram, but the subprogram must be called and entered first at that point.

If a variable name is listed as being called by location at one entry point, it must be listed as called by location at any other entry points at which it is specified. The same is true for calls by value. If a variable is called by value (which is the usual case for simple variables in FORTRAN), then a value determined for that variable by one execution of the subprogram is present when a subsequent execution is required. This is not true of variables specified as called by location or of arrays since they are always called by location. The value of any variable called by location is the current value of the corresponding actual argument in a calling program.

When ENTRY statements are used within a function subprogram, the entry point names are treated like variables, just as the name specified in the FUNCTION statement is. If default characteristics that would be assumed for an entry point name according to a governing first-letter rule are not correct, its type and size must be declared in the function and in any calling program.

The function name and entry point names may differ in type and size. Upon return from a function, the return value is the value most recently assigned to the function name or to any of its entry names, irrespective of the name by which the function was called. If the type and size of the value differ from that assigned to the variable in the current function reference, an error is likely. The function name and its entry point names are equivalenced by the FORTRAN system. After one of the names has been assigned a value, the other names have indeterminate values.

A subroutine subprogram, TESTE, is shown in figure 8.11. Three alternate entry points, each having a different set of dummy arguments, are specified. Comments included in figure 8.11 point out sections of code where variable names are known or unknown and differences between call by location and call by value.

```
      SUBROUTINE TESTE (A,B,K1,K2,I,J,R)
      DIMENSION A(100), B(K1,K2)
      X1 = 0.
      X2 = 0.
      RETURN
      ENTRY PROCES (A,B,K1,K2,I,/NAME/)
C     I IS RESET BY THIS ENTRY.
             .
             .
             .
      B(I,1) = A(1)
             .
             .
             .
      NAME = K1 * K2
      IF (I.EQ.0) GO TO 100
      ENTRY PROC2 (/NAME/)
C     A AND B CANNOT BE REFERRED TO IF ENTRY WAS AT PROC2
C     SINCE ARRAYS ARE CALLED BY LOCATION.  NAME IS
C     RESET IF PROC2 IS CALLED.
      NAME = K1 − K2
      RETURN
100   K = K + 1
      ENTRY PROC3 (B,K1,K2)
C     B CAN BE REFERENCED SINCE IT IS DEFINED ON ALL PATHS
C     REACHING HERE.  NAME IS NOT VALID IF ENTRY POINT
C     PROC3 WAS USED, SINCE IT IS CALLED BY LOCATION.
      B(1,1) = 10.0
      B(K1,K2) = 10.0
      RETURN
      END
```

FIGURE 8.11

REF

STATEMENT FUNCTIONS

When the same computations are required repetitively (remember our proposed example, matrix multiplication, at the beginning of this chapter), an alternative to either writing the same arithmetic expressions over and over or writing a separate subprogram is to define a *statement function*. This approach works only for arithmetic or logical expressions, but it allows a programmer to set up a convenient shorthand for use in his program. To do so, he writes a *statement function definition* preceding the first executable statement in the program unit in which the arithmetic computation or logical expression evaluation is frequently required. Having done so, he need only write the statement function name and specify actual arguments wherever the expression evaluation is needed in that program unit. As with a function subprogram, a single numeric or logical value is returned as a result. The statement function name cannot be referred to in other program units like a function or subroutine name can, however, unless the statement function is defined in the other program units as well.

```
        .
        .
        .
    FIRSTR (A,B,C) = ((−B + SQRT (B**2−4.*A*C)) / (2.*A)) + Q
        .
        .
        .

    X = Y * 2
    Z = Y * FIRSTR (XA,XB,XC)
        .
        .
        .

    Z2 = FIRSTR (M,N,P)
    Z3 = FIRSTR (R,S,T) / 3.
        .
        .
        .

    END
```

FIGURE 8.12

The statement function FIRSTR is defined and then referred to three times in the program in figure 8.12. Since FIRSTR is defined to accept three values, its name and three actual arguments are specified in each function reference. As with function or subroutine subprograms, each actual argument must agree in type and size with its corresponding dummy argument. It may be an expression. Obviously, the first assignment statement containing a reference to FIRSTR is much easier to write (and less apt to contain errors) than its equivalent, without FIRSTR:

REF

$$Z = Y * (((-XB + SQRT (XB**2 - 4.*XA*XC)) / (2.*XA)) + Q)$$

The dummy arguments A, B, and C in figure 8.12 are just placeholders that show the compiler how to use the actual arguments specified in the calling sequence when the statement function is referred to. As figure 8.12 demonstrates, variables other than those used as dummy arguments (Q, in this example) may be included in a statement function definition. FORTRAN built-in functions (such as SQRT in figure 8.12) and other statement functions can also be referenced. If another statement function is referenced, it must be defined by a preceding statement function definition in the program unit. A statement function definition cannot refer to itself or to any other function leading back to itself. That is, recursive definition of statement functions is not allowed.

A statement function definition is not executable. It only gives a "skeleton" to use whenever the function name appears in an executable statement. In form, it resembles an assignment statement:

name (a1,a2,a3, . . .) = expression

The *name* is the statement function name, each *a* is a dummy argument, and *expression* is an arithmetic or logical expression. The statement function name can be any valid FORTRAN symbolic name. Its type and size (and, hence, the type and size of the return value) must be declared in a statement physically preceding the function definition or are determined by default according to the governing first-letter rule and standard lengths for the implementation. The dummy arguments must be unique within the statement. All names used as dummy arguments in a statement function definition are local to the single statement in which they appear. Variables having the same names may appear elsewhere in the program unit; they have no relation to the dummy argument names in the statement function definition.

In IBM 360/370 FORTRAN, a statement function definition cannot include subscripted variables. WATFIV permits subscripted variables to be used in the arithmetic or logical expression, that is, on the right-hand side of the definition.

Additional examples of valid statement function definitions are

```
SUM (A,C,D,F) = A + C + D + F
FUNC (Z) = (A+X**Z) / Z
TWOF (I,J) = I * FUNONE (J)
```

Given these definitions, the following function references are valid.

```
SUM (R,S,Q**4,T)
FUNC (D*4.+6.3)
TWOF (V(I),N)
```

But the following definitions are invalid, for the reasons indicated.

SUBPROG (A,B,C) = 3.*A + B * C   Statement function name cannot exceed six characters.

3RDF (A,I) = A**I   Statement function name must begin with alphabetic character.

FUNC (X,Y,Z(3)) = X/Y + Z(3)   Dummy argument cannot be subscripted variable.

FUNC (4.,C) = (4.*(Z+3))/6.   Dummy argument must be variable.

MYF (C,D) = MYF (R,S) + C   Recursive definition is not allowed.

REF

The following definition is invalid in IBM 360/370 FORTRAN because subscripted variables are not permitted in a statement function definition.

THISF (A,B) = A*B**2 + C(I)   Expression cannot contain subscripted variable.

Since WATFIV systems permit use of subscripted variables on the right-hand side of a definition, this definition is valid in WATFIV.

EXERCISES

QUEST

1. (TUT)
   a) Write the SUBROUTINE statement for a subprogram that finds the largest element of a vector.
   b) What arguments are required?
2. (TUT)
   a) Write the FUNCTION statement for a subprogram that finds the largest element of a vector.
   b) What arguments are required?
3. (TUT) Write two CALL statements transferring control to the subroutine in exercise 1.
4. (TUT) Write two function references transferring control to the function in exercise 2.
5. (TUT) How are values returned by a subroutine subprogram?

§ 5.3 6. (TUT)
   a) How many values can be returned by a function subprogram?
   b) How does the return occur?
7. (REF) Write an ENTRY statement to be added to the subroutine described in exercise 1 to permit a program to call the subroutine to obtain the smallest element in the vector as well.
8. (REF)
   a) What subprograms might you include in a system designed to compute the standard arithmetic operations on polynomials?
   b) Suggest arguments and/or return values for the subprograms that you proposed above.

PROGRAMMING PROBLEMS

1. Assume that you have a vector of sorted elements. Write a function that searches the vector for a given value. If it finds the value, it returns an index showing the relative location of the value; otherwise it returns zero.

2. (TUT) Write a subprogram to sort the elements of a vector. Check to see whether the first two elements are in order. If they are, compare the second element to the next one. If they are out of order, switch them before making the next compare. Make that compare, switch elements if necessary, and check to see whether the previous pairs are still in order. Continue this procedure until you make it through the list without finding any elements out of order. Then you are done.

§ 5.3   3. (TUT) The smallest common multiple (SCM) of two integers I and J is defined to be the smallest integer such that both I and J divide it exactly. Devise the algorithm to find the SCM and express it by means of a flow-chart for a function subprogram that defines ISCM (I,J) to be the SCM of I and J. Do not worry about efficiency.

§ 5.3   4. (TUT) If you already have a function IGCD (I,J) which finds the greatest common divisor efficiently, how can it be used to find the SCM efficiently?

§ 5.4   5. (TUT) Write a subroutine NORM (AM,SD,A,N) that computes the mean AM of the array A(I), I=1, . . . , N, and the standard deviation SD of the same array, where

$$AM = \frac{1}{N} \sum_{I=1}^{N} A(I)$$

$$SD = \sqrt{\frac{1}{N} \sum_{I=1}^{N} (A(I) - AM)^2}$$

In doing so, you may want to refer to the program that you created in response to programming problem 2 in chapter 5. For that problem, you wrote a single main program using simple variables to find means and standard deviation.

§ 5.4   6. (REF) Write a subroutine STNDRD (A,W,T,N,M) which has the following actions:
The array A(I,J) contains the score of the Jth test for the Ith student. There are M tests and N students. Normalize the scores on each test to a mean of zero and a standard deviation of 1.0 by first forming

$$AM = \frac{1}{N} \sum_{I=1}^{N} A(I,J)$$

and

$$SD = \sqrt{\frac{1}{N} \sum_{I=1}^{N} (A(I,J) - AM)^2}$$

and then forming

$$B(I,J) = \frac{A(I,J) - AM}{SD} \quad \text{if } SD \neq 0, \left.\begin{matrix} \\ \\ \end{matrix}\right\} I = 1, \ldots, N$$

and B(I,J) = 0, if SD = 0.

Repeat these steps for J = 1, . . . , M.

Then form the weighted sum of the normalized scores and return the result in T.

$$T(I) = \sum_{J=1}^{M} B(I,J) \times W(J)$$

§ 5.5   7.   (REF) Write a subroutine GROUP (A,B,I) to be called each time a new value of A is calculated. The subroutine should accept five successive values of A and form their sum and the sum of their squares. It should then store these sums in B(I,1) and B(I,2) and increment I by one.

§ 5.5   8.   (REF) Write a print subroutine PRSUB (A) to be called each time a new value of A is calculated. The subroutine should print three numbers across a line, but there is a snag: The numbers are computed in a diagonal order, that is, as indicated below. Therefore, the partial contents of several lines must be saved. State what the initial values of any variables must be if it is important.

etc.

§ 9.2   9.   (REF) Write a program that computes

$$A(1) \times X^2 + A(2) \times X^6 + A(3) \times X^{10} + \ldots + A(N) \times X^{4 \times N - 2}$$

as rapidly as possible.

§ 9.2   10.   (REF) Write a program to evaluate exp(x). This program should form $x = z + N$ where $|z| \leq 1/2$ and N is an integer. You may assume that the array A(I) contains exp(I) for I = 1, . . . , 50, and that $|x| < 50$.

INTRO One of the most difficult tasks that confronts any programmer is getting started with a new project and working out its design. A time-worn rule is that good design makes for easy programming and successful systems; but, with poor design, most systems are stillborn. This chapter presents techniques for easing into the design process and generating a good design with no "dark spots"—undefined areas that are not exposed until the program is coded.

The emphasis in this approach is on breaking the system to be defined into small logical modules, each of which has a single discernible function and a simple relation to the rest of the system and its users (the outside world). The phrase *information boundary* is used to describe the information items (variables, arguments, input data, output data, storage areas, and the like) that a module shares with the outside world. This boundary should be as simple as possible, including only a few data items with simple structures. It should be regarded as a contract between the module and the rest of the world: When provided input items with appropriate structures, the module provides output items with proper structures to the rest of the world.

You will find it helpful to read one or more references on flowcharting before studying this chapter. Chapters 3 and 5 of C. W. Gear, *Introduction to Computer Science*, and *Flowcharting Techniques*, a paperback by Marilyn Bohl, provide guidelines in using flowcharts as suggested in this chapter. Flowcharts are extremely valuable in helping you to analyze the processing operations needed to solve a problem.

Debugging refers to the steps in checking a program for correctness after it has been compiled successfully (i.e., without generating error messages from the compiler). If the program is large and consists of several subprograms, debugging may be carried out for each subprogram as a separate unit. After each subprogram has been debugged, the complete program can be subjected to debugging. The second portion of this chapter

Chapter

9

Design and Debugging

indicates some of the common types of errors (bugs) in FORTRAN programming and how to look for them. It also explains debugging statements of WATFIV and of FORTRAN as implemented on IBM 360/370 computers.

Step-by-step procedures of program design are followed in a sample design problem, which is explained in detail in the reference section.

DESIGN STRATEGIES

The first rule of effective programming is to understand a problem as completely as possible before beginning to code. As the following outline shows, other steps in design are important as well. This outline is intended as a general guideline of the steps that you should follow.

Step 1. Make a complete list of the functions the system, or problem solution, is to perform. Most FORTRAN programs, or systems of FORTRAN subprograms, perform more than a single function. In general, they perform a variety of functions under a variety of different conditions. This initial list of functions should be the maximum set of functions that the system may have to perform. It will probably include some functions that are not included in final coding. The list helps you to get some feeling for the maximum range of possibilities that the system must encompass. It is in a sense the horizon, the most distant boundary.

Step 2. Write a complete list of the information items that the system must receive from the outside world in order to perform the functions listed in step 1. Make a second list of the information items that the system should provide as output to the outside world. Both should be maximum sets of information items. Do not, at first, attempt to structure these information items or to indicate their interrelationships. Simply listing them serves to delineate the maximum horizon. Each list is a part of the information boundary between the system and the outside world. You may discover that certain functions that the system must perform cannot be performed with the information items provided.

Step 3. Identify a command language for the system. All systems with multiple functions have some kind of command language through which relations are established. Perhaps it is an explicit set of commands such as the job-control statements or macro instructions usually found in operating systems. Sometimes the commands are given implicitly by choosing one of several entry points to the system. In any case, these various commands should be identified explicitly and the information items associated with each command should be recognized. You should understand, in a general way, how the system is to perform each command that you list. You must make sure that the system has sufficient information to perform each command, and you should list the output information associated with each one. At this point, you are making the design of the system more specific. In setting up these commands, you may decide that some of the functions that you listed in step 1 should be omitted from the system.

Step 4.   Specify the data elements that will constitute the information items listed in step 2 and the ways in which those data elements will be organized. That is, define the data structures involved. You should specify the overall information flow into and out of the system. Since it is extremely important that the content and organization of data on all input and output files (i.e., the file structures) be established, you should write the data definition statements for these files before writing any executable statements. You may even wish to compile them separately at this point. You must define the structures of all tables or other information items that are maintained by the system in a common storage area accessible to multiple functions. It is wise to plan the data structures for all subprograms in the system before beginning to code.

FURTHER ANALYSIS

The steps above will get you started and give you an overall view of the design for a system. However, these steps do not provide a sufficient basis for coding. One must look at a system as one looks at an onion. The purpose of the design process is to peel the sections of the system, going from the greatest level of generality to the smallest level of detail. After a layer is removed, the system should be broken into modules (subsystems) at the new level. The design process should be done in detail for each subsystem; hence, the four steps listed below should be carried out for each. Continue this process until you have defined modules that can be coded as single subprograms without further design.

There is always a question about how deep into the design segmentation process to go and how small the final modules should be. This is up to the judgment and experience of the programmer. Generally one errs in the direction of making modules too big. One always begins coding too soon.

Step 5.   Determine the information boundary for the module—the information items that come to or go from it. Note that the functions of a given module will have been defined by the design step executed previously. For example, the last design step may have been the definition of a multiaccessed table, a fourth step as listed above. The design of a table leads to the definition of modules to process the table data.

Step 6.   Define in detail the data structures for all tables used internally and externally to this module. This means determining the arrays, common areas of storage, and equivalence structures used within this module. (Chapter 6 explains how to provide for these in FORTRAN programs.)

Step 7.   Determine the algorithmic process by which this module is to perform its function. This means understanding clearly the basic set of FOR-TRAN statements or subprograms that must be executed to deliver the output information items that form a part of the information boundary of this module.

Step 8.   Flowchart the process by which this module will execute its function. In doing so, you will break this module into submodules, each of which has a particular function. Each module becomes a module at the next layer in the design phase. Each of these steps (5–8) is repeated for each module. Only when the final modules are small enough for programming, should actual writing of FORTRAN statements begin.

Notice that steps 5, 6, 7, and 8 define an information boundary for each module. It is extremely important that all communication between one module and another be within the information boundary defined for it. Always, there is the temptation to reach from one module to another to access data that is not defined to be common to both. This makes the system hard to document and difficult to maintain. Experience indicates that this sort of sneaking one's hand under the fence always catches up with one eventually. An advantage of modular systems is that they are easier to code than large never-ending programs. When coding a given module, if its information boundary has been defined correctly, the programmer does not have to worry about what effect his next FORTRAN statement will have on some other part of the system. The only effect it can have is through the information items that are common to this module and other modules. If the items have been designed properly, the programmer need not fear the influence of his statement. As long as the module/outside-world contract is kept (only specified information items are transmitted and only in the structures agreed upon), errors will not be generated.

The modular approach recommended above leads to a system that is both flexible and easy to program. It reveals dark spots that must be clarified in the design of any complex programming system. One always assumes that poorly understood areas are small, relative to the whole, and that they will clarify themselves eventually. Experience indicates that what appear to be small areas of misunderstanding eventually grow to exceed the total size of the parts of the problem that are understood. Ignoring dark areas, rather than investigating them in a recursive way, leads to difficulty, if not disaster.

A FEW IMPORTANT RULES

Basic guidelines to good design are given below. Some are familiar but worth repeating; others have not been stated elsewhere in this text.

1   Remember that computer programs model reality. Your modules should be broken down as the real situation breaks down. Your data structures should pattern extant relations of data.

2   Always code and check your data descriptions and declarations first.

3   Separate your modules into primary and secondary ones. The primary ones are those which are essential. The secondary ones are peripheral; no other modules are dependent on them. Code and debug the primary modules first.

4   Separate input/output functions from process functions. Include each in a different module, and perhaps, even in a different subsystem, having component modules of only one type.

5   Isolate the repetitive portion of a process from the process itself. Create one module that keeps track of the iterations and prepares the data for the code that actually does the process on a single data structure.

DEBUGGING

After a program has been designed, coded, and compiled successfully, at least one major task remains: The programmer must make certain that his program performs as intended. This part of a programmer's job is known as *program debugging*.

The debugging of a program or system of programs may be broken down into the following steps:

1   Desk checking, which involves a careful examination of the source-program listing after coding or compilation and before actually submitting the program for execution.

2   Creating separate debugging environments for each subprogram.

3   Bringing the total system to the point where it can execute without creating machine interrupts.

4   Testing the total system with a large variety of inputs to try to force machine interrupts.

5   Testing the total system with a wide variety of inputs for which correct results have been determined and are available for comparison with actual outputs.

DESK CHECKING

Before executing your program on the computer, you should sit down with the source-program listing produced from an error-free compilation run and follow each flow of control through the program. In other words, you should step through the program manually, pretending to be the computer. If the compiler available to you is a load and go compiler (in which case, compilation and execution are initiated by a single request), you should check and recheck your program coding before submitting it to the computer.

As an example, assume that you have written a program to process payroll data. In desk checking, you should pose questions such as "What will happen when an input value of 51340 for man number and 44.50 for salary are provided as input to this program?" Then, you should assume that exactly this happens and follow each processing step as it will be followed by the computer executing the program. Determine whether the output created from this input is correct.

Unless a program is very short or very simple, it contains many flows of control (also called paths of program logic) that must be followed. You should attempt to follow all of them. In doing so, you will need to assume not only correct inputs but also incorrect ones—those that cause error-handling routines to be performed. Remember that you are pretending to be the computer, so you can assume nothing; you can only carry out instructions, exactly as they have been prepared by you, the programmer. The program flowchart should be referred to during desk checking as a means of ensuring that all flows of control are checked out.

Desk checking is a technique of careful scrutiny. Although you have eliminated errors of the types that can be detected by the compiler, there are many types of errors that may still exist in your program. Some kinds of errors to look for when desk checking are listed below.

1   Variables that are the wrong type or size.

2   Array subscripts that might be zero for some paths through the program, or that might be too large (exceed the maximum for the dimension) in some cases.

3   Loops that will be executed too many times, or too few times. Look for loops that should sometimes be avoided altogether, but will be executed at least once as the program now stands. Such loops usually result in using zero for a subscript, or doing arithmetic with values that haven't been defined.

4   Subroutine calls containing incorrect numbers of arguments. Look for arguments that are of the wrong type. Use of arithmetic expressions as arguments is particularly dangerous because the compiler picks the type and size of the result.

5   Equivalenced arrays that cause storage to be used for multiple purposes at the same time.

6   Arithmetic expressions with incorrect parenthesization or that are not interpeted as you intend.

7   Conversion errors in handling data, first as floating-point, then as integer. Check that the floating-point values don't have to be exact in order for your program to work correctly.

8   FORMAT statements that do not correspond to card layouts and input data. Make sure that the field descriptions specified in FORMAT statements are correct.

9   Incorrect handling of the first input or the last input. Even experienced programmers often fail to provide correct routines for processing required at end of file.

10   Failure to initialize variables. You cannot assume that locations in storage contain blanks, zeros, or any other particular values unless statements in your program have caused such values to be placed therein.

11   Failure to detect or provide for the handling of invalid input.

As you have probably decided, desk checking is not a quick, easy task. But it is a vital one. A few hours of programmer time spent wisely at this point can prevent needless waste of both programmer time and computer time later. Some programmers work in teams, checking not only their programs but programs of others as well. Often a new viewpoint is a more objective one. The programmer who is extremely familiar with his program may unconsciously read into it logic that is not there. For this reason a friend can sometimes more aptly play the role of the computer.

DEBUGGING ENVIRONMENTS

It is best to have the parts of a system working independently before you put them together. To do this, it is wise to write a small main program to call each subroutine that you want to check and to call the subroutines repetitively, with several different sets of argument values. Use of a small main program allows you to be sure that any errors that occur are in the subroutine rather than in the calling program. If, instead, you try to debug the system as a whole, you will be forced to spend much of your time determining which subroutine is causing an error before you can even attempt to eliminate it.

In a similar vein, most systems have a single main routine, or driver, that coordinates the execution of subroutines. (See figure 9.1.) It is good practice to test this routine with dummy subroutines before testing it with actual subroutines. The objective is again to establish a working piece before putting that piece together with other system components.

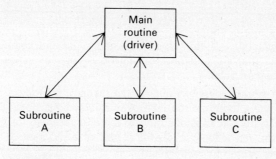

FIGURE 9.1

A common method of system organization is shown schematically in figure 9.1. The system comprises a main routine and three subroutines, A, B, and C. In debugging this system, we must set up dummy subroutines for A, B, and C to test the main routine. We must also set up dummy main routines to call A, B, and C with one or two data setups before putting the system together. Data that would normally be generated for a subroutine by other routines can be put in DATA statements (explained in chapter 6) in the dummy main routine to create the proper information boundary for the subroutine.

MACHINE-INTERRUPT ERRORS

Programming errors are of two types. Errors of the first type are fatal to the program. They force termination of a program because the computer cannot understand what needs to be done; it cannot act upon a situation that has arisen during execution. Errors of the second type cause incorrect output to be provided by a program, but they do not stop its execution by the computer.

One of the goals in debugging is to reach the stage where you can bombard your program with many different input possibilities on one computer run. Before you can do this, however, you must eliminate errors of the first type mentioned above, since your program executes no further when one of these occurs.

Most fatal errors are machine-interrupt errors. Such errors occur whenever your program executes a statement that is invalid as far as the computer is concerned. Probable causes of machine interrupts are listed below.

1   Mismatch of subroutine arguments
    If arguments listed in a CALL statement are the wrong size, type, or dimen-
    sion, or if an incorrect number of arguments is given, a machine interrupt
    usually occurs.

2   An infinite loop
    If you are incrementing a floating-point value, then testing it for equality
    with another value, the result of your arithmetic may be very close, but never
    equal, to the compared value. If failure of the test for equality causes a loop
    to be executed, you will never exit from the loop. Testing for a condition
    other than equality (e.g., ABS(A − B).LE..005) is one way to avoid this
    problem.

3   Dividing by zero or some small value
    Division operations of this type frequently cause the computer to try to
    store results that are outside the numerical range of values that can be
    stored in the computer.

4   Addressing storage locations outside the range of an array
    If you execute a loop one too many times, array subscripts within the loop
    may address storage locations outside the area reserved for the array. This
    kind of error can lead to overwriting part of a program or trying to use
    memory that isn't in the machine.

5   Using variables that have not been assigned values or are zero as subscripts
    Both FORTRAN and WATFIV have features that can be used to find errors
    resulting from invalid subscripts. (See below.)

    Reading invalid characters or constants of invalid form frequently causes
errors that are regarded as fatal by FORTRAN systems. Although machine
interrupts do not occur in such cases, the system does not allow program execution to continue.

    What can one do about machine interrupts? Desk checking is a notable
"ounce of prevention." By careful desk checking, you can eliminate many
machine-interrupt errors before they occur. Should one occur, use of the
debugging statements and techniques described later in this chapter is advisable.

    As you probably realize by now, most programs initially contain numerous
errors. When you are beyond this stage, you should be able to find many of the
remaining errors on each computer run. Beginning programmers are often
embarrassed by making errors, but they need not be, because this is the norm.
The important thing is to test a program thoroughly so that no (or almost no)
errors remain.

TESTING WITH A VARIETY OF INPUTS

You should plan your method of testing and your test data at the time you
design your system. By establishing simple input data structures, you simplify
both coding and debugging tasks. When input data structures are simple, you
can form many test cases with relative ease. Some guidelines to follow when
generating test cases are listed below.

1   Make sure that all statements in each program under test are executed by at
    least one of your test cases.

2   When testing a program that performs more than one function, be sure to test each function.

3   For each function under test, use test values at the extreme ends of the range for which the function was designed, and at least one middle value.

4   Provide invalid as well as valid input to each program under test to check its error-handling procedures. Each program should check the validity of its input. The programs are easier and more efficient to use. They are also easier to debug because they check each other.

DEBUGGING STATEMENTS

As you gain experience in programming, you will learn to use the FORTRAN statements that we have studied in debugging as well as in meeting the problem-solving requirements of problem statements. Most systems also include statements designed especially for debugging purposes. Some techniques for both are explained below.

TRACING PROGRAM EXECUTION

One of the simplest and most powerful techniques for debugging is to create a trace of the execution of a program, printing both "where it's been" and the values of important variables in each area. You can do so by inserting PRINT statements at strategic points in the program. (See figure 9.2.) Each statement should print a unique constant and the values of selected variables.

```
      INTEGER TFLOW, TVALUE
      COMMON TFLOW, TVALUE
C     THESE ARE THE TRACE VARIABLES.
      READ, TFLOW, TVALUE
         .
         .
         .
      IF (TFLOW.NE.0.) PRINT, 'BEGIN COMPUTE'
         .
         .
         .
      CALL B(I,K)
      IF (TVALUE.NE.0.) PRINT, 'B RETURNED VALUE OF ', K
         .
         .
         .
      END
```

FIGURE 9.2

A common problem is that statements inserted for debugging get in the way when a program is used in a production mode. Another problem is that if you trace everything, the test output is so voluminous and complex that you can't interpret it—at least not without devoting weeks of concentrated effort to the task. One way to avoid these problems is to include several switches in a program for use in debugging. Each switch controls the output of one kind of debugging trace or of debugging in a certain section of the program. For example, one switch can force a trace of the flow of the program; another can permit tracing of the values of one or two important variables; and a third can control the printing of output by a particular subprogram. When this approach is used, the first action of a program or system of programs under test is to read the values for these trace switches and place them in a common storage area where they can be referred to by statements in all subprograms. After the system is thoroughly tested, DATA statements can be inserted to set all of these switches off. The READ statement at the beginning and the PRINT statements associated with tracing can be removed.

WATFIV FEATURES

Because WATFIV is designed to be a student-oriented program development and debugging system, it offers many special features at program execution-time. If you use a subscript that is too large or too small, WATFIV detects the invalid reference immediately and prints the number of the statement where it is used. The same is true for most of the machine-interrupt conditions. WATFIV cannot detect infinite loops, but since time limits can be specified for debugging runs, any program that enters such a loop eventually uses up its time. Then you can at least tell where you were at that particular moment. WATFIV can be directed to check for references to variables that have not been given values. The method of invoking this check is system-dependent, but it normally involves use of the $JOB (or $COMPILE) control card. (See appendix C.) This check increases the amount of output provided by a program and lengthens program execution-time, but it is very useful in early stages of testing, when you are still trying to eliminate machine interrupts.

THE ON ERROR GO TO STATEMENT

WATFIV allows you to go to a particular statement in your program if an error occurs. You do so by executing an *ON ERROR GO TO statement* in which the number of that statement appears. This enables you to recover from the error by taking some alternate or corrective action, print a message describing the error, diagnose the specific cause of the error, branch to a call to a system-provided subroutine that takes action for your program, or initiate other special action as advisable.

Any number of ON ERROR GO TO statements may be included in a program. To avoid infinite loops on recovery attempts, only one ON ERROR GO TO statement—the last one encountered before an error occurs—can be executed per program. Use of an ON ERROR GO TO statement to monitor and recover from invalid input is shown in figure 9.3.

```
        DIMENSION A(10)
        ON ERROR GO TO 100
  10    READ, A
         .
         .
         .

  100   PRINT, 'ERROR IN INPUT.   PLEASE TRY AGAIN.'
        GO TO 10
         .
         .
         .

        END
```

FIGURE 9.3

Generally, an ON ERROR GO TO statement can be placed anywhere in a program. It is not advisable to include an ON ERROR GO TO statement in the range of a DO statement because no checking is performed to determine whether the transfer at execution-time will be valid. Indefinite looping may result.

THE DUMPLIST STATEMENT

The *DUMPLIST statement* of WATFIV is another debugging aid. It works in much the same way as the general-purpose NAMELIST statement except that the word DUMPLIST replaces the word NAMELIST, and a list of names appearing in a DUMPLIST statement need never appear in READ or WRITE statements in the program. (See "The NAMELIST statement" in chapter 10.) Some sample DUMPLIST statements are

```
DUMPLIST /LIST1/A,B,ARR1
DUMPLIST /LIST2/ROOT1,ROOT2/LIST3/AVE
```

The general form of the DUMPLIST statement is

```
DUMPLIST /n1/a[,b, . . .] [/n2/c[,d, . . .] . . .]
```

where $n1$, $n2$, . . . are the names of lists, and a, b, c, d, . . . are the simple variables or array variables which constitute the list whose name they follow.

A DUMPLIST statement has no effect if the program in which it appears executes normally. If execution of the program is terminated because of an error condition, however, WATFIV generates NAMELIST-like output of all DUMPLIST statements appearing in subprograms that have been entered. The printed values are the values of the named variables at program termination.

To avoid producing too much output, you should select only a few important variables when constructing DUMPLIST statements. Array variables, in particular, should be used only with forethought, because the values of all elements in a selected array are printed if abnormal termination occurs. By including the name of each subprogram in a DUMPLIST statement in that subprogram, you can determine which subprograms were executed prior to program termination. Usually, a bug in a program can be detected by examining the final values of a few carefully chosen variables.

FORTRAN DEBUGGING

FORTRAN as developed for IBM 360/370 computers also includes a debug facility. To ensure that debugging routines do not become intermixed with problem-solving functions and to permit them to be removed easily when checkout of a program unit (single main program or subprogram) is completed, the designers of FORTRAN determined that these routines should be grouped in one part of the program unit. Hence, the FORTRAN programmer specifies debugging actions to be taken at various points in his program by means of groups of statements called *debug packets*. A source-program deck consists of the source-language statements that comprise the program unit, followed by a DEBUG statement, followed by any debug packets, followed by the END statement for the unit.

A debug packet is preceded by an AT debug packet identification statement and consists of one or more executable debug facility statements (explained below) and/or FORTRAN source-language statements. The packet may contain any FORTRAN source-language statements except SUBROUTINE, FUNCTION, IMPLICIT, BLOCK DATA, and statement function definitions. It is terminated by either another AT statement or the END statement of the program unit.

```
        REAL A, B, C
        N100 = 0
          .
          .
          .
100     A(I) = 4.7 * FUNC1(T,K,L)
          .
          .
          .
        DEBUG TRACE
        AT 100
        TRACE ON
        N100 = N100 + 1
        DISPLAY A(I), N100
        END
```

FIGURE 9.4

The subprogram in figure 9.4 contains one debug packet. The statements between AT and END are executed prior to each execution of statement 100. These statements ensure that tracing of statement labels is effected, add one to a count of the number of times the packet has been executed, and print that count and the current value of the subscripted variable A(I) on the debug output data set.

There may be statement labels in a debug packet but they must not duplicate those in other packets or in the main body of the program. There may also be declarations in the packets, but the names in a packet must not duplicate names used elsewhere in the program. To avoid confusion, you can qualify the names in a packet by beginning them with a letter that you do not use as the first letter of other variables. Similarly, statement labels should be made unique; using only labels from 80000 to 89999 in debug packets works well.

The main program or subprogram cannot branch to a label in a debug packet, but the packet may branch to any label in the program. There may be several packets per program, but they cannot communicate across program units except through variables in common storage. DO loops within a packet must be wholly within the packet.

THE DEBUG STATEMENT

A DEBUG statement must immediately precede the AT statement for the first debug packet in a program unit. It sets the general conditions for the debug facility and establishes debugging operations that apply to the entire unit. The general form of the DEBUG statement is

DEBUG *option1* [, *option2*, . . .]

where each *option* is one of the following, in any order:

- UNIT(*i*)
  This option allows the output of debugging to go onto a data set other than the standard output data set. The integer *i* is a FORTRAN logical unit number, the identifier associated with a certain input/output file (data set). If this option is not specified, debugging output is routed to the standard output data set. (To learn how logical unit numbers are assigned to files, and which logical unit numbers are assigned to what files at your installation, you should consult programming and operations documentation for the system in use.)

- SUBCHK [(*ar1* [, *ar2*, . . .])]
  This option causes the FORTRAN system to ascertain that array subscripts are within the dimension bounds declared for the named arrays, just as WATFIV does automatically. The parameters *ar1*, *ar2*, . . . are the names of arrays for which subscripts are to be checked. If an invalid subscript is generated, an error message is placed on the debug output data set and execution continues, using the invalid subscript. If the list of array names is omitted, the subscripts of all arrays in the program unit are checked. If the option is not used, no subscripts are checked.

- TRACE
  This option must be present if you expect to use tracing in this program unit. It does not actually initiate tracing, but it warns the compiler that TRACE ON statements may be included in debug packets of this unit.

- INIT [(*v1* [, *v2*, . . .])]
  This option causes the value of any of the variables *v1*, *v2*, . . . to be displayed whenever a new value is assigned to the variable (via an assignment, READ, or ASSIGN statement). If an array name is specified, and one or more values in the array are changed, only the changed values are displayed. If the option is specified but the list is omitted, a display occurs whenever the value of any variable or array element in this program unit is changed.

- SUBTRACE
  If this option is specified, the name of the subprogram is printed on the debug output data set whenever the subprogram is called. RETURN is printed whenever a return is executed. This option holds only for the subprogram containing the DEBUG statement. If you want similar tracing in another subprogram, you must include the DEBUG statement with the SUBTRACE option in that subprogram. The option is of no value when the program unit is a single main program.

  DEBUG UNIT(7), SUBTRACE, TRACE, INIT(INPUT)

This statement indicates that debug output is to be routed to the data set assigned to logical unit 7; the subprogram name is to be printed whenever the subprogram is entered; tracing may be requested; and the value represented by the variable INPUT is to be displayed whenever it is changed.

THE AT STATEMENT

The AT statement identifies the beginning of a debug packet and indicates the point in the program at which the debugging operations in that packet are to be performed. The debugging statements are executed just prior to execution of the statement identified. The general form of the AT statement is

AT *statement number*

where *statement number* is the label preceding any executable statement in the single main program or subprogram being debugged. AT statements in a given test unit may not contain the same statement number.

THE TRACE ON STATEMENT

The TRACE ON statement, used in figure 9.4, initiates the tracing of program flow by statement number. Each time a statement identified by a statement number is executed, the statement number is recorded on the debug output data set.

This statement has no effect unless the TRACE option is specified in the DEBUG statement for this program unit. Once invoked, however, tracing continues until a TRACE OFF statement is executed in some debug packet. Its effect holds through any levels of subprogram calls and returns and causes tracing in all of those subprograms in which the TRACE option is specified.

Some programmers give statement numbers to important statements for tracing purposes, even if they need not be labeled for branching. It is not wise, however, to retain numerous unneeded labels in fully checked-out programs.

THE TRACE OFF STATEMENT

The TRACE OFF statement may appear in any debug packet. It cancels the effect of a TRACE ON statement; that is, it stops the recording of program flow by statement number. Its form is

TRACE OFF

THE DISPLAY STATEMENT

The DISPLAY statement (seen in figure 9.4) causes the current values of specified simple variables and array variables to be recorded on the debug output data set. The variable names are printed along with their values as aids to identification. The form of the output is the same as that described for the NAMELIST statement in chapter 10. The use of this statement is a convenience, eliminating the need for FORMAT, NAMELIST, or WRITE statements to display values for debugging. The general form of the statement is

DISPLAY *list*

where *list* is a series of simple variables and/or array variables, separated by commas. Subscripted variables and dummy arguments cannot appear in the list.

A SAMPLE DESIGN

REF

Now we are ready to tackle a problem. In solving it, we shall follow steps 1 through 4 (page 154) and do steps 5 through 8 (page 155) recursively to define the modules at all levels and complete their design.

Assume that we are to draw outline maps on a printer. The maps will be specified as a series of lines, each of which will be indicated by its endpoints. Each endpoint will be given as an ordered pair of numbers, the first representing the horizontal displacement of the point, and the second representing its vertical displacement. There should be no need to know the actual scale of a map. We must scale the values so that the map fits on one page. Since the user may want to overlay one map on another, we must be able to use different character symbols for different maps.

Do you fully understand this mapping problem? Or do you have questions immediately? Usually, a programmer is presented with a problem that is no more specific than this. His task is not only to write the program, but also to define the problem—to discover what kind of a system should be created to satisfy what needs.

STEPS 1–4

Function list for map problem

We start with step 1, listing the functions of the system.

1 Read in map.
2 Scale current set of maps.

REF

3   Change map coordinates (ordered pairs) from floating-point values to integers in the range from 1 to 132, assuming there are 132 characters per print line.

4   Print current set of maps.

5   Overlay a new map on old maps.

6   Read commands entered by a user.

Information items

The second step is to list the information items the system must receive to perform each function and the output that it will provide. We define the information boundary for each function.

Input

1   Title for map
Format for map coordinates
Print character used for this map outline
Number of points in the outline of a single map
Point values

2   Maximum and minimum horizontal values of points to scale to the width of the print line

3   Same items as in 2

4   Current list of maps
Number of maps
Title for each map
Number of points for each map
Point values for each map as integers
Print character for each map outline

5   Variable or information item to record fact that next map should be overlayed on current maps

6   Elements of command language
Name, format, and function of each command

Output

The output of the system is a single map, or a set of maps printed as overlays. A set of two maps should look something like the sketch in figure 9.5.

Commands

The next step is to define the command language. In this case, we use an actual command set, since a series of requests is to be entered by the user. In other cases the command language might be expressed in the information items themselves, or by the use of input parameters or entry points. We consider the command language in correspondence with our function list of step 1.

1   Reading of a map can be initiated by a card with the word READ in columns

REF

1 through 4. The balance of the required information items should be on succeeding cards. (Their structure is specified in step 4, which establishes the data structures.)

2 Scaling should not be initiated by a command. The program should perform scaling automatically as part of the map printing function.

3 Conversion of point values should not be requested by the user. It, too, should be done automatically.

4 PRINT in columns 1 through 5 should initiate a print operation. All other required information items should have been saved by earlier operations.

5 OVERLAY in columns 1 through 7 should suffice.

6 Reading of commands should be the first function of the system and is basic to its operation; it is not desirable that a special command be entered to enable the command-reading function.

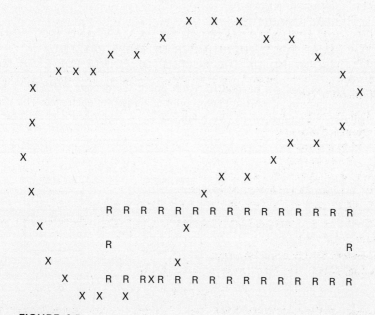

FIGURE 9.5

Data structures

The fourth step is to define the data structures involved in each function.

1 The input structures should be as flexible as possible. One suggestion follows:

    a) 'label for map output'
        one card; quotes required but not read into storage

REF

b) format
   execution-time format for use with FORTRAN execution-time format facility (discussed in chapter 10); parentheses enclosing data list but no word FORMAT or statement label required

c) map print character

d) number of points in map
   integer in columns 1 through 5 (with WATFIV, format-free input can be used)

e) cards with points
   as many cards as necessary; program reads correct number of cards because it knows the format and number of points

2 Now we have to decide how to store the coordinates and other information about the current set of maps.

```
         DIMENSION POINTS(1000,2), NPOINT(10)
         INTEGER NMAP/0/
         REAL CHAR(10)
C        WE ASSUME A MAXIMUM OF 10 MAPS AND 1000 POINTS.
C        NMAP TELLS THE NUMBER OF MAPS PRESENT.
C        NPOINT HOLDS THE NUMBER OF POINTS FOR EACH MAP.
```

Since two values are needed for each point, we declare POINTS, a two-dimensional array. CHAR holds the print character for each map. The use of these data structures when two maps are to be processed is shown below. (See figure 9.6.)

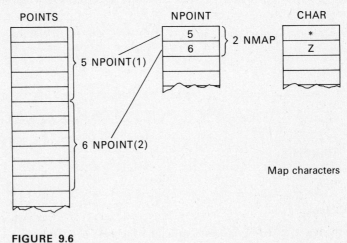

FIGURE 9.6

For internal processing, we require two additional data structures.

REF

```
          DIMENSION PCHAR(132)
C         LINE TO PUT CHARACTERS FOR PRINTING
          DIMENSION ISCALE(1000,2)
C         ARRAY FOR SCALED INTEGER VALUES
C         WILL ALSO BE USED BY THE PRINT FUNCTION
```

3   Same data structures as 2 above.

4   In printing the current set of maps, we need one additional data structure.

```
          DIMENSION CLABEL(20)
C         AN ARRAY FOR THE LABEL OF THE CURRENT MAP
```

5   To record an OVERLAY command so that the next map is not read in atop the preceding map, but rather is inserted in addition to it, we declare

```
          INTEGER IOVER
```

6   To read in the command line, we need

```
          REAL COMM(20)
```


STEPS 5–8

We have completed the first four steps of design. Now we must organize the above functions into modules and do the secondary design steps. As we look at the commands, we see that they break down naturally into several basic modules. These are:

1   Command read module
    Checks command for accuracy and transfers control to proper submodule.

2   Map read module
    Reads titles, formats, print characters, points, and the OVERLAY command.

3   Print module
    Scales and creates integers. Puts points in print line and prints them. Prints label.

The command read module

1   Information items
    Command names and module name corresponding to each command

2   Data structures
    Array of command names
    Input line

3   Algorithm
    Check for command name in array. Give error message if name is not present. Transfer to proper entry for the given command. Each command returns after it has been executed. See flowchart in figure 9.7.

    Each box in the flowchart is now a candidate for submodule analysis. The 'search for name in table' box should certainly be subjected to such analysis. You should pursue this investigation as a programming problem.

REF

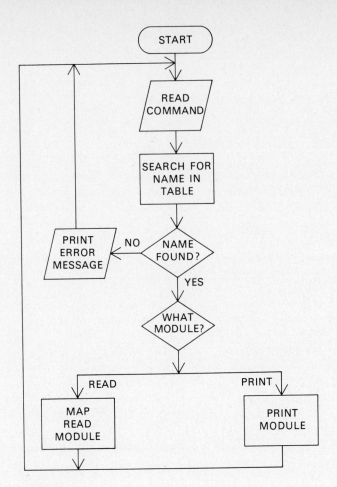

FIGURE 9.7

The map read module

1　Information items
　Same as listed under functions 1 and 5, which this module encompasses

2　Data structures
　Same as 1 above

3　Algorithm
　Check overlay switch. If it is zero, set NMAP to zero. Read the map title, the format, the map print character, and the number of points. Then read the points into the next available locations in POINTS array. Return to command read module. See flowchart in figure 9.8.

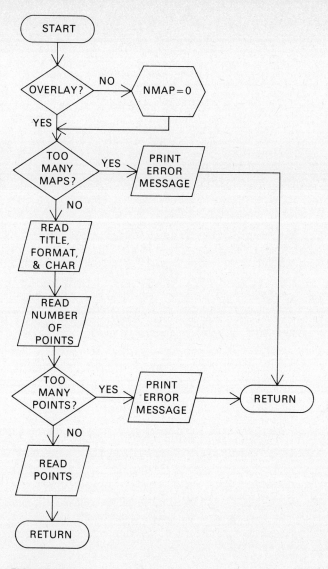

FIGURE 9.8

You are likely to find a dark spot in the procedure for reading in points for a new map when there is an overlay. If you do not understand how to index into the middle of the array POINTS, you should break the 'read points' box into another stage of design. Otherwise, you can begin coding.

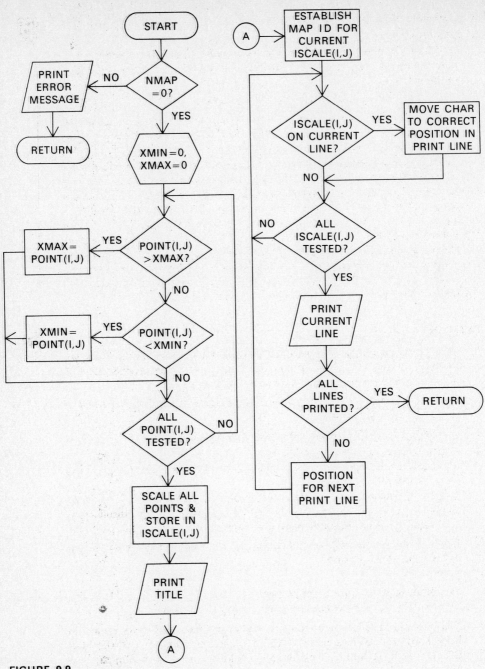

FIGURE 9.9

The print module

1   Information items (All those listed under functions 2, 3, and 4)

2 Data structures (Same as 1 above)

3 Algorithm

First find the lowest and highest horizontal point values. Use them to compute the integer values by the following formula, where X is the initial form of the value

$$IXNEW = (X-XMIN) \ / \ ((XMAX-XMIN) * 132.) + .5$$

Print the title. For each line, identify the points falling on that line and insert the correct character for each pair of points in the line. Print the line. Return to command read module. (See figure 9.9.)

REF

The .5 in the formula above is for rounding. If the maps might be large, then a sort of the new points should be introduced so that they appear one line at a time. They must be marked as to which map they came from so that the correct print character is printed. Otherwise, the 132 lines can be printed by finding the points corresponding to each line from each map and inserting the correct print character in the output line. This formula assumes that there are ten horizontal characters per inch so that the map is square. If your printer has ten horizontal characters per inch but only six or eight lines per inch, then your formula for scaling in the vertical direction must be slightly different. (Use the formula above as a guide in determining an equivalent.)

EXERCISES

QUEST

1. (TUT) Explain what is meant by the term *information boundary*. In doing so, identify possible components, indicate when it must be established, and show why it is an important programming consideration.

2. (TUT) What are some advantages and disadvantages of a modular approach to system design?

3. (TUT) Distinguish between debugging and desk checking.

4. (TUT) Discuss with fellow students
    a) some of the errors in your programs that have been detected by the compiler during compilation
    b) errors causing abnormal termination of your programs
    c) errors that you detected only after discovering that the results provided by your programs were not correct

5. (TUT) Refer to the preceding exercise. In what ways might some of the errors have been avoided?

6. (TUT)
    a) What is meant by a program trace?
    b) Explain one way of causing such tracing to be performed.

7. (TUT) Suggest a problem-solving application that might be coded in FORTRAN as implemented in WATFIV systems and how the ON ERROR GO TO and DUMPLIST statements could be used in debugging the program.

8. (TUT) Construct a debug packet causing the value of the variable DIV to be printed and tracing to be initiated prior to each execution of statement 300.

PROGRAMMING PROBLEMS

Any of the following topics may be used as design problems and as projects for programming.

1. (REF) Design a system to read matrices from cards and store them on files. Each matrix should have an input form which includes its format and dimensions. Implement operations on the files for each of the common matrix operations (inverse, product, sum, difference, and so on). Include some additional operations for convenience (such as changing the diagonal of a matrix into a vector). Permit the user to give a simple set of commands for the operations he wants to do. Each command should include the command name (perhaps as an integer) and the locations of the matrices involved, plus any special parameters for the specified operation.

2. (REF) Design a system to project a person's income, taxes, outflow, and so on, for a given month or set of months. Allow a variety of inputs, such as current wage, doctor bills, car payment, house payment, and the like. Create special subprograms to compute the values of interest, taxes, insurance, and so on, for each type of transaction. Emphasize a design that allows you to expand your program, adding new types of transactions or new request types.

3. (REF) Write a program to control a set of elevators where the input is an initial set of positions for the elevators, and a series of requests from different floors, along with a time at which each request is made. Do not spend too much time trying to generate the optimum schedule; just write a system to do a reasonable job.

4. (REF) Design a system to give information about a ferry schedule. There should be several different types of requests, as well as a method for inputting the schedule to your program.

5. (REF) Design a system for hotel reservations; it should keep track of room numbers, room types, individuals, and current occupancy.

6. (REF) Design a system to schedule the classes at a grade school, high school, or college. Try to think of the ramifications of your system on grading, attendance, and the like.

7. (REF) Design a system to record the mileage of a fleet of trucks as a basis for determination and scheduling of preventive maintenance. It should indicate which types of maintenance must be performed at which times and on which trucks.

8. (REF) Design a system to keep track of the production of a set of fields over several years. You must record seed types, planting times, fertilizer usage, and so on. To enhance the system, record also the gross characteristics of the weather during the period.

9. (REF) Design a system to keep track of customers' orders handled at a warehouse. You must monitor levels of stock and reorder any stock that drops below its established minimum level.

The problems following chapters 10 (input/output) and 11 (logical and character variables) are also both design and programming problems.

INTRO

Most, if not all, of the programs we have written or examined thus far have used format-free input and output (input/output, or I/O). Values to be read or written have been identified in READ or PRINT statements, respectively. Sometimes, however, we need to read input that is not in a form suitable for format-free input. At other times, we want to write output (say, a report) in a form other than that provided by format-free output. To do so, we usually accept a dual responsibility: We identify the values to be read or written, and we describe those values. We do the former by means of an I/O list in a READ or WRITE statement. For the latter, we use a FORMAT statement. You will learn about these statements in this chapter.

The reference section explains how flexibility in I/O operations can be obtained by reading I/O lists as data at program execution time. Core-to-core I/O, a special feature of WATFOR/WATFIV whereby data can be moved in storage under format control, is explained and illustrated. The IBM 360/370 FORTRAN programmer who uses formatted I/O should be aware of a format-free I/O capability available to him with NAMELIST statements. Hence, the chapter concludes with discussion of NAMELIST, a FORTRAN statement that causes default formatting to be applied.

HOW TO USE THIS CHAPTER

FORTRAN offers a wide variety of input/output capabilities, but many of these are not needed for basic programming applications. The beginning programmer can concentrate initially on those features that meet his immediate input/output requirements. If you are a beginner, you should read the explanation of the FORMAT statement in this chapter but study only the integer (I) and floating-point (F) field types, or format codes. Then read the discussions of the READ and WRITE statements and of reading and writing with format control. Having done so, you will be able to code programs that read single card images and write single lines of formatted numeric data.

Chapter

10

INPUT/OUTPUT

Although this level of programming skill is sufficient for basic programming applications, there are many other input/output features that you can learn to use advantageously. After you become familiar with other data types (discussed in the reference section of chapter 2), you should study the other format codes explained in this chapter. Some of them help you to read or write data of other types. Others help you to deal more precisely with spacing considerations. Before reading or writing data to be stored as arrays, learn to use implied DOs as explained here. Knowledge of additional material presented in the reference section is essential for many types of programming applications.

INPUT/OUTPUT—CHARACTERS VERSUS INTERNAL CODING

TUT

There are two basic types of input and output in FORTRAN. In one, characters of the internal coding scheme used in computer memory are converted on output to characters with which we are familiar (the letters A through Z, digits 0 through 9, and special characters such as *, &, and /). Conversely, on input, characters in familiar form are read and converted to the internal coding scheme used for computation and manipulation by the computer itself. This type of input and output is called *formatted*, or *character*, *input/output*. In the second type, values are transferred from memory to some external medium, or vice-versa, in their internal forms. No conversion to the external character form occurs. This type of input and output is called *unformatted*, or *record*, *input/output*.

The main advantage of the character form of input/output is that a person can create input by punching data onto cards or keying it at a terminal and can read characters printed as output. The WATFIV format-free input and output statements PRINT and READ, as discussed in chapter 3, are of the character input/output type. The primary advantage of record input/output is that the computer does not have to spend time converting back and forth from the internal representation to the character representation. A typical use of unformatted input/output is in writing out data that need not be examined by people, then reading that data back into computer storage for additional processing. Formatted input/output is discussed in detail in this chapter. Unformatted input/output is discussed in chapter 12.

A SIMPLE EXAMPLE

Formatted input/output can be controlled by READ, WRITE, and FORMAT statements. Perhaps the best way to understand the functions of these statements is to consider a simple example in which they are used. Hence, the example below is intended to give a feeling for formatted I/O. You need not understand each detail of the example at this time; the details will become meaningful to you as you study this chapter.

Assume that an input line contains three integers, each a maximum of ten characters long. The first integer appears in a field comprised of columns 1 through 10 of the input line. It is right-justified in this field, so any unused columns are at the left end of the data. The second integer is right-justified in columns 11 through 20, and the last is right-justified in columns 21 through 30. Further assume that our task is to read this data into main-storage locations reserved for the variables I, J, and K, change the integers to floating-point form, and divide each by 10. The results of the division operations are to be printed as floating-point numbers having one place to the right of the decimal point, in ten-column fields of an output line. Figure 10.1 shows one way this can be done.

```
      READ (5,99) I, J, K
      A = I
      B = J
      C = K
      A = A/10.
      B = B/10.
      C = C/10.
      WRITE (6,98) A, B, C
99    FORMAT (3I10)
98    FORMAT (3F10.1)
      STOP
      END
```

FIGURE 10.1

In the READ statement, the integer 5 identifies the source of the input data; the integer 99 is the label of a FORMAT statement; and the variables I, J, and K are the I/O list telling the locations in memory into which the input data is to be moved.

The types and sizes of variables in this program are determined by default. Hence, the three assignment statements following READ cause conversion from integer to floating point to occur. We do not perform the division operations until after converting the values to floating point because integer arithmetic would truncate decimal places. For example, if the value of I were 55, then I/10 would be 5, but, after conversion, A/10. is 5.5. The WRITE statement is analogous to READ but controls output operations rather than input.

In the FORMAT statements, the characters 3I10 and 3F10.1 describe the fields that contain or will contain data. Each numeral 3 tells how many fields of a given type there are. The I and the F are format codes that tell the types. The 10 gives the number of character positions in each field, and the .1 gives the number of those positions to be printed to the right of a decimal point on output. Since the FORMAT statements are nonexecutable statements, they may appear anywhere in the program. Some programmers feel that it is wise to group them—usually, with other nonexecutable statements at the beginning of a single main program or of each subprogram. If each FORMAT statement is referred to by only one READ or WRITE statement, you may prefer to place each FORMAT statement immediately following the statement that refers to it.

WHY USE FORMATTED READ AND WRITE?

Why bother with READ, WRITE, and FORMAT statements as shown in figure 10.1? Why not just use format-free READ and PRINT and concentrate on the problem-solving required in a program?

A major reason for using READ, WRITE, and FORMAT is that format-free I/O is not available in most FORTRAN systems. The format-free READ and PRINT statements are special statements of WATFOR and WATFIV, designed to make input/output programming easy for students. Those of you using these statements with FORTRAN systems should note that you have had to include a FORMAT statement (provided for you in chapter 3 in a somewhat cookbook approach) in each program. Perhaps you are beginning to understand why.

Even when format-free I/O is available, it is not always sufficient. As noted in the introduction to this chapter, there may be situations where you need to read input data that is not in the form required for format-free input. At other times, you may want to print output in other than the form established for format-free output.

Fields that are read or written using format-free I/O must be separated by commas or blanks. In contrast, when FORMAT statements are used to specify field widths, no separating characters are required. When large volumes of data must be processed, saving space on the external medium is important.

Format-free I/O does not lend itself to reading or printing some types of data. For example, it does not provide for long strings of characters. Have you tried to print a report heading using format-free output?

Suppose that data is to be sorted. A sort program arranges data according to the content of one or more fields of each input line. These fields must appear in the same, fixed positions within every line. Generally, to be compatible with other languages and data-processing methods, the lines must be in a format other than that of format-free I/O.

Finally, there is the weak historical justification for using READ, WRITE, and FORMAT: That is the way I/O has always been done in FORTRAN.

REPORT WRITING

FORMAT statements can be used advantageously to lay out headings for reports. This is done by including the headings as literal constants in FORMAT statements. An example is

200   FORMAT (1X,'HEADING',13X,'COLUMN 1',13X,'2')

Execution of a WRITE statement referring to this FORMAT statement causes the literal constants HEADING, COLUMN 1, and 2 to be printed, thirteen spaces apart, on a print line.

FORMAT statements can also be used to lay out data represented by variables in rows and columns on a report page. If array data are to be printed, but the array elements will not fit across a single page, list features of the FORMAT statement can be used to list the subscripted variable names with both row and column indices in columns, or strips, down one page. The array elements can be printed in lists on another page. Then the lists of subscripted variable names and current element values can be laid side by side to form a single report.

By printing alphabetic characters to describe rows, along with the numeric values in those rows, we can print out titles for rows as well as for columns. The alphabetic characters can be put into an array with a DATA statement, and one array element can be printed out at the beginning of each line.

In most systems, the first character position of the print line is used for carriage control. It can be set to a specific value causing a skip to a new page, single space, double space, or other action appropriate for report formatting. This facility is a convenience for the programmer.

THE FORMAT STATEMENT

The FORMAT statement must be used when formatted input/output in other than format-free form is desired. The data to be read or written is viewed as a continuous stream of characters. The characters may include letters, digits, special characters, and blanks. The purpose of the FORMAT statement is to break the stream into lines, to break the lines into fields, and to specify the characteristics of the data to be placed in (or taken from) each field. (See figure 10.2.)

The action of the FORMAT statement

Given a stream of characters:

1. Break it into lines.

2. Break the lines into fields.

3. Specify the types, sizes, and (if necessary) the number of positions to the right of the decimal point in each field.

literal constant HEADER

2-digit integer I(2)

floating-point F(4.1)

HEADER 47 00.1

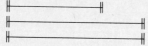

3-digit integer I(3)

character data A(10)

1-digit integer I(1)

logical data L(1)

floating-point F(3.2)

001 CAT 1 T .11

002 DOG 4 F .12

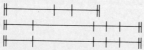
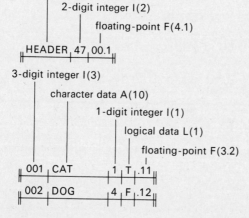

FIGURE 10.2

Within a particular line, a given field always starts at the same character position. That character position is the number you get by starting at the beginning of the line and counting characters (including blanks) until you reach the field in question. Fields cannot extend over lines, and a single data item cannot cross field boundaries. However, one FORMAT statement can describe the formats of several lines.

A *line* as referred to in this chapter may be a line as we often think of it, say, entered from a user terminal or printed on a report. It may also be in other form, for example, a single punched card. For purposes of this discussion, the terms *record* and *line* are synonymous.

A MORE FORMAL DESCRIPTION OF THE FORMAT STATEMENT

Basically, the FORMAT statement is a map that gives a series of descriptions of data items to be read as input or written as output. Each description tells how a data item is represented in memory and its corresponding size as a character string. For example, a value may be stored internally in floating-point form and represented externally by the character string 47.9. Fortunately, the FORTRAN programmer rarely needs to understand machine-level details of how variables are represented internally as long as he remembers which type of internal coding is used for a given variable. He should observe that any card image or print line is simply a sequence of characters; the character positions can be numbered from left to right, starting with the numeral 1. The most common punched cards have eighty columns, numbered from 1 through 80. Most print lines are 132 characters in length, but there are some variations from system to system. The FORMAT statement, in effect, groups these characters across the input/output line.

The general form of the FORMAT statement is

nnn FORMAT ($f1$ [,$f2$,...])

where *nnn* is a statement number (the label of the FORMAT statement) and *f1*, *f2*,... are *field descriptors*. Each field descriptor specifies one field or a set of fields of the same type and size. Examples are 8I4, F4.1, and 2P3F10.3.

The general form of a field descriptor is

srtw.d

This general form looks complicated until you understand what each character means. Most of them are optional and are not often used. Their meanings and the valid entries for each are explained below.

s   is optional and is a *scale factor*. It has the form *n*P where *n* is an unsigned or negatively signed integer—the power of ten by which an internally stored value is divided or multiplied to equal the input or output representation of the value. (See "The scale factor" in this chapter.)

r   is optional and is a *repetition factor*. When consecutive fields on a line are the same, the number of consecutive identical fields can be indicated by an unsigned integer. This eliminates the need to write the same field description many times. If *r* is omitted, a value of 1 is assumed.

t   is a *format code*. In most cases, it specifies the type of a data value in memory so that conversion takes place as required. (The format codes and their meanings are discussed below.)

w is an unsigned integer indicating the number of character positions in a field. The total number of characters specified by a field descriptor is *w* (the width) times *r* (the repetition factor).

d is an unsigned integer indicating the number of character positions to the right of a decimal point. The positions are already included in the field width. This entry is valid only when using F, E, D, or G format code. For other format codes, the decimal point and entry for *d* are omitted.

FORMAT CODES

A wide variety of format codes can be specified in FORMAT statements. Those available in most FORTRAN systems are listed and then explained in greater detail below. A specific system may offer additional types, in which case, installation documentation should be consulted to learn about those types.

Format code	Meaning
I	Integer
F	Floating point
E	Floating point in exponential form
D	Floating point in double-precision form
G	General format
L	Logical
A	Character format
Z	Hexadecimal
H	Literal data
X	Skip
T	Fixed position

I—INTEGER

[*r*]I*w*

The I format code is used in transmitting integer data. The unsigned integer *w* tells the number of characters in the field. The repetition factor *r* may be specified. On input, all blanks are treated as zeros. Therefore, each blank to the left of the integer in the field has no effect but each blank to the right of the integer multiplies the integer by a factor of ten. On output, any zeros preceding the leftmost nonzero digit (leading zeros) are suppressed. A sign, if present, must precede the integer on input and is written before the integer on output.

The statements

```
      WRITE (6,340) J, K, L
340   FORMAT ('1',3I6)
```

provide output such as the following on one print line (b̸ means blank):

$$\underbrace{\not b \not b \not b 456 \not b \not b}_{I6}\underbrace{-300 \not b}_{I6}\underbrace{12345}_{I6}$$

Note the character 1 enclosed in single quotes at the beginning of the format list. Note also that this character does not appear in the printed line. In most systems, the first character of any line to be printed is used to control vertical spacing of the printer. Before coding FORMAT statements for print operations, you should read "Carriage control" in this chapter.

F—FLOATING POINT

$[r]$F$w.d$

The F format code is used in transmitting floating-point data. The unsigned integer w is the total number of characters in the field; d is the number of those characters to the right of the decimal point. On input, if no decimal point is present, it is assumed to be positioned as specified by d. If a decimal point is present, but at a position other than d indicates, the actual point overrides d. In effect, d is ignored. If no sign is present, the value is assumed to be positive. If a sign is present, it must immediately precede the first digit of the numeral. On output, leading zeros are suppressed; if the output value is negative, a minus sign precedes the first digit of the numeral. The number of characters specified for the field must provide for a sign if the value is negative and for the decimal point, as well as for at least all digits to the left of the decimal point. If insufficient positions are provided for the integer portion, including the decimal point and the sign (if any), asterisks are written instead of data. The fractional part of the number is rounded to fit if the number of digits to the right of the decimal point exceeds d, the number of character positions declared for it.

The statements

```
      WRITE (6,470) I, A, B
470   FORMAT (' ',I5,F9.4,F6.1)
```

provide output such as the following on one print line:

$$\underbrace{\not b \not b \not b 34 \not b}_{I5}\underbrace{\not b \not b 1.4321}_{F9.4}\underbrace{\not b \not b 23.9}_{F6.1}$$

E—FLOATING POINT IN EXPONENTIAL FORM

$[r]$E$w.d$

The E format code is generally used for reading or writing floating-point data when the magnitude of the values is large or is unknown at the time the program is written. This format code is similar to F. The exponential form described in chapter 4 can be used for input values, but it is optional. If no exponent is included in the input, the data is handled as for F format code. The number of decimal positions to the right of the decimal point is assumed to be that specified by d if no decimal point is included in the input.

On output, d is not only the total number of decimal positions to the right of the decimal point, but also the total number of significant decimal digits. Each output field contains a minus sign if the value is negative, a zero, a decimal point, the first d significant digits, an E, and a two-digit exponent preceded by a minus sign or a blank. Thus, it appears as follows:

w characters

$$\overbrace{\pm 0.\underbrace{xxx...x}_{d \text{ digits}}E \pm xx}$$

Unless w is greater than or equal to $d + 7$, a format error may occur.

The statements

```
        WRITE (5,100)  A, B, C
100     FORMAT ('0',F9.2,E13.5,E15.7)
```

provide output such as the following on one print line:

$$\underbrace{\not b\not b\not b234.22\not b}_{F9.2}\underbrace{-0.12345E\not b08}_{E13.5}\underbrace{\not b\not b0.9876543E-28}_{E15.7}$$

D—DOUBLE PRECISION

$[r]Dw.d$

The D format code is used for reading and writing values stored internally as double-precision data. In general, double precision is used when more significant digits are needed than can otherwise be represented in floating-point form in computer memory. The D format code works much the same as E except that more significant digits can be read or written, and D is used instead of E to denote exponentiation on output. (See the examples above.) To learn more about double-precision features of FORTRAN, refer to the discussion of double precision in chapter 5.

Because of the way most FORTRAN compilers are designed, preparing floating-point input is not difficult for the user. He need not be concerned about whether an F, E, or D format code appears in the field descriptor for an input data item. Input such as 12.345 and .33344 can be read into storage locations reserved for variables described by F, E, or D format codes. Similarly, values such as 12.09E+04 and 0.045678E−03 can be provided as input for variables described by F, E, or D. The compiler interprets the values as dictated by the format codes in the program.

G—GENERAL

$[r]Gw.d$

The G format code is a generalized code used to transmit integer, floating-point, complex, or logical data, as determined by the type of the corresponding variable in the I/O list.

On input, G works exactly as I, F, E, D, or L. If the data is of INTEGER or LOGICAL type, d and the point preceding d are optional and, if present, ignored. For floating point (F, E, or D) or complex (a pair of F, E, or D, or a combination of F and E or F and D in two consecutive field descriptors), both w and d are required.

On output, G is treated just like I or L for variables in the I/O list that are of INTEGER or LOGICAL type. For real or complex data, d is the total number of significant digits to be printed, but not necessarily the number of digits after the decimal point. The d is also used to determine whether the value is to be written with or without an exponent. If the output value is between .1 and $10**d$, it is written without an exponent; it appears as d significant digits with a decimal point in the proper place. Otherwise, the value is printed in E or D format, depending on its size in storage (single- or double-precision form). For real and complex data in E or D format, w must provide a position for a leading zero, the decimal point, four positions for an exponent, and a position for a minus sign if the value may be negative, as well as d positions for significant digits. It is wise to have w greater than or equal to $d + 7$.

L—LOGICAL

$[r]Lw$

The L format code is used in transmitting logical data. The unsigned integer w tells the number of characters in the field, just as it does in an $[r]Iw$ field descriptor (for integer data). On input, the first T or F in the field determines whether the value is true or false. On output, the letter T or F is written to indicate the current value of the logical variable. For further details, see chapter 11.

A—CHARACTER FORMAT

$[r]Aw$

The A format code is used in transmitting data that is stored internally in character format. The unsigned integer w is, in effect, the maximum number of characters (other than system-provided blanks) that may be transmitted; the actual number of characters transmitted depends on the length of the corresponding variable in the I/O list of the READ or WRITE statement. In IBM 360/370 FORTRAN, that variable may be of INTEGER, REAL, COMPLEX, or LOGICAL type. In WATFIV, it may also be of CHARACTER type. Numeric as well as alphabetic and special characters can be transmitted, but numeric data is converted digit by digit to internal form, rather than as a field containing one binary number. The converted value cannot be used in arithmetic operations. For additional details, see discussion of character strings in chapter 11.

Z—HEXADECIMAL

$[r]Zw$

The Z format code is used to transmit data in a form that corresponds directly to the pattern of binary digits (bit pattern) used in computer storage to represent a data value. Generally, the programmer uses Z format code to set up a particular bit pattern in storage (on input) or to display internal-format data in a print form that he can read easily (on output). This format code is machine-dependent since the structure and organization of main storage differ somewhat from one type of machine to another, but most FORTRAN implementations provide some method of reading and writing core-image patterns.

In IBM 360/370, main storage is structured as eight-bit units called *bytes*. Four binary digits, or bits, can be represented conveniently by one hexadecimal digit as shown in figure 10.3. (See "Hexadecimal constants", particularly figure 4.2, in chapter 4 to review binary and hexadecimal equivalents.) Two hexadecimal digits represent the contents of one byte.

	Byte		Byte		Byte		Byte	
Binary	1111	1010	1111	0010	0000	0000	0001	0100
Hexadecimal	F	A	F	2	0	0	1	8

FIGURE 10.3

The Z format code is generally used to set or display numeric values. An INTEGER*2 data item can be expressed as four hexadecimal digits, an INTEGER*4 or REAL*4 data item can be expressed as eight hexadecimal digits, and so on. (See figure 10.4.)

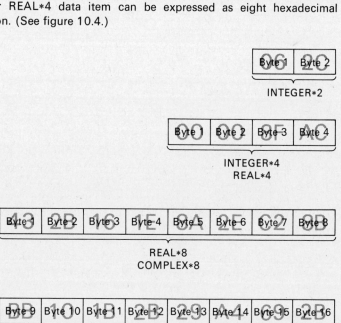

FIGURE 10.4

If an input data item does not include as many hexadecimal digits as can be stored in the locations reserved for the variable into which data is being moved, the data item is padded on the left with zeros. If it contains too many hexadecimal digits, excess digits are truncated from the left. Leading, embedded, and trailing blanks in the input field of length w are treated as zeros. Only the hexadecimal digits 0 through 9 and A through F may appear in the data item.

On output, if the number of hexadecimal digits (say n) required to represent the data item exceeds w, only the w rightmost digits are written; $n-w$ digits are truncated. If w exceeds the number of hexadecimal digits, the leftmost $w-n$ positions of the output field are set to zeros.

This method of reading or writing data should not be confused with the unformatted transmission of data to and from main storage, which is discussed in chapter 12. We can easily read or write hexadecimal digits; that is, data in this form is man-readable and either has been or will be converted to bit patterns for the computer. In contrast, with unformatted I/O, data is expressed and remains in machine-readable form. In general, we neither prepare nor interpret unformatted data.

H—LITERALS

nHabc...

'abc...'

There are two ways to introduce literals in a FORMAT statement: following the H format code or enclosed in single quotes. These literals are strings of characters. Literal data is read or written directly into or from the FORMAT statement; no entry in the I/O list of a READ or WRITE statement is referred to in transmitting literal data.

Literals are used primarily for headings and identification in reports. In the first method, nH, n is the number of characters in the literal and the characters immediately follow the H.

99   FORMAT (20H THIS IS THE HEADING)

In the second method, the literal is enclosed in single quotes. The following statement is equivalent to the one above.

99   FORMAT (' THIS IS THE HEADING')

An advantage of using quotes is that you need not count the number of characters in the literal data. This eliminates a potential cause of error. If you need to include a single quote within such a string, you must represent it by two single quotes. An advantage of using the H format code is that you can specify the number of character positions to be used for the literal, and this number need not be the same as the number of characters specified for the literal.

When a FORMAT statement containing literal data is referred to in a READ statement, the literal data is replaced by an equivalent number of characters (either n or as many as are enclosed in quotes) from the input data stream. On output, either n characters or the characters enclosed in quotes are written on the external medium. For example, if R is a floating-point variable whose current value is 1.384, the statements

```
        WRITE (6,50) R
50      FORMAT (' THE RESULT IS',F8.3)
```

cause the following line to be written as output:

```
THE RESULT IS    1.384
```

As this example indicates, field descriptors for other data items may appear in a FORMAT statement that contains literal data. Note that the first character of the literal is a blank, the carriage control character. Use of one character of literal data, either by itself or at the beginning of literal data to be printed, is a convenient way of specifying that character. (See also "Carriage control" in this chapter.)

Since the same FORMAT statement can be referred to for both input and output, a literal is an easy means of reading data for a report title as input, then printing out that report title without having to even mention it in other statements in the program. For example, the READ statement below causes the first twenty characters of the next input line from logical unit 5 to be read into the FORMAT statement in storage, replacing the blank and HEADING, and filling twelve succeeding positions as well. The WRITE statement causes the first character of that data (i.e., the contents of the first of twenty storage locations reserved by 20H) to be used for carriage control and the contents of the next nineteen positions to be printed as output.

```
        READ (5,200)
200     FORMAT (20H HEADING)
        WRITE (6,200)
```

Input data to be read into literals need not be enclosed in single quotes. No enclosing quotes are printed when literal data is provided as output.

X—SKIP

*w*X

The X format code is used to skip *w* characters on input or to insert *w* blank characters on output. For example, if a card contains five ten-column fields of integer data, but the second of those fields is not to be read, we can write

```
        READ (5,40) I, J, K, L
40      FORMAT (I10,10X,3I10)
```

On output, an important function of X is to control horizontal spacing. Assume three floating-point values are to be printed. If we use the statements

```
        WRITE (6,45) R, S, T
45      FORMAT (1H1,3F8.2)
```

we might print, for example,

```
12345.78 − 4561.3412345.67
```

If we replace the FORMAT statement above by

       45   FORMAT (1H1,5X,F8.2,5X,F8.2,5X,F8.2)

the same values appear as

       12345.78   −4561.34   12345.67

T—FIXED POSITION

T*w*

The T format code is used to specify the position of the first character of the next field to be read or written. It is used in the following statements to cause the first 30 columns of each input card to be ignored. The characters in columns 31 through 80 are read as numeric data.

       READ (5,40) A, B, C, D, E, F, G
    40   FORMAT (T31,5F6.1,2E10.2)

On output, the T format code is similar to the tabulation key of a typewriter. Repetitive execution of

       WRITE (6,50) ARR, L, T
    50   FORMAT (T15,2A4,T35,I6,T60,F8.2)

causes three columns of data to be printed; these columns begin in the 15th, 35th, and 60th character positions of the output record. Note that these correspond to columns 14, 34, and 59 of the print line, since the first character position of a record to be printed is used for carriage control.

A common use of the T format code is in positioning report headings. For example,

       WRITE (6,70)
    70   FORMAT ('1',T35,'MONTHLY PROFIT REPORT')

causes the heading MONTHLY PROFIT REPORT to be printed, beginning in the 35th character position (print position 34) of the first line of a report page.

Because the T format code is used to specify absolute positioning, we do not have to read or write data in the order that it appears on the external medium. The following statements are permissible:

       WRITE (6,50) L, T, ARR
    50   FORMAT (T35,I6,T60,F8.2,T15,2A4)

Furthermore, we can read data more than once, or we can overwrite data written previously in the current line. For example, we can fill a field with zeros, then replace only the rightmost zeros by significant digits of an output value.

THE SLASH (/) CHARACTER

The simplest form of the FORMAT statement is the one we have been using thus far; it contains field descriptors separated by commas and enclosed in one set of parentheses. One FORTRAN record (print line or punched card, for example) is defined. We can complicate this form by using a slash within the

FORMAT statement to indicate the end of one FORTRAN record and the start of a new one. This means, for example, that more than one print line can be described by a single FORMAT statement. The following statement describes two FORTRAN record formats.

    100   FORMAT ('0',I3,F5.2/X1,I5)

Consecutive slashes can be used to skip input records or to introduce blank output records. If there are *n* consecutive slashes at the beginning or end of a FORMAT statement, *n* input records are skipped or *n* blank records are inserted on output. If there are *n* consecutive slashes within a FORMAT statement, $n-1$ input records are skipped or $n-1$ blank records are inserted on output. For example, the statement

    100   FORMAT (' ',3X,F5.2//' ',I3,2F5.2)

describes three FORTRAN record formats. The second of three records written according to this format is blank. In effect, the format specification causes double spacing between a line written according to the format ' ',3X,F5.2 and a line written according to the format ' ',I3,2F5.2.

GROUP FORMAT SPECIFICATIONS

One way to simplify the writing of FORMAT statements is to use a repetition factor whenever identical field descriptors apply consecutively. For example, we have considered statements similar to

        WRITE (6,40) A, B, C, D
    40   FORMAT (4F5.2)

Another means of simplification that is sometimes appropriate involves use of a *group repeat count*. For example,

        WRITE (6,40) I, A, J, B, K, C, L, D
    40   FORMAT (4(5X,I6,F5.2))

The group repeat count 4 in this FORMAT statement causes succeeding characters of the output line to be interpreted as though described by (5X,I6, F5.2,5X,I6,F5.2,5X,I6,F5.2,5X,I6,F5.2). Obviously, use of the group repeat count is more convenient from the programmer's point of view.

A group repeat count is similar to a repetition factor except that (1) it applies to any number of field descriptors immediately following it and enclosed in parentheses, rather than to only one; and (2) it serves somewhat differently in controlling the order in which field descriptors are used. To understand this second point, consider the following statements:

    60   FORMAT (I3,2(I4,I5),I6)
    70   FORMAT (I3,(I4,I5,I4,I5),I6)
    80   FORMAT (I3,I4,I5,I4,I5,I6)

If no group repeat count is specified before inner parentheses but such parentheses are included (as in the second statement above), a group repeat count of 1 is assumed. Hence, if not more than six values are read or written according to any of these FORMAT statements, their effects are identical. If there are more than six items in the I/O list of a READ or WRITE statement referring to one of these statements, then some of the field descriptors must be reused. The rule is: If the closing right parenthesis of the FORMAT statement is reached before all items in the I/O list have been processed, control returns (1) to the first field descriptor of the FORMAT statement if there are no group repeat counts, or (2) to the group repeat count associated with the left parenthesis that corresponds to the second rightmost right parenthesis otherwise. We see that statements 60 and 70 above are still identical in effect; the seventh data item is interpreted as a four-digit integer (I4). However, the seventh data item transmitted according to statement 80 is a three-digit integer as described by I3.

The depth to which group format specifications can be nested is system-dependent. WATFOR, WATFIV, and IBM 360/370 FORTRAN allow a maximum depth of two.

CARRIAGE CONTROL

When generating lines for printing, we need a way to skip to a new page when all information that belongs on the current page has been printed, or to skip to a new line when we have written all that belongs on the current line. In most systems, we specify such actions by putting a certain character at the beginning of each output record, or line. This character is not printed; instead, it serves as a code to control the carriage on the printer. Usually, it is entered as a literal, either with the H format code or enclosed in single quotes. (See "Literals" in this chapter.) There are some variations from system to system as to the permissible code values and their meanings, but the representations shown in figure 10.5 are common. Some printers also have controls for one-half-page skips and one-third-page skips.

Character		Effect
∅	(i.e., blank)	Advance one line before printing (single-space).
0	(zero)	Advance two lines before printing (double-space); this causes one blank line.
1		Skip to a new page before printing.
+		Do not space before printing; this causes overprinting.

FIGURE 10.5

Assuming the carriage control codes shown in figure 10.5, either of the following statements causes a skip to a new page before printing.

```
50    FORMAT (1H1,X20,'THIS IS THE HEADING')
60    FORMAT ('1',X20,'THIS IS THE HEADING')
```

Look again at the FORMAT statements shown in preceding examples in this chapter. What printer actions are initiated by the FORMAT statements set up to control print operations?

If one fails to specify a value for the carriage control character, page skips and line skips occur erratically, depending on the first character of the output line. Also the first character of the line is not printed, whether or not the programmer considered its use for carriage control.

THE SCALE FACTOR

Sometimes it is convenient to scale real or complex values by multiplying them by powers of ten when they are transmitted to/from main storage. One reason for this scaling is to treat numbers such as 108.63 and .245 as floating-point numbers without decimal fractions internally. By doing so, we avoid the approximation that occurs when converting the fractional portions to hexa-decimal or binary, the form in which floating-point numbers are stored in the computer. If we have the value 45.67, the integer 45 can be represented exactly in the internal coding scheme, but the fraction .67 can only be approximated by the closest binary fraction. If we do not scale, a floating-point value with a fractional portion may be changed in the process of simply being read into memory from one external medium and written out to another. If several approximated values are used in computations, intolerable inaccuracies may result.

Another reason for scaling may be to change input values expressed as percentages to equivalent decimal fractions for internal computations. Conversely, we may wish to scale to express decimal fractions as percentages on output.

Conversion is effected by the scale factor nP according to the formula:

$$\text{external value} = \text{internal value} * 10**n$$

where n is an unsigned or negatively signed integer in the expression nP that precedes the repetition factor or, if there is no repetition factor, the F, E, D, or G of a field descriptor for real or complex data.

For example, if input data is in the form x.xxxx and is to be used internally in the form xxxxx., the field descriptor −4PF6.4 can be used to effect this change. If this value is used in computation and the result is to be scaled to the original form for output, the field descriptor −4PF6.4 can also be used to describe this value.

Although sometimes advisable, scale factors must be used with caution. A scale factor may be specified for any real or complex data; but, on input, if the external form of the data contains an exponent, the scale factor is ignored. Only F-type input is scaled, but various forms of input are otherwise acceptable and apt to be selected. Some examples are:

Field descriptor	Input form	Internal form
−4PF6.4	8.4163	84163.
2PF5.2	13.42	.1342
−2PE11.2	13.08	1308.
−2PE11.2	130.8E−01	13.08

On output, the scale factor applies to any real or complex value, but in different ways. For numbers without an exponent, its effect is analogous to that for similar input. Scaling occurs. For numbers with an E or a D exponent, the decimal point may be moved as directed by a scale factor, but the exponent of the input/output value is adjusted to account for the move. The input/output value is not changed; that is, no scaling occurs. Some examples are:

Field descriptor	Internal form	Output form
2PF3.0	134.	13400
0PE10.3	238.	0.238E 03
1PE10.3	238.	2.380E 02
2PF7.4	14.3841	1438.41
−2PF7.0	143841.	1438.41
0PG13.5	5.2461	0.52461E 01
3PG13.5	5.2461	524.61E−02

Another consideration is that a scale factor, once introduced, applies to all subsequently interpreted F, E, D, and G field descriptors in the FORMAT statement until another scale factor is encountered. The scale factor 0P can be used to restore normal, nonscaling interpretation.

The following FORMAT statement can be used to change four consecutive percentages to fractions on input and back to percentages on output. The value transmitted according to the field descriptor 0PF4.5 is unchanged.

77   FORMAT (2P3F3.0,F4.0,0PF4.5)

READ AND WRITE STATEMENTS

A READ or WRITE statement tells what FORMAT statement to use, which values to transmit, and where to put them or take them from. A READ statement may also identify statements to which transfer is to be made when there is no more data to be read or if an error occurs on transmission. The general forms of these statements are

READ (*unit,fmt,*END=*label1,*ERR=*label2*) *list*
WRITE (*unit,fmt*) *list*

where the user-specified entries are as explained below. One or more of the entries may be optional, depending not only on the input/output operation required but also on the compiler that will translate the program and the computer system on which it will be run.

The *unit* is an integer constant or integer variable that represents a *logical unit number* (sometimes called a *file reference number*). This number indicates the file to or from which I/O is to take place. (The file must have been associated with the logical unit number, perhaps by a CALL to OPEN, a FORTRAN-supplied subprogram, or perhaps by a system-established default.) The assignments of logical unit numbers to input/output devices is system-dependent and should be checked at each installation where your program is run. Generally, 5 means card input, 6 means printer output, and 7 means the card punch. However, other numbers may be defined for these devices and for magnetic tape, disk, or drum units and user terminals. In some systems, the specification of a logical unit number is optional if an established default (say, the number of a particular card reader for input or of a particular printer for output) applies. If the unit number is omitted, the surrounding parentheses may be omitted also. Again, you should check details of input/output at your installation. (See also appendix E.)

In WATFIV systems, formatted input/output statements in which unit numbers and parentheses are omitted are similar to those in figure 10.6. Note that the keyword READ is used for input but that PRINT rather than WRITE is used for output.

```
       REAL  A,  B,  C
       READ  99,  A,  B,  C
       PRINT 98,  A,  B,  C
99     FORMAT (3F5.0)
98     FORMAT ('1',3F5.0)
       STOP
       END
```

FIGURE 10.6

As you have probably decided, the *fmt* entry in the general form of the READ or WRITE statement is the statement number of a FORMAT statement that provides descriptions of the fields from or to which data is being moved. To read or write with programmer-specified format control, a FORMAT statement must be identified.

The END and ERR options may appear in a READ statement. The END option contains the label of an executable statement (*label1*) to which control should be transferred when there is no more data to read. The ERR option specifies an executable statement (*label2*) to which control should be transferred if an input error occurs. If either of these options is omitted, a default system action is taken if the condition occurs; generally, program execution is terminated. Some examples are:

```
       READ  (5,200,END=900)  A,  B,  C
200    FORMAT (F5.3,2G8.3)

       READ  (5,25,END=900,ERR=950)  ARR
25     FORMAT (3I6)
```

The *list* in a READ or WRITE statement is an I/O list containing simple variable names, array names with or without subscripts, or implied DOs (explained later in this chapter). With WATFOR or WATFIV, the I/O list of a WRITE statement may also contain expressions, but an expression cannot begin with a left parenthesis since this character might also signal the beginning of an implied DO. If the I/O list is omitted, a line is skipped on input, or a blank line is inserted on output, unless data was transmitted directly between the FORMAT statement and the file. (See "Literals" in this chapter.) Skipping a line may mean not reading one card on input; a blank line on output may show up as a blank print line.

READING AND WRITING WITH FORMAT CONTROL

Execution of a READ statement containing a FORMAT statement number initiates a formatted read operation. Each action of format control depends on information provided jointly by the I/O list of the READ statement, if one exists, and the format specification of the FORMAT statement. The leftmost entry in each is the first to be used. Whenever a field descriptor containing an I, F, E, D, G, L, A, or Z format code is encountered, a check is made to see whether there is an I/O list entry for which no value has been transmitted. If there is, appropriately converted information is transmitted. If there is no unused entry in the I/O list, the read operation is terminated. Field descriptors containing an X, T, or H format code or literal data enclosed in single quotes are not paired with I/O list entries. If one of these is encountered in a format specification before all I/O list entries have been used, it causes I/O action independently.

If format control reaches the rightmost right parenthesis of the format specification, but there are remaining entries in the I/O list, field descriptors in the format specification are reused until data has been transmitted for all I/O list entries. If there are fewer entries in the I/O list than there are field descriptors, any unused field descriptors are ignored. Thus, data is transmitted for each entry in an I/O list. Field descriptors are used once, repetitively, or not at all, depending on when the I/O list is satisfied. The READ statement, not the FORMAT statement, determines the number of read operations required. And whether or not all field descriptors are used has no effect on a subsequent execution of READ or WRITE referring to the FORMAT statement. An I/O operation always begins with the leftmost field descriptor of the FORMAT statement.

Some examples are

```
      READ (5,100) N, A, B, C
100   FORMAT (I3,F5.3,2F7.3)

      READ (5,30) ARR, J, K
30    FORMAT (10G8.3,I5,I2)
```

A WRITE statement that refers to a FORMAT statement directs writing with format control in a similar manner. As with READ, the number of entries in the I/O list, if any, determines the number of data items transmitted. Examples are

```
      WRITE (6,250) A, B, C
250   FORMAT (A1,F5.3,D10.3)

      WRITE (6,100) R, S, T
100   FORMAT (' ',2I8,F8.5)
```

REF

IMPLIED DO

Consider the program in figure 10.7. The READ statement causes eight values to be read from the file associated with logical unit number 5 into the main-storage locations reserved for the first eight elements of array AR. The characters of the input stream are interpreted as floating-point values and are stored internally in floating-point form. The WRITE statement refers to the same FORMAT statement, but deals with different data. All elements of array AT and values of two simple variables are provided as output.

```
        REAL AR(20), AT(6)
        INTEGER I
        READ (5,100) (AR(I),I=1,8)
            .
            .
            .
        WRITE (6,100) AT, X, Y
            .
            .
            .
100     FORMAT (8F10.4)
        STOP
        END
```

FIGURE 10.7

The READ statement contains a feature that we have not seen in previous examples, although the I=1,8 part may look familiar. The construction (AR(I),I=1,8) is called an *implied DO;* it is a means of setting up a looping action within the READ statement. This statement is equivalent to the more cumbersome statement

READ (5,100) A(1), A(2), A(3), A(4), A(5), A(6), A(7), A(8)

The parameters of an implied DO have the same meanings as similar parameters of the DO statement. We have, here,

READ (*unit,fmt*) (*list,variable*=1,*integer constant*)

where *unit* and *fmt* are as explained above, and *list* is a subscripted variable followed immediately by a comma, then the integer variable used as a subscript, for which start and end values are specified. We might also include another comma and an increment value following the integer constant; since we have not, an increment value of 1 is assumed. The entire DO notation must be enclosed in parentheses.

Although we have directed our attention thus far to use of an implied DO in a READ statement, we could just as well have used an implied DO in the WRITE statement. To print a table formatted as shown in figure 10.8, for example, where XXXXXX represents the contents of BARR(1), BARR(2),..., BARR(50), we use the statements shown in figure 10.9.

REF

```
        1              XXXXXX
        2              XXXXXX
        3              XXXXXX
        .                 .
        .                 .
        .                 .
       50              XXXXXX
```

FIGURE 10.8

```
        INTEGER BARR(50), K
          .
          .
          .
        WRITE (6,200) K, (BARR(K),K=1,50)
200     FORMAT (' ',15X,I2,10X,I6)
          .
          .
          .
        END
```

FIGURE 10.9

The WRITE statement below causes data to be written from the variables A, B(1,3), B(3,3), B(5,3), B(7,3), B(9,3), and C onto the file associated with logical unit number 6 in the format specified by the FORMAT statement identified by statement number 80.

```
        WRITE (6,80) A, (B(I,3),I=1,10,2), C
```

Note that this WRITE statement causes the odd elements of the third column of the two-dimensional array B to be written as output.

```
        REAL ARR(5,10)
        INTEGER I, J
          .
          .
          .
        WRITE (6,400) ((ARR(I,J),J=1,10),I=1,5)
400     FORMAT (' ',X3,10F9.3)
          .
          .
          .
        END
```

FIGURE 10.10

REF

The use of implied DOs becomes somewhat complex when we want to read or write values from multiple dimensions of an array. To print a matrix having five rows and ten columns, one row to a line, we write statements such as those in figure 10.10. The innermost DO notation varies most rapidly. An inner implied DO is executed completely for each change in the subscript value of the next innermost implied DO. Each set of implied DO parameters is enclosed in a separate set of parentheses, with a comma following the right parenthesis of all but the outermost set.

Output data from the program in figure 10.10 is written line by line, positioned as shown in figure 10.11. You should assume the role of the computer, desk checking the anticipated execution of this statement to verify that such results will occur.

```
ARR(1,1)     ARR(1,2)     ARR(1,3) ... ... ARR(1,10)
ARR(2,1)     ARR(2,2)     ...              ARR(2,10)
ARR(3,1)     ...                               .
ARR(4,1)     ...                               .
ARR(5,1)     ...                           ARR(5,10)
```

FIGURE 10.11

In WATFIV systems, implied DOs may also appear in format-free READ and PRINT statements and in DATA statements. For discussion of their use in these statements, see chapters 3 and 6, respectively.

EXECUTION-TIME FORMAT CONTROL

Values for repetition factors, field widths, and decimal places must be specified in FORMAT statements as positive nonzero integer constants not greater than 256. When group repeat counts or scale factors are used, they must also be specified as integer constants. The programmer who uses the FORMAT statement as described thus far cannot define or change these values at program execution-time.

Suppose data to be read as input is punched into cards, but is not positioned on the cards as the controlling FORMAT statement describes. What can be done? Either the cards must be repunched, or the FORMAT statement must be changed and the program recompiled.

To prevent such a situation, the FORTRAN programmer can take another approach. He can read the format specification of a FORMAT statement as alphabetic data (A format code) into an array in storage at program execution-time. In effect, a suitable FORMAT statement can be coded after input data has been prepared, and both the FORMAT statement and the data can be read as input by the program. An example is shown in figure 10.12.

REF

```
        DIMENSION FMAT(20)
C       POSITIONS OF I, J, AND K ON INPUT CARD
C       ARE READ INTO ARRAY FMAT AS DATA.
        READ (5,99) FMAT
C       FMAT NOW CONTAINS THE FORMAT SPECIFICATION.
99      FORMAT (20A4)
        READ (5,FMAT) I, J, K
C       USES ARRAY NAME INSTEAD OF STATEMENT NUMBER.
        PRINT I, J, K
        STOP
        END
```

FIGURE 10.12

The field descriptors read into an array must have the same forms as field descriptors coded in any FORMAT statement. As in any FORMAT statement, the complete set of descriptors must be enclosed in parentheses. Only the statement number and the word FORMAT are omitted. The array name (FMAT, in figure 10.12) must be specified: first in the I/O list of a READ statement that reads the format specification into the array; then in place of a FORMAT statement number in any READ or WRITE statements using that format specification.

An execution-time format must be stored in an array, declared as such in a DIMENSION, type, or COMMON statement, even if the array consists of only one element. A format specification containing double quotes within a literal field defined by quotes should be used only for output. If the format specification is used for input, the field for the literal should be defined using the H format code.

There are other approaches to achieve format flexibility. Some of them use a format specification placed into an array specified in a DATA or type statement. As you gain FORTRAN programming experience, you will see that execution-time formats can be constructed and modified by a program as well as read as input data.

CORE-TO-CORE I/O

We have used READ, WRITE, and FORMAT statements in this chapter to transmit data between locations in main storage and an external I/O device. In doing so, we identify a particular device by including its logical unit number in the READ or WRITE statement (e.g., 5 for the card reader; 6 for the printer). WATFIV also allows us to read and write with format control between one area of main storage and another. To use this feature, we replace the logical unit number in the READ or WRITE statement with an area name. The area name must be a variable of CHARACTER type. The main-storage locations reserved for that variable are treated as an I/O device. Using this facility, we can read data, interpreting it in one way, then reread it, interpreting it another way. In effect, we can transform data from one form to another.

One case where core-to-core I/O is useful is the reading of cards of

REF

different data formats. We don't know the format of a card before we read it, so we don't know what the FORMAT statement that describes the data should say. Yet we have to use the FORMAT statement when reading the data. Let us assume, as in figure 10.13, that the first position of each input card holds a one-digit code. The code value may be either 1 or 2, indicating that the format specification of FORMAT statement 97 or 98, respectively, is appropriate for the card. We read the data into memory as a character string, equivalence the first character to the one-character variable COTYPE for reference purposes, then reread the data as it is to be handled in the program.

```
        DIMENSION F(5), I(2)
        CHARACTER CARD*80, COTYPE, STR*16
        EQUIVALENCE (CARD,COTYPE)
        READ (5,99) CARD
99      FORMAT (A80)
        IF (COTYPE.EQ.'1') GO TO 1
        IF (COTYPE.EQ.'2') GO TO 2
        PRINT, 'INVALID CARD TYPE ', COTYPE
        STOP
1       READ (CARD,97) F
97      FORMAT (1X,5F5.0)
        GO TO 3
2       READ (CARD,98) STR, I
98      FORMAT (1X,A16,2I4)
3          .
           .
           .
        END
```

FIGURE 10.13

You must be careful not to overflow the area being written, on output, or to read from an area larger than the area specified on input. For example, the statements in figure 10.14 are in error.

```
        CHARACTER*10 INAREA
           .
           .
           .
        WRITE (INAREA,40) R, S
40      FORMAT (F8.3,F5.2)
           .
           .
           .
        END
```

FIGURE 10.14

REF

Another point to remember is that characters in the string in a core I/O area must be valid for the type of variable that you describe them to be. A string consisting of ABC123 cannot be converted to satisfy the field descriptor I6, whether that string is read from an area of storage or from an input card.

Data must be read into, or written from, a core I/O area represented by a simple variable as one line, or record. To allow for reading or writing multiple records when using core-to-core I/O, we can set up a core I/O area as an array of character variables. An example is shown in figure 10.15. The READ statement causes data to be read from IN(1) and IN(2). To write data into IN(3) without affecting IN(1) and IN(2), we use the WRITE statement as shown.

```
        CHARACTER*20  IN(4)
        .
        .
        .
        READ  (IN,70)  I,  J,  R,  ARR(6)
70      FORMAT  (2I5,F10.6/X2,6I3)
        .
        .
        WRITE  (IN(3),80)  FIG,  INT
80      FORMAT  (F13.8,I7)
        .
        .
        .
        END
```

FIGURE 10.15

WRITE statements referring to an area name can be used to build print-line images without writing them to an output file. It might be, for example, that at a given point in a program you have some, but not all, data required for output lines. No carriage control character need be used in the FORMAT statement that controls the writing of data into a core I/O area, since no actual printer need be controlled. If the content of a core I/O area is eventually written to a printer, however, the usual carriage control is required.

Generally, core-to-core I/O would be useful in standard FORTRAN as well as in WATFIV. However, this feature is system-dependent. To do this kind of formatting within main storage, one usually has to resort to assembler language and use routines provided by a particular installation.

THE NAMELIST STATEMENT

IBM 360/370 FORTRAN and WATFIV allow a list facility whereby we can read or write values without describing their formats in a FORMAT statement. This capability is similar to WATFOR/WATFIV format-free I/O in that specific descriptions of values to be read or written are not required. The compiler supplies formatting automatically according to the type and size of the variable to or from which a value is being moved. A nonexecutable statement, the *NAMELIST statement*, contains a list name, enclosed in slashes and followed by a list of variables. The list of variables effectively replaces the I/O list of a READ or WRITE statement of formatted I/O. And the name of the list rather than the statement number of a FORMAT statement appears in the READ or WRITE statement. (See figure 10.16.)

```
DIMENSION I(2,2)
NAMELIST /OUTPUT/A,I,Z,T
    .
    .
    .
Z = 100000.
    .
    .
    .
A = T + Z
    .
    .
    .
WRITE (6,OUTPUT)
STOP
END
```

FIGURE 10.16

The names as well as the values of variables specified in a NAMELIST statement list are printed when a WRITE statement referring to the name of the list is executed. In the case of an array, the name of the array is printed once, followed by values of array elements, separated by commas. Output such as produced by the WRITE statement in figure 10.16 is shown as an example in figure 10.17.

```
Column 2
  ┌
  ↓
&OUTPUT
A=500000.00,  I=11,21,12,22,
Z=100000.00,  T=400000.00,
&END
```

FIGURE 10.17

The general form of the NAMELIST statement is

NAMELIST /n1/a[,b,...] [/n2/c[,d,...]...]

where *n1*, *n2*,... are the names of lists, and *a, b, c, d,*... are the simple variables or array variables which constitute the list whose name they follow.

More than one NAMELIST statement can appear in a program, and a variable name can appear in more than one NAMELIST list. The name of a list is declared to be a NAMELIST name by its appearance in a NAMELIST statement; it can and must appear in one, and only one, NAMELIST statement before it is used in a READ or WRITE statement. A NAMELIST name cannot appear in any other kinds of statements in the program. A NAMELIST statement must follow any declaration statements giving type, size, or dimension information for a variable specified in a list in the NAMELIST statement. The variables may be of any type; but array names cannot be subscripted, and names used as dummy arguments in FUNCTION or SUBROUTINE statements cannot be specified.

Output data written with reference to a NAMELIST name is in a form that can be read by a READ statement referring to the same NAMELIST name. (See figures 10.17 and 10.19.) NAMELIST input can also be prepared manually. The first position of each line (card) of the data set to be read must be blank. The second position of the first line must contain an ampersand (&), immediately followed by the NAMELIST name, followed by one or more blanks. Following this is a list of data items. Each data item has one of the forms shown below.

- *variable name = constant*
  where *variable name* is a simple variable name or a subscripted array name with integer constants as subscripts and the *constant* may be integer, real, complex, literal, or logical.

- *array name = set of constants*
  where *array name* is an unsubscripted array name and the *set of constants* comprises constants of one of the forms mentioned above, separated by commas. Successive occurrences of the same constant can be specified as *k*constant* where *k* is an unsigned integer (recalling the repetition factor of a field descriptor when using formatted I/O).

```
DIMENSION A(2,3), B(2), C(3)
LOGICAL L
NAMELIST /INPUT/A,L,T,I,J,B,C
READ (5,INPUT)
  .
  .
  .
END
```

FIGURE 10.18

A program in which the list of names specified in a NAMELIST statement is referred to as an input list is given in figure 10.18. Data to be read by the program is shown in figure 10.19. Embedded blanks are not permitted in the names or constants. Each constant should obey all rules for the type of the variable to which it is being assigned. Trailing blanks after integers and exponents (before a separating comma) are treated as zeros.

REF

Column 2
↓ ——————
&INPUT
L=.TRUE., T=.5, I=4,
A=11., 21., 12., 22., B(1)=47.6, B(2)=3.1416,
C=3*0.0,
&END

FIGURE 10.19

An input data set need not contain values for all variables in a referenced NAMELIST list. (See J in figures 10.18 and 10.19.) But all variable names appearing in an input data set for a NAMELIST name must appear in the list identified by that name. The order in which the data items appear need not be the same as that of the names in the list. (See A in figures 10.18 and 10.19.) When array values are read as input, either each element can be mentioned explicitly (for example, B in figure 10.19) or the array name can be specified, followed by a series of values separated by commas (for example, A). In the latter case, the number of constants must be less than or equal to the number of elements in the array. The order in which values are assigned is the usual FORTRAN order, created by varying the leftmost subscript, then the next left-most, and so on. If an array is only partially filled, a value for another variable must follow as a delimiter on the same input line. If values for an array are specified on more than one line, the values must be specified as a series (rather than for specific elements) and the first value on a continuation line must begin in column 1 of the line. The characters &END mark the end of the input data set.

The NAMELIST statement is general-purpose, but many FORTRAN programmers find it particularly useful as a means of producing output for debugging purposes. The execution of WRITE statements referring to NAMELIST statements can serve as a program trace facility, since both the names and the values of NAMELIST variables are displayed as output. DUMPLIST, a statement similar in form to NAMELIST but designed especially for program debugging, is available in WATFIV systems. A DUMPLIST statement automatically provides NAMELIST-format output of the values of specified variables if abnormal program termination occurs. Further details of this statement are given under "The DUMPLIST statement" in chapter 9.

EXERCISES

QUEST

1. (TUT) Write FORMAT statements to be referred to when reading the following input:
    a) Five five-digit integers in columns 1 through 25 of a card, followed by five floating-point values, each having two digits to either side of a decimal point that is also punched in the card.
    b) Five sets of values in a card. Each set is a single-column integer,

followed by a four-column floating-point value having two decimal places, but the decimal point is not punched.

c) The same as (b) except that the last two values are on a second card.

d) The same as (b) except that each set includes a complex value—a pair of numbers with one position to the right of a point (not punched) in the next ten columns. The value is to be stored with double precision.

e) A character string containing 100 characters.

f) Five floating-point values, each four columns long with two decimal places, to be multiplied by 100 on input; followed by three pairs of numbers, the first of which is an integer in two columns, and the second a floating-point value in two columns with no decimal places. The pairs are not to be scaled.

g) Five logical values, the first three of which are six columns long, and the last two of which are one column each.

h) A hexadecimal value 22 columns long.

2. (TUT) Write FORMAT statements to describe the following output:

a) Six floating-point values, each having twelve positions, two of which are to the right of a decimal point.

b) A four-digit integer followed by six floating-point values like those of (a) above.

c) Three five-digit integers, each on a separate line, with two blank lines following the second line. The integers should begin in print positions 10, 20, and 30 of their respective lines.

d) Eight sets of three values, reusing the following pattern: one integer (3 columns), one logical value (1 column), and one floating-point number (5 columns, no decimal point).

e) Two complex values. The real part of each is a six-position floating-point value with three decimal places. The imaginary part of each requires twelve positions, has six decimal places, and is in exponential form. Assume that the values are stored with double precision.

PROGRAMMING PROBLEMS

1. (TUT) Write a program to print the following information, in the format indicated.

```
          1.0
       3.0 3.0 3.0
    5.0 5.0 5.0 5.0 5.0
  6.0 6.0 6.0 6.0 6.0 6.0
  6.0 6.0 6.0 6.0 6.0 6.0
          1.0
          1.0
       3.0 3.0 3.0
```

2. (TUT) Write a program to print the following information. Use only one FORMAT statement in the program.

```
    1
  1.11
    T1F
```

3. (TUT) Write a program to read the data characters punched in the odd-numbered columns of an input card. Print the characters in the order read, in every third print position of an output line.

4. (REF) Write a general matrix print routine to print a title, and row and column headings as integers, and, optionally, row and column headings as character strings supplied by the user. See chapter 11 if you want to use variables of CHARACTER type in your subprogram.

5. (REF) Write a general matrix input routine that reads the dimensions, format, and values for a matrix into a storage area specified by the user. It should be a subroutine.

6. (REF) Write a subprogram to print a polygon and shade it with a print character specified by the user. (See chapter 11 for character-string handling.)

7. (REF) Write a subprogram that analyzes a vector of numeric values and decides which of three FORMAT statements to use for printing, depending on the sizes and ranges of the values in the vector. Make available a general FORMAT that fits anything, one that handles numbers from 1 to 1000, and one that prints values with fractional parts.

8. (REF) Write a subprogram that maintains a print area for the user and writes out a line when the area is full. The user should call the subprogram with a single value to be placed in the area and an indication of its type. Create the image in core. Establish a secondary entry point so that the user can call the subprogram to print a line even if it's not full. Use WATFIV core-to-core I/O if it is available at your installation. Otherwise, store the values as an array and build an appropriate FORMAT statement as a character string.

INTRO This chapter discusses manipulation of logical and character quantities in FORTRAN and in WATFIV. Logical constants and variables can have the values .TRUE. and .FALSE. They can be connected with other logical constants and variables by means of logical operators to form complex logical expressions having either of these values. They can also appear with logical expressions involving relational operators (explained in chapter 7). Again, the final result of expression evaluation is a single logical value. Such expressions (and more complex forms) can be used in assignment statements involving logical variables and in logical IF statements as introduced in chapter 7 and explained in detail in this chapter.

Three basic operations associated with character data are performed in FORTRAN and WATFIV:

- input and output of character strings
- assignment of character strings to variables
- comparison of character strings

We look at techniques for setting up these operations in this chapter. A significant difference between IBM 360/370 FORTRAN and WATFIV is that the latter permits declaration of variables of CHARACTER type. Related programming considerations are discussed in the reference section.

TUT **LOGICAL DATA** There are two logical constants: .TRUE. and .FALSE. (See chapter 4.) A value of .TRUE. or .FALSE. can be represented by a variable declared to be of LOGICAL type. (See chapter 2.) As an example, the first statement in figure 11.1 is a type statement that declares S1 and S2 to be logical variables and L to be a logical one-dimensional array having three elements. The logical constant .TRUE. is assigned to S1 when the logical assignment statement is executed. The first logical IF statement causes the real variable A to be set to 40 if S2 and L(1) have the logical value .TRUE. The second logical IF causes a branch to statement 100 if the current

Chapter

11

Logical and Character Variables

value of A is greater than the current value of B. You will learn more about these kinds of statements in this chapter.

```
        LOGICAL  S1,  S2,  L(3)
        REAL  A,  B
        COMPLEX  C
        S1 = .TRUE.
        READ,  A,  B,  C
            .
            .
            .
        IF  (S2.AND.L(1))  A = 40.
        IF  (A.GT.B)  GO  TO  100
            .
            .
            .
100     PRINT,  A,  B
        STOP
        END
```

FIGURE 11.1

Those of you who are using WATFOR or WATFIV should be aware that either of these systems uses only the high-order byte of a logical quantity in logical operations. Logical variables may be declared of size 4 or size 1 (LOGI-CAL∗4 or LOGICAL∗1). They are of size 4 by default. But only the leftmost byte of any storage area reserved for logical data is used to store the logical value. A string of eight 1 bits represents .TRUE.; a string of eight 0 bits represents .FALSE. The remaining three bytes are ignored in logical operations. If a program makes extensive use of logical values, especially of large logical arrays, it is advisable to declare them to be of size 1 to avoid wasting storage space.

LOGICAL OPERATORS

Logical quantities are manipulated using any of three *logical operators* : .AND., .OR., and .NOT. To understand the use of these operators, assume that X and Y are logical variables. We define the logical operators as follows :

- The expression

     X.AND.Y

  has the value .TRUE. if and only if both X and Y have the value .TRUE. Otherwise, the expression has the value .FALSE.

- The expression

     X.OR.Y

  has the value .TRUE. if either X or Y or both X and Y have the value .TRUE. The expression has the value .FALSE. if, and only if, both X and Y have the value .FALSE.

- The expression

    .NOT.X

has the value .TRUE. if X is .FALSE. The expression has the value .FALSE. if X is .TRUE.

We summarize our definitions in tabular form in figure 11.2.

X	Y	X.AND.Y	X.OR.Y	.NOT.X
.TRUE.	.TRUE.	.TRUE.	.TRUE.	.FALSE.
.TRUE.	.FALSE.	.FALSE.	.TRUE.	.FALSE.
.FALSE.	.TRUE.	.FALSE.	.TRUE.	.TRUE.
.FALSE.	.FALSE.	.FALSE.	.FALSE.	.TRUE.

FIGURE 11.2

LOGICAL EXPRESSIONS

Any expression which, when evaluated, produces a logical result is a *logical-valued expression*, or *logical expression*. In our definitions above, X and Y were assumed to be logical variables, but the operands in a logical expression may have any of a wide variety of forms. The forms are summarized below.

Examples	Description
.TRUE. S1 L(2)	A single logical primary, which can be a logical constant, logical variable, logical subscripted variable, logical function reference, or logical expression enclosed in parentheses
S1.NOT.L(2) S2.AND..NOT.S3	Logical primaries combined with logical operator
A.NE.B B.LE.A*7.	Arithmetic expressions whose type is INTEGER or REAL combined with relational operator
A.NE.B.OR.S1	Logical operators combined with logical expressions of any of the forms above

Two logical operators may appear in sequence only if the second of those operators is .NOT. Remember that the compiler is not sensitive to blanks; hence, spacing adjacent to a logical operator (or the lack of it) is optional. Only expressions which have the value .TRUE. or .FALSE. may be used with logical operators. You may need to review the use of relational operators in logical expressions. If so, see chapter 7.

Assuming the declarations of figure 11.1, the examples above are valid logical expressions. But the following expressions are invalid, for the reasons indicated.

A.LT..FALSE..OR.S1   Logical constant cannot be compared with real variable.

A.GT..AND.S2	Logical operator cannot follow relational operator.
.OR.S1.AND.L(3)	.OR. must have two operands.
A.AND.L(2)	A is not a logical expression.
C.LT.B.AND.S2	Complex variable cannot be used with relational operator.

OPERATOR HIERARCHY

So that we can evaluate any logical expression and anticipate how the computer will do so, we must become familiar with precedence levels of all FORTRAN operators. A hierarchy is established for relational and logical operators, just as for arithmetic operators. (Recall "Operator hierarchy" in chapter 5.) The complete hierarchy of FORTRAN operators is shown in figure 11.3.

(Highest)

		Precedence level
**	Exponentiation	1
*, /	Multiplication and division	2
+, −	Addition and subtraction	3
.LT. .GT. .EQ. .NE. .LE. .GE.	All relational operators	4
.NOT.		5
.AND.		6
.OR.		7

(Lowest)

FIGURE 11.3

The operators at the top of the list in figure 11.3 are evaluated before the ones below. All relational operators are at the same level of precedence, and relational operations are done before logical operations. .NOT. is evaluated before .AND., just as * is evaluated before +. .OR. is the last of any sequence of operations to be performed.

Applying this order of precedence, we see that the logical expression

A .GT. B .OR. C .LE. D .AND. E .EQ. 0.

is evaluated as

((A .GT. B) .OR. ((C.LE.D) .AND. (E.EQ.0.)))

This expression is true if C is less than or equal to D and E is equal to zero, or if A is greater than B.

We used parentheses above to describe the order in which the relational and logical operations are carried out by the computer when the normal order of precedence applies. If this normal order is the order desired, the parentheses can be used but are not required. We can use parentheses in logical expressions, just as in arithmetic expressions, to force an evaluation order. For example, can you suggest values for the variables A, B, C, D, and E such that the logical value of the following expression differs from that of the expression above?

(A.GT.B .OR. C.LE.D) .AND. E .EQ. 0.

Compare the values of the expressions when E is not equal to zero. The first expression may be true, but the one that includes parentheses can only be false. Obviously, a knowledge of operator hierarchies and of the order in which expressions are evaluated is essential to FORTRAN programming. An additional point to remember is that when operators of equal precedence appear in an expression, the leftmost of the equal-precedence operators is evaluated first. We could write "expressions in parentheses" and then "evaluation of functions" at the top of the list in figure 11.3 to further document the order in which the computer performs its work.

THE LOGICAL ASSIGNMENT STATEMENT

By now, you are quite familiar with the arithmetic assignment statement; it is used in numerous programs throughout this text and was discussed in detail in chapter 5. A statement that is very similar in form but deals with logical quantities rather than arithmetic data is the *logical assignment statement*. Recall the following logical assignment statement from figure 11.1:

S1 = .TRUE.

The general form of this statement is

logical variable = logical expression

where *logical variable* is a subscripted or nonsubscripted variable declared to be of LOGICAL type and *logical expression* is any valid logical expression. Assume that G and H are logical variables, and L and M are integers. The following assignments are valid.

G = .NOT. H
H = L .GT. M
H = L .GT. M .AND. H
G = 3. + L .NE. 16 .OR. H

MULTIPLE ASSIGNMENT IN WATFIV

In WATFOR and WATFIV, several logical variables can be assigned values in one assignment statement. For example, the following statement is permissible:

G = H = L .GT. M

It has the same effect as the sequence of statements:

H = L .GT. M
G = H

For more about multiple assignment statements, see the reference section of chapter 5.

THE LOGICAL IF STATEMENT

The use of logical IF statements containing logical expressions involving relational operators was introduced in the tutorial section of chapter 7. Recall

```
IF (A.GT.B) GO TO 200
IF (I.NE.4) SUM = SUM + ARR(4)
```

Having learned about other forms of logical expressions, we can now use logical IF statements such as the following (assuming again that G and H are logical variables, and L and M are integers).

```
IF (G .OR. H) GO TO 35
IF (L .LT. M .AND. G) TOT = TOT / 5
IF (M − 5 .EQ. L .OR. .NOT. H) V = 0.
```

The first of these statements causes a branch to statement 35 if either G or H has the value .TRUE. when the IF statement is encountered. The second causes TOT to be divided by 5 if the current value of L is less than M (L .LT. M has the value .TRUE.) *and* G has the value .TRUE. The third causes V to be set to zero if the value of M − 5 is equal to the value of L (M − 5 .EQ. L has the value .TRUE.) *or* .NOT. H has the value .TRUE. (i.e., the current value of H is .FALSE.).

SAVING THE RESULTS OF EVALUATION

Often we need to ask the same questions about the values of variables at several points in a program. For example, assume that sequences of instructions are executed or skipped on the basis of whether or not the input value for A is greater than the input value for B. At each branch point, we can use a logical IF statement of the form

```
IF (A.GT.B) GO TO n
```

where *n* is a statement number. In such cases, it is convenient and efficient to modify this approach somewhat by saving the result of the test (i.e., of the expression evaluation) in a variable. If the input value for either A or B may be replaced by a value calculated during program execution before one or more of these logical IF statements is encountered, such saving is mandatory. There is no need to re-evaluate the logical expression each time, at each branch point. Since the result of the test is either 'yes' or 'no' (more accurately, .TRUE. or .FALSE.), it can be stored in a logical variable. We store it by executing one logical assignment statement. (See figure 11.4.) Having done so, we need only refer to the current value of the logical variable whenever the result of the test must be known. Figure 11.4 shows this retention of a result.

Remember that the logical IF statement expects a logical-valued expression, but the arithmetic IF statement expects an arithmetic quantity. If the following statement appeared in figure 11.4, an error would occur.

```
     IF  (LRES)  10,20,30
```

You must understand the difference between the logical IF and the arithmetic IF and use them accordingly.

```
        LOGICAL  LINE,  LRES
        REAL A,  B
        READ,  LINE,  A,  B
        LRES = A.GT.B
        .
        .
        .

        IF  (LRES)  GO  TO  100
        .
        .
        .

        IF  (LRES)  GO  TO  200
        .
        .
        .

100     PRINT,  LINE,  .TRUE.,  A,  B
        STOP
        END
```

FIGURE 11.4

FORMAT-FREE I/O OF LOGICAL VALUES

REF

As figure 11.4 indicates, we can read and write logical data using WATFIV format-free I/O. A logical input value may be expressed as T, F, .TRUE., or .FALSE. Other rules for preparing format-free logical input are as described in chapter 3. Either of the examples below is acceptable input to the program in figure 11.4.

```
     .FALSE.,26.5,14.3
     T              3.342          16.9
```

The value of a logical variable that appears in a PRINT statement is printed as T or F, indicating .TRUE. or .FALSE., respectively. Logical expressions can be specified in PRINT statements. (See .TRUE. in the PRINT statement in figure 11.4.) Entire arrays of logical values can be printed. Additional examples are shown in figure 11.5.

```
        LOGICAL  LTAB(4,3),  E
        REAL  C,  D
        READ,  E,  ((LTAB(I,J),I=1,4),J=1,2)
        READ,  LTAB(3,3),  LTAB(1,3),  C,  D
```

REF

```
        LTAB(2,3) = .NOT.LTAB(3,3)
                .
                .
                .
        PRINT, .TRUE., D
        PRINT, ((LTAB(I,J),I=1,3),J=1,3)
        PRINT, C.GT.D, .NOT.E
        STOP
        END
```

FIGURE 11.5

FORMATTED I/O

When logical data is read or written using formatted I/O, a field descriptor of the form Lw appears in the FORMAT statement that gives the format of the data on the external medium. On input, a field of w character positions is scanned from left to right. The first T or F encountered in the field determines whether a value of .TRUE. or .FALSE. is assigned to the corresponding logical variable. If the field is blank, the logical variable is set to .FALSE. On output, a value of T or F is printed right-justified in a field of length w; any unused left-most positions are set to blanks. Arrays of logical data values as well as simple variables or specific array elements can be written or read. (See figure 11.6.)

```
        LOGICAL LONE, LTWO, LS*1, LV*1
        DIMENSION LV(4)
        INTEGER I, J, K, U
        READ (5,60) I, J, K, LONE, LTWO
 60     FORMAT (3I4,2L7)
        LV(1) = I.LT.J
        LV(2) = LONE.OR.J.NE.K
        U = I + J
                .
                .
                .
        WRITE (6,100) LV(1), LV(2), LONE, U
100     FORMAT (2(L1,1X),L4,I4)
        STOP
        END
```

FIGURE 11.6

DECLARATION AND INITIALIZATION OF CHARACTER VARIABLES

Both FORTRAN and WATFOR/WATFIV systems permit manipulation of character data. The basic difference between FORTRAN and WATFIV with respect to character data is that FORTRAN permits no CHARACTER declaration. Therefore, any character manipulations in FORTRAN have to occur as though the data were of other types. This means that only groups of characters of sizes equivalent to the sizes allowed for LOGICAL, INTEGER, or REAL data can be manipulated. We must deal with 1, 2, 4, or 8 characters.

In FORTRAN, logical, integer, and real variables can be initialized to character-string values in type statements as shown below.

```
INTEGER A/'FISH'/
REAL*8 X2/'HEADING'/
LOGICAL*1 C/'C'/,D/'D'/,E/'E'/
REAL HOL/4HABCD/
REAL X(4)/'REPO', 'RT F', 'IFTE', 'EN  '/
```

Since the character-string HEADING fills only seven of the eight storage positions reserved for X, a blank character is stored in the rightmost position. The fourth declaration illustrates use of the H-type, or Hollerith, constant. (See chapters 4 and 10.) The last example shows how a relatively large amount of data can be stored in consecutive locations as an array.

In WATFIV, we declare character variables in a straightforward manner, just as we declare variables of any other data type. Examples are

```
CHARACTER*3 A, B, C
CHARACTER D*3, E*2/'MY'/
CHARACTER*5 I(4)/'JOHN', 'JERRY', 'KATHY', 'SAM'/
```

WATFIV character strings may range from 1 to 255 characters in size. We need not program around size restrictions because we can declare variables of the sizes we want to use and use them as declared throughout our program. (To review WATFIV declaration of variables of CHARACTER type, see the reference section of chapter 2.)

In both FORTRAN and WATFIV, character strings may contain alphabetic characters (A–Z), numeric characters (0–9), and any of numerous special characters (#,@,.,(, etc.) that can be read or written on the computer system in use.

INPUT AND OUTPUT

Character strings may be read as input or written as output using formatted I/O or, in WATFIV, format-free I/O.

When formatted I/O is used, the A format code appears in the field descriptor that indicates the format of the data on the external medium. The characters may be read into or written from a variable of any type. First, consider the statements in figure 11.7, a portion of an IBM 360/370 FORTRAN program.

In the first read operation in figure 11.7, the input values fit exactly in the storage locations to which they are moved. In the second, two rules must be applied:

- If the number of characters read is greater than the length of the receiving variable, excess characters are truncated at the left.

- If the number of characters read is less than the length of the receiving variable, the unused rightmost positions are filled with blanks.

REF

```
          REAL*8 B, P
          INTEGER M
          READ (5,30) B, P, M
     30   FORMAT (2A8,A4)
              .
              .
              .
          READ (5,60) B, P, M
     60   FORMAT (A3,A8,A6)
              .
              .
              .
          END
```

FIGURE 11.7

The next three characters in the input stream are read into the leftmost positions of B, and the five remaining positions are filled with blanks. The next eight are read into P. The next two characters are effectively skipped, because only the rightmost four of six characters can be stored in M.

The actions controlled by these two sets of statements are summarized schematically in figure 11.8. (b̸ means blank.) Misfits are not recognized as errors. On the contrary, the compiler assumes that characters are to be skipped or that locations need not be used, just as readily as it accepts perfect fits.

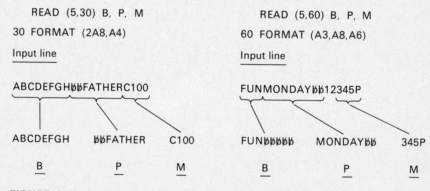

FIGURE 11.8

An example showing both formatted input and formatted output of character data is given in figure 11.9. The rules stated above are applied on input, and reading occurs as pictured in the upper portion of figure 11.10. Two similar rules govern printing of output:

● If the number of positions in the output field is greater than the size of the variable from which data is written, the data is right-justified, preceded by leading blanks.

REF

- If the output field is smaller than the size of the variable from which data is written, excess characters are truncated from the right.

```
        REAL*4  A,  B,  C
        WRITE  (6,1)
1       FORMAT ('THIS  IS  A  LITERAL')
        READ  (5,2)  A,  B,  C
2       FORMAT  (A4,1X,A6,1X,A2)
        WRITE  (6,3)  A,  B,  C
3       FORMAT  (1X,3(1X,A4))
        WRITE  (6,4)  A
4       FORMAT  (1X,A6)
        WRITE  (6,5)  B
5       FORMAT  (1X,A2)
        STOP
        END
```

FIGURE 11.9

FORMAT statement 4 enacts the first of these rules in formatting the value of A for printing. FORMAT statement 5 uses the second in formatting B.

Input line

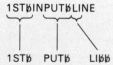

1STɓPUTɓ   LIɓɓ

Output lines

THIS IS A LITERAL
1STɓPUTɓɓLI
ɓɓ1STɓ
PU

FIGURE 11.10

FORMAT-FREE I/O OF CHARACTER VALUES

When WATFIV format-free input and output are used, strings of any size up to 255 characters can be read into or written from a single variable of CHARACTER type. The rules for input strings that are too long or too short are the same as the rules governing formatted I/O. On output, the size of the variable from which data is written determines the length of the string, so there is no such thing as a string that is too long or too short.

REF

The WATFIV program in figure 11.11 reads and prints ten names, each of which is up to twenty characters in length. The names are punched as character strings, either one to a card, or with multiple strings on each card. Each input character string must be surrounded by single quotes and separated from the next string by a comma or by one or more blanks. As many cards as necessary are read, until ten strings have been stored as elements of A. The first PRINT statement prints three character strings, separated from one another by blank characters as a one-line output identifier. The second PRINT statement displays the ten values of array A. In neither case are we limited to groups of 1, 2, 4, or 8 characters.

```
CHARACTER*20 A(10)
CHARACTER B*10/'THE FIRST '/,C*9/'TEN WERE '/,
1D*4/'BEST'/
READ, A
PRINT, B, C, D
PRINT, A
STOP
END
```

FIGURE 11.11

Rather than initializing character variables, then printing their values, we might have used the statement

PRINT, 'THE FIRST TEN WERE BEST'

As an exercise, you should run both forms of this program and compare their outputs.

One important distinction must be kept in mind when preparing format-free or formatted input. For the former, single quotes must enclose character strings as delimiters, but they are not actually read into storage. For the latter, enclosing single quotes should not be used. To cause a single quote to be read as data when using WATFIV format-free input, two successive single quotes must be entered in the input stream.

Character strings can be stored in variables of types other than CHARACTER in WATFOR and WATFIV. But in general this is neither necessary nor advisable. If you use format-free PRINT statements to print out data represented by a variable of other than CHARACTER type, the output is apt to surprise you. The data is stored in the form declared for it and is interpreted as a variable of that type. A character string represented by a variable of INTEGER type is printed as an integer (containing only digits), which is the way the computer has been instructed to interpret the value.

ASSIGNMENT OF CHARACTER STRINGS

Character values, whether stored in character variables or in variables of other types, can be moved to other variables using assignment statements. In IBM

360/370 FORTRAN, the receiving variable may be INTEGER, REAL, or LOGICAL as appropriate for the type declaration used for the character variable being assigned, or any of these if a character-string constant is assigned. In WATFIV, the receiving variable may also be of CHARACTER type. When using variables of mixed types, such as INTEGER and REAL, one type may not be assigned to another if it contains characters. Similarly, one size cannot be assigned to another size, such as an INTEGER*2 data item to an INTEGER*4 receiving variable. The compiler attempts to make the standard conversions from one type or size to another. These conversions are designed to work for data stored in whatever form is required by the particular size and type, not for character data. Data of different sizes and types can be equivalenced if you need to refer to part of a string of characters, or to refer to a character string as though it were of one size and type for one reference but of another size and type for another reference. Figure 11.12 illustrates placing character data in a real variable, moving (copying) it into another real variable, then accessing it there and in its original locations as a four-element array of logical values of size 1.

```
      REAL  CHAR, B
      LOGICAL*1  SINGLE(4)
      EQUIVALENCE  (CHAR,SINGLE)
      DATA CHAR/'READ'/
      B = CHAR
      WRITE  (6,1) CHAR, B, SINGLE(2), SINGLE(4)
1     FORMAT  (1X,A4,A4,A1,A1)
      STOP
      END
```

FIGURE 11.12

The output provided by this program is shown and explained in figure 11.13.

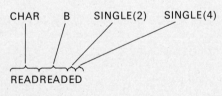

FIGURE 11.13

COMPARISON OF CHARACTER STRINGS

There are times when you want to know which of two character strings should appear first in a list. This consideration arises when sorting character strings, say, a list of names, or when searching an ordered (already sorted) list. Usually, special characters come before letters, and letters come before numerals; but the established order, or *collating sequence*, varies somewhat from system to system.

REF

Comparison operations are performed character by character, beginning with the leftmost characters of the quantities being compared, just as we arrange values. An ordered list of character strings as established in IBM 360/370 computer systems is shown in figure 11.14.

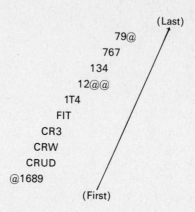

(Last)
79@
767
134
12@@
1T4
FIT
CR3
CRW
CRUD
@1689
(First)

FIGURE 11.14

The most common comparison is a simple determination of whether or not two strings have identical values. The FORTRAN relational operators .EQ. and .NE. may be used, no matter what type was declared for the variables

```
        INTEGER I/'DATE'/, J, K1/'PARK'/, K2/'SON'/
        INTEGER INPUT(2)
        READ (5,2) INPUT(1), INPUT(2), J
2       FORMAT (3A4)
        IF (I.NE.J) WRITE (6,1)
1       FORMAT (' DATE NOT EQUAL')
        IF (INPUT(1).NE.K1) GO TO 10
        IF (INPUT(2).NE.K2) GO TO 20
30      WRITE (6,200)
200     FORMAT (' NAMES EQUAL')
        STOP
20      IF (INPUT(2).GT.K2) GO TO 40
50      WRITE (6,3)
3       FORMAT (' INPUT NAME LOW')
        STOP
40      WRITE (6,4)
4       FORMAT (' INPUT NAME HIGH')
        STOP
10      IF (INPUT(1).GT.K1) GO TO 40
        GO TO 50
        END
```

FIGURE 11.15

representing the character strings being compared. In sorting and searching, the relational operators .LT., .GT., .GE., and .LE. are useful. Because of the way variables are stored, these operators work correctly for character strings represented by integer variables but may not work correctly otherwise. Variables of the same length and type should be specified in any comparison. Otherwise the compiler performs conversions to establish quantities of the same data type, and results are not as expected. The string 'AB12' represented by a variable of INTEGER type is not equal to the string 'AB12' represented by a variable of REAL type.

The FORTRAN program in figure 11.15 compares I and J. It then compares an input name with the name PARKSON. Since the strings are represented by integer variables, they are stored and manipulated as quantities of length 4. Note that the last half of each name must be compared to 'SON' only if the first half and 'PARK' are equal.

COMPARISONS WITH VARIABLES OF CHARACTER TYPE

Using WATFIV, variables of CHARACTER type can be compared. Any of the relational operators work correctly with these variables, just as they do with integer variables containing character strings. If two compared variables of CHARACTER type have different lengths, the shorter one is treated as though it is the same size as the longer with blank characters added at the right as necessary. A warning message is issued at compile-time when operands of different lengths are compared. The general guideline is that comparisons should involve only variables of identical type, and this applies to variables of CHARACTER type just as to variables of other types. A variable of CHARACTER type should be compared only with another variable of CHARACTER type.

The comparisons in figure 11.16 are much easier to express than those in figure 11.15 because the strings need not be manipulated in groups of 4. Using 15 as the size for the variables in figure 11.16 emphasizes that the CHARACTER type declaration offers flexibility not available otherwise.

```
      CHARACTER K1*15/'PARKSON'/, INPUT*15
C     NOTICE THAT K1 IS AUTOMATICALLY FILLED OUT WITH
C     BLANKS.
      READ, INPUT
      IF (INPUT.EQ.K1) PRINT, 'NAMES EQUAL'
      IF (INPUT.LT.K1) PRINT, 'INPUT NAME LOW'
      IF (INPUT.GT.K1) PRINT, 'INPUT NAME HIGH'
      STOP
      END
```

FIGURE 11.16

In this WATFIV example, there is some redundant testing since each variable is tested three times, but the programming is simple. GO TO statements branching to a labeled STOP statement are an alternative.

EXERCISES

1. (TUT) Which of the following are valid logical expressions (and what assumptions must you make about the types of the variables involved)?
   a) K
   b) 1 .GT. K
   c) D.OR.H
   d) H .AND..NOT.P
   e) E .LT. .AND. Q
   f) (A.GT.B.OR.L).AND(I .OR.L3)
   g) A.AND.B.OR.C.AND.(C.OR. D.LT.C)
   h) (L.AND..NOT.(B.LE.C.ANDB.LT.D).OR..NOT.(.GT.TIME)

2. (TUT) Rewrite each invalid expression in the preceding exercise to form a valid expression.

3. (TUT) Write an IF statement that causes FOUND to be printed when each of the following sets of conditions is met.
   a) A is 47. or 46. or between 99. and 101.
   b) L is true.
   c) Either L2 is false or I is between 5 and 9.
   d) L3 and L4 are true.

4. (TUT) Refer to the preceding exercise. Write one IF statement that causes FOUND to be printed if either (a), (b), and (c) are true, or (d) is true.

5. (REF) Read in five logical values. Print true if the first three are false and the last two are true; otherwise print false.

6. (REF) Read in four logical values representing the colors of four frogs (T if green; F if yellow). Write statements to give the value .TRUE. to L1 if there are exactly two green frogs.

7. (REF) As in 6, but give the value .TRUE. to L1 if there are exactly three green frogs.

8. (REF) Using standard FORTRAN, declare variables to represent three character strings, up to 3, 8, and 12 characters in length respectively. Initialize the first variable to 'AMT'.

9. (REF) Repeat the preceding exercise, but assume WATFIV character declaration and handling capabilities.

10. (REF) Using standard FORTRAN, read three character strings; then print them, separated by *'s. The first variable should be three characters long, and the second and third should be five characters each.

11. (REF) Repeat the preceding exercise, but assume WATFIV character declaration and handling capabilities.

PROGRAMMING PROBLEMS

§ 3.6

1. (REF) Assume that $A(I,J), I=1,...,M, J=1,...,N$ contains the Jth score of the Ith student. Assume that $W(J)$ contains the weight of the Jth problem. Write a program to rank order the students by sorting into $K(I)$ the position of the Ith student in the class. In doing so, you may find it useful to review

the subroutine subprogram that you constructed in response to programming problem 6 of chapter 8.

§ 5.1   2.   (REF) An array $X(I), I=1, ..., M$ contains floating-point numbers. Write a program to find the sum of the N largest. Assume that $1 \leq N \leq M$.

3.   (REF) Write a program to read an array of logical values as input. Use the array elements to represent connections between cities. If city I can be reached directly from city J, the corresponding array element should have the value .TRUE. The program should be able to answer questions about whether two cities are directly connected. If not, it should print a series of steps to get from one to the other.

4.   (REF) Write a program to implement a binary add. Use arrays containing five logical values. (Those of you studying C. W. Gear, *Introduction to Computer Science*, can refer to the discussion of machine addition in that text as a guideline.)

5.   (REF) Write a program to search for a certain character string in an array of character-string values. Read the search argument and array as input, assuming the array values are sorted. (Terminate the program immediately if they are not.)

6.   (REF) Refer to the preceding programming problem. Write a program to achieve the same end objective, but assume that the array values are read in random order. Use either of two approaches:
    a)   Sort the array values before searching
    b)   Search the array without sorting

7.   (REF) Compare the programming techniques and efficiency of programs created in response to 5 and 6 above.

8.   (REF) Rewrite the tic-tac-toe program that you wrote in response to programming problem 13 in chapter 7 to use logical variables to represent the state of the game. (Two variables will be needed for each square.) Use logical expressions in deciding which move to make next.

[11] INTRO In general, input/output statements are used to move data between main storage and an external device such as a card reader, printer, card punch, magnetic tape unit, or disk storage unit. The programmer uses the input/output statement to specify the kind of I/O operation required.

As explained in the tutorial section of chapter 10, there are two basic types of input and output in FORTRAN: (1) formatted, or character, I/O and (2) unformatted, or record, I/O. Formatted I/O, discussed in detail in chapter 10, comes up again in some portions of this chapter. Also, unformatted I/O is explained and applied in problem solving.

The formatted I/O operations discussed previously and the unformatted I/O operations discussed in the tutorial section of this chapter are sequential operations. Data items are written or read in sequence, in the same order that they appear on the external medium (usually, punched card, printed page, or magnetic tape). The input/output statements that control sequential I/O are READ, WRITE, REWIND, BACKSPACE, and END FILE. FORMAT and NAMELIST statements may be referred to by READ and WRITE statements controlling sequential I/O.

Sometimes, direct-access rather than sequential I/O operations are appropriate for a particular problem situation. When direct-access I/O is used, data items are written and read in an order specified by the user. The input/output statements that control direct access I/O are DEFINE FILE, READ, WRITE, and FIND. Direct-access I/O is explained in the reference section of this chapter.

[11] TUT SEQUENTIAL OPERATIONS The WATFIV format-free READ and PRINT statements (explained in chapter 3) and the formatted READ and WRITE statements of IBM 360/370 FORTRAN (explained in chapter 10) look at card input or print output as strings of characters. Generally, each card or line constitutes one FORTRAN *record*, and groups of related records form a *file*, or *data set*. Each file is *sequential*, since I/O operations

Chapter

12

MORE ABOUT INPUT/OUTPUT

begin with the first character on the file and proceed toward the last character. Once a card has been read, we cannot back up and reread the card during a single processing run. Once a sequence of characters has been written to the printer, it cannot be rewritten. Use of this approach for sequential files on punched cards, printer paper, and magnetic tape is illustrated in figure 12.1.

Sequential files

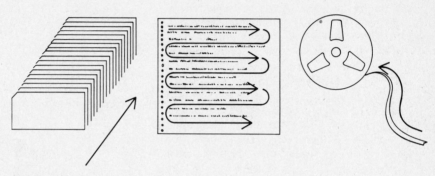

FIGURE 12.1

UNFORMATTED I/O

Sometimes, although we want to read or write records in sequence, it is appropriate to use unformatted, rather than formatted, I/O. The unformatted I/O operations are sequential operations, but the data items moved to or from main storage are viewed as strings of values, rather than as strings of characters. With unformatted I/O, we need not specify the lengths of items being read or written because their lengths for input/output are the same as their lengths in storage. We need not specify their types because no conversion of data from one form to another occurs.

As stated in chapter 10, the primary advantages of unformatted I/O are that no time is required for conversion operations and that data placed on an external medium in internal form takes up less space than it would if converted to external (character) form. Usually, data provided as output of unformatted I/O operations is intended to be used as input for a subsequent processing run.

UNFORMATTED READ AND WRITE STATEMENTS

Unformatted read and write operations, like formatted, are controlled by READ and WRITE statements. An I/O list is given in the READ or WRITE statement, but no FORMAT statement number is specified. In this case, there is a one-to-one correspondence between main-storage locations (bytes, in IBM 360/370) and positions for data on the external medium. A single READ or WRITE statement is used to move a single record of information. The length of the record is dependent upon the number and size of variables in the I/O list.

```
        DIMENSION  A(10,40)
        DO 10  I=1,10
10      WRITE  (8)  (A(I,J),J=1,40)
        REWIND 8
        DO 20  I=1,10
20      READ  (8)  (A(I,J),J=1,40)
            .
            .
            .
        END
```

FIGURE 12.2

Unformatted input/output operations, sequential in nature, are used in figure 12.2. The program writes an array row by row; each row is a single record. It then reads the array back into storage in the same order in which it was written initially.

IDENTIFYING DATA SOURCES AND DESTINATIONS

Notice that the WRITE, REWIND, and READ statements in figure 12.2 contain the numeral 8. This is a logical unit number such as the ones used in formatted READ and WRITE statements in chapter 10. It identifies the file to or from which data is moved. Generally, this form of sequential file can be stored on any of several external media available in a system. Magnetic tapes and magnetic disks are common. Because the external coding scheme of the data is retained, the data cannot be written as printed output.

At the time a FORTRAN program is executed, logical unit numbers must be associated with specific input/output devices available on the computer system in use. The method for establishing this association is system-dependent, so you must become familiar with programming and operational procedures at the installation where your programs are run. You must be aware of what logical unit numbers are usually assigned to what types of devices so that you can code input/output statements correctly.

The system design (chapter 9) should indicate which logical files the system programs use and what each of the files is used for. The files may be overwritten by new data immediately, saved for a day or a week in system libraries, or kept for months or years in large storage vaults. Since magnetic tapes are easy to dismount and store, they are a common way of saving FORTRAN unformatted files for a length of time.

LOGICAL RECORDS

Normally, data to be read as unformatted input has been created by execution of the same program or another program that provided the data as unformatted output. The information written as the result of one execution of a WRITE statement is one *logical record*. A READ statement can read all or part of a logical record.

One way to understand the term *logical record* is to compare a logical record to a card image or print line of formatted input/output. When using FORMAT statements to read data from a card, the maximum amount of data that can be read from a card (in most systems, 80 characters) is determined by the physical characteristics of the card itself. If you read past the end of one card (record), you begin reading the next card (record); if you stop reading in the middle of a card (record), you begin reading a new card (record) on the next READ.

When reading without reference to FORMAT statements, the amount of data that is read is the amount of data in the next record in sequence. The amount of data in that record was determined previously by the list of variables included in the I/O list of the WRITE statement that created the record. If a READ statement reads only part of a logical record, the next READ statement starts at the beginning of the next logical record. The balance of an incompletely read logical record is skipped.

When writing output with format control, you can begin a new line by including a /, the slash character, at the appropriate point in the referenced FORMAT statement, or by exhausting the list of field descriptors in that statement. When writing without format control, one execution of a WRITE statement creates one logical record (line) of output.

A series of WRITE statements creating logical records is shown at the left in figure 12.3. Together, all logical records written by execution of WRITE statements referring to logical unit 9 form one file. READ statements such as might be used to access this file during subsequent processing are shown at the right in figure 12.3. Each execution of a READ statement causes data to be retrieved from the next logical record in sequence. There need be no correspondence between variable names; relative position determines which values are assigned to which variables.

DIMENSION D (4)		DIMENSION X1 (3)
WRITE (9) A, B, C	A / R1	REWIND 9
	B / R2	READ (9) R1, R2, R3
	C / R3	
WRITE (9) D	D (1) / X1 (1)	READ (9) X1
	D (2) / X1 (2)	
	D (3) / X1 (3)	
	D (4) skipped	
WRITE (9) E	E / X	READ (9) X, Y, Z
WRITE (9) F, G	F / Y	
	G / Z	

FIGURE 12.3

PROCESSING OPTIONS

When reading logical records without format control, there are three ways to detect when the last record is read. One way is to place a count of the number of records in the first logical record of a file when it is created. Then we can read that number of records from the file.

However, it is not always possible to determine this count before writing the records. If one record is to be written for each card read as input, but the number of input cards is not known beforehand, there is no way of knowing how many records will be written to the file.

Another way of recognizing end of file is to set up a convention that a record of a certain type (dummy record) indicates the end of the file. This approach may not be reliable. It depends upon special input procedures that are often difficult to establish or enforce, and it is invalid if a normal data record has the form of the dummy record.

A third, more reliable way is to include the END option in any READ statement referring to an input file. This option permits us to specify a statement in the FORTRAN program to which control is to be transferred when a read attempt fails because there are no more records in the file. An example is

READ (8,END=999) A, B, C

When this READ statement is executed but there are no more records in the file assigned to logical unit 8, control is transferred to statement 999. Presumably, statement 999 is a STOP statement or the first statement of a special sequence of statements to be executed only at end of file.

A second option that can be specified in the READ statement is the ERR option. It allows the FORTRAN programmer to regain control if an input/output error occurs while reading a record. Such a problem may arise, for example, if dust particles are encountered on a magnetic tape.

In practice, most FORTRAN systems have automatic error recovery procedures so that control is transferred to the statement named in the ERR option only after the system has determined that the input/output error cannot be corrected. The statement or routine beginning at the label specified in the ERR option is the programmer's choice of action, should such a situation occur. To cause control to be transferred to statement 998 if an input/output error is encountered on logical unit 8, we expand our READ statement above to

READ (8,END=999,ERR=998) A, B, C

You may recall that either or both of these options can be specified in READ statements that control formatted I/O operations. (See chapter 10.) The order in which they are specified is not significant. If either is omitted and the end-of-file or error condition occurs, a system default action is taken. Generally, the program is terminated.

THE REWIND STATEMENT

The REWIND 8 statement in figure 12.2 is a typical use of the *REWIND statement*. The general form of this statement is

REWIND *unit*

where *unit* is the logical unit number associated with the file to be rewound. The REWIND statement is designed for use with magnetic tape files. Its effect is to position a tape to the starting marker on the tape so that the first reading or writing on the tape occurs at a known fixed position—the first logical record of the file.

One use of the REWIND statement is to start over, reading a file from the beginning after it has been written as in figure 12.2 or rereading logical records from the beginning of the file. Many programmers include a REWIND statement for every magnetic tape file before moving any data to or from the file. It is not wise to assume that a tape is in the rewound position, ready for read or write operations, just because the computer operator has mounted the tape for a run.

THE BACKSPACE STATEMENT

The *BACKSPACE statement* is somewhat similar to REWIND in that it is used to position a sequential file. Instead of returning from any point in a file to the beginning of that file, however, we move backwards only one logical record. The general form of this statement is

BACKSPACE *unit*

where *unit* is the logical unit number associated with the file to be backspaced. If the file is already at its beginning, execution of the BACKSPACE statement has no effect; you cannot backspace to a point preceding the first logical record of the file. Examples are

BACKSPACE 6
BACKSPACE 8

THE END FILE STATEMENT

The *END FILE statement* is intended for use with a sequential file when it is created (i.e., written as output). Usually, the END FILE statement is included in a sequence of statements to be executed only after all data records have been written to a file. It causes an *end-of-file mark* to be written following the last data record on the file. When this file is subsequently read as input, the end-of-file mark will be sensed automatically and prevent any attempt to read more records than have been placed on the file. The statement

END FILE 6

causes an end-of-file mark to be placed at the current position of the file on logical unit 6.

You should adopt the convention of using END FILE statements for all magnetic-tape files created by your programs. The end-of-file mark is the means by which the END option of a READ statement gains control when one of the files is read as input by a FORTRAN program.

AN EXAMPLE

Figure 12.4 demonstrates the use of sequential input/output statements. The program creates a file, then reads and re-reads the file that it has created. What values are written and read by the WRITE and READ statements? What are the values of the variables when processing is completed? How many input files are used by the program? How many output files? How many records are contained in the file on logical unit 9? What file is referred to by the PRINT statement?

```
        INTEGER*4 I, J
        I = 9
        B = 7.0
        WRITE (I) B
        END FILE 9
        E = 14.0
        REWIND 9
        READ (I) A
        BACKSPACE I
        READ (9) C
        REWIND I
        READ (I) D
        READ (I,END=999) E
        PRINT, 'THIS WILL NOT BE PRINTED'
        STOP
999     PRINT, 'END OF FILE AFTER ONE RECORD'
        STOP
        END
```

FIGURE 12.4

REMARKS

With sequential I/O, you can read or write all or part of a file, rewind it, and either read or write from its beginning. You cannot read several records and then choose to write a record to the same file at its current position. You cannot decide to read from a file that you have been creating without first repositioning the file to its beginning. Either of these attempted operations causes an input/output error to occur. Some systems allow you to space to the end of a file you have been reading (past the end-of-file mark) and write data there. If you have set up multiple files within one batch of data by writing end-of-file marks therein, you cannot add data to any file other than the last file.

It is in relation to input/output that most system-dependent features of computer processing appear. As noted earlier, you must know what types of input/output devices are available at your installation and what logical unit numbers are associated with the files on those devices. You must also know how the files are organized and what system controls govern access to the files.

Obviously, answers to such questions are not within the scope of a FOR-TRAN program. And techniques or features for accomplishing such tasks are not within the scope of this book. To learn of them, you should consult operating-system documentation at your installation. System-dependent information pertaining directly to FORTRAN programming is usually available in a FORTRAN programmer's guide.

REF

DIRECT-ACCESS I/O

Sometimes it is useful to have a file to or from which data can be transferred in any order. For example, suppose a file contains records for a large airline. Each record shows flight number, schedule, and available space. We want to know when flight 689 is leaving and if we can obtain reservations for two. It is desirable to access the record for flight 689 directly; we gain nothing by reading all physically preceding records in the file. IBM 360/370 FORTRAN and WATFIV provide this capability through *direct-access I/O*.

DEFINING A DIRECT-ACCESS FILE

When using direct-access I/O, a first step is to set up direct-access files. Each file consists of a number of records, and each of those records has an *index* which indicates the relative position of the record in the file. The first record has index 1, the second has index 2, and so on. Thus we might compare the file to a large one-dimensional array, with the index serving the same purpose as an array subscript. But instead of referring to only one array element, we refer to a complete record on the file. That record can hold the values of all variables we might choose to include in the I/O list of a READ or WRITE statement. We must specify the number of records in the file and the size of the records just as we must specify the number of elements in an array and the type and size of the elements.

THE DEFINE FILE STATEMENT

Suppose we decide to set up a direct-access file for a stock status report program. Each item in stock is identified by a five-digit part number. For each item, a card containing the item number and the current quantity in stock has been punched to serve as input to our file creation program. Figure 12.5 shows how we can create a direct-access file containing the current status of 5000 different kinds of items.

The *DEFINE FILE statement* in figure 12.5 causes a portion of direct-access storage space available on logical unit 8, most likely magnetic disk or magnetic drum, to be allocated for this file. The file comprises 5000 records, each of which is up to 60 characters in length. The letter E indicates that any read or write operations to the file will be made with format control. INDEX is an integer variable selected by the programmer to serve as the *associated variable* for the file. Whenever a read or write operation refers to this file, INDEX is set to a value that points to the next sequential record in the file. Thus, INDEX can be

REF

useful in reading or writing a direct-access file sequentially from a given point in the file.

```
          INTEGER NUM, QTY
          DEFINE FILE 8 (5000,60,E,INDEX)
    10    READ (5,90,END=100) NUM, QTY
          WRITE (8'NUM,90) NUM, QTY
          GO TO 10
    90    FORMAT (I5,I7)
    100   STOP
          END
```

FIGURE 12.5

The general form of the DEFINE FILE statement is

DEFINE FILE *unit* (*numrec,size,f,assoc*) [, *unit* (*numrec*, . . .), . . .]

where *unit* is the logical unit number associated with the file, and *numrec* is the number of records in the file. The *size* is an integer constant that indicates the maximum size of each record on the file, but the unit of measurement for *size* depends on the value specified for *f*. We provide a value for *f* indicating whether the file is to be accessed with or without format control, as follows:

f	Meaning
E	The file is to be read or written with format control. The maximum record size is measured in number of characters (for IBM 360/370, this is equivalent to bytes).
U	The file is to be read or written without format control. The maximum record size is measured in number of storage units, or words. In IBM 360/370, each word consists of four bytes.
L	The file is to be read or written either with or without format control. The maximum record size is measured in number of storage locations (bytes).

As noted above, the fourth entry within the parentheses of a DEFINE FILE statement, *assoc*, is an integer variable that serves as an associated variable for the file. It must be a simple variable and cannot appear in the I/O list of a READ or WRITE statement referring to this file.

Several direct-access files can be defined in one DEFINE FILE statement, and several DEFINE FILE statements may appear in a program. Each direct-access file must be described once, and this description may appear once in each program or subprogram. Subsequent descriptions are ignored. The DEFINE FILE statement must be executed prior to any input/output statement referring to a file described in the statement. Only direct-access READ and WRITE statements and FIND statements may refer to a file defined in a DEFINE FILE statement. By specifying an index, or relative record number, as well as a logical

REF

unit number in these input/output statements, we can perform operations on any record we choose within the direct-access file. Other input/output statements which refer to direct-access files are ignored.

READING A DIRECT-ACCESS FILE

In figure 12.5, we wrote logical records to a direct-access file, but we read input data used to create the file from a sequential punched-card file. There are situations, of course, where we need to read data from a direct-access file. Figure 12.6 shows use of a direct-access READ statement to move selected records from a direct-access file. The associated variable named in the DEFINE FILE statement for the file is used to locate and print the data from a selected record and nineteen physically succeeding records on the file. Note that in this program we use WATFIV format-free READ and PRINT statements as well as direct-access I/O.

```
      INTEGER NUM, QTY
      DEFINE FILE 8 (5000,60,E,INDEX)
      READ, INDEX
      DO 30 I=1,20
      READ (8'INDEX,90) NUM, QTY
30    PRINT, NUM, QTY
      STOP
90    FORMAT (I5,I7)
      END
```

FIGURE 12.6

The general form of the direct-access READ statement is

READ (*unit'rel,fmt*,ERR=*label*) *list*

where *unit* is the logical unit number, and *rel* is an integer expression that represents the relative position of a record within the file associated with *unit*. Specification of *fmt* is optional; it is appropriate only if a file is being read with format control. If specified, it is the number of a FORMAT statement that describes the data being read or the name of an array that is being used for execution-time format specification. The ERR option is as explained earlier for both formatted and unformatted sequential I/O operations, and the *list* is an I/O list as used in either of these kinds of operations. Note that we are not concerned with an END option, that is, with encountering an end-of-file condition, when using direct-access files.

UPDATING A DIRECT-ACCESS FILE

You may have wondered why we declared a maximum size of 60 bytes for each record in our stock status file when we included only two entries in each record of the file. Let us suppose now that we want to add the number of a preferred vendor as a third entry in certain records of the file. To do so, we read each record

REF

to be changed, then rewrite it to contain the new information. Reading and writing selected records to modify them is called *updating the file*. Figure 12.7 shows how this can be done.

```
        INTEGER NUM, QTY, VENDOR
        DEFINE FILE 8 (5000,60,E,INDEX)
10      READ (5,90,END=100) INDEX, VENDOR
        READ (8'INDEX,91) NUM, QTY
        WRITE (8'INDEX,92) NUM, QTY, VENDOR
        GO TO 10
90      FORMAT (I4,I5)
91      FORMAT (I5,I7)
92      FORMAT (I5,I7,I5)
100     STOP
        END
```

FIGURE 12.7

The general form of the direct-access WRITE statement is similar to that of the direct-access READ statement. It is

WRITE (*unit'rel,fmt*) *list*

where *unit, rel, fmt,* and *list* are as defined for READ above.

Of course, neither a READ nor WRITE statement can cause more data to be moved than can be stored in a record of the maximum size declared for records in the referenced direct-access file. Thus, the WRITE statement in figure 12.8 causes an input/output error to occur.

```
        DIMENSION IARVEN(6), IARLOC(6)
        INTEGER NUM, QTY
        DEFINE FILE 8 (5000,60,E,INDEX)
             .
             .
             .
        WRITE (8'INDEX,90) NUM, QTY, IARVEN, IARLOC
90      FORMAT (I5,I7,6I5,6A4)
             .
             .
             .
        STOP
        END
```

FIGURE 12.8

The WRITE statement in figure 12.8 controls formatted I/O. If the file were being written without format control, the data that would not fit in the first record would be written into the next adjacent record. This may or may not be

REF

what the programmer intends. When using formatted I/O, if the data being written fills only part of a record (as ours have previously), unused positions are filled with blanks. When using unformatted I/O, unused positions are filled with zeros. Until a record is written, its contents are undefined.

THE FIND STATEMENT

When a direct-access read operation is performed, two actions are required. First, the desired record must be located on the direct-access file. Then the data must be transferred from the file to main storage. Since the first of these usually requires physical positioning of an input/output device, for example, moving a disk read/write head to a proper position, significant amounts of time may be required.

To reduce or eliminate delays due to I/O activity, the *FIND statement* can be used to locate the next record to be read before a READ statement is actually encountered during processing. Furthermore, the locating can be done while other processing steps in the program are being carried out. The program has no access to the record until the READ is executed, but the read operation can be performed faster if the desired record has already been found.

```
            .
            .
            .
        FIND  (8'50)
            .
            .
            .
10      READ (8'50) A, B, C
            .
            .
            .
        END
```

FIGURE 12.9

While the statements between FIND and READ in figure 12.9 are being executed, record 50 in the file associated with logical unit 8 is being located. If the record has been located by the time the READ is executed, data transfer occurs immediately. If the record has not been found, a slight delay occurs ; but it is shorter than would otherwise have been necessary.

The general form of the FIND statement is

FIND (*unit′rel*)

where *unit* is the logical unit number of the file containing the record identified by *rel*, an integer expression indicating the relative position of the record to be read. Obviously, the same relative record number should be specified in FIND and READ statements intended to correspond. After execution of a FIND state-

REF

ment that locates a record in a specified file, the associated variable for the file points to the record specified in the FIND statement. There is no advantage to using a FIND statement for a write operation.

AN EXAMPLE

WATFIV format-free input/output, formatted sequential read, and formatted direct-access read and write operations are used in figure 12.10. Study this example to identify the general objective of the program, the files that it accesses, and the read and write operations that move data between main storage and external files.

```
        DIMENSION A(50)
        DEFINE FILE 8 (100,200,E,INDEX)
        DO 100 INDEX=1,20
        READ (5,99) A
C    CREATES DIRECT-ACCESS FILE.
100     WRITE (8'INDEX,99) A
        READ (8'10,99) A
C    READS ONE COMPLETE RECORD.
        PRINT, A(1)
        READ, I
        IF (I.LT.1.OR.I.GT.18) GO TO 1000
        FIND (8'I)
        DO 200 J=1,3
C    SEQUENTIAL READ OF PARTIAL RECORD.
        READ (8,99) A(1), A(2)
200     PRINT, A(2)
        STOP 1
1000    PRINT, 'INVALID INTEGER'
        STOP 2
99      FORMAT (25F3.0)
        END
```

FIGURE 12.10

PROGRAMMING CONSIDERATIONS

As you may have decided, direct-access operations are somewhat more complex than sequential operations. The programmer has to be much more aware of the general characteristics of files accessed by his programs. Since he must specify the maximum size in terms of characters, bytes, or words, he must know how the data that is being moved maps into main storage on the type of machine on which his programs will be run. It is in relation to direct-access I/O that the greatest variations in ways of implementation from system to system arise.

Obviously, an installation that permits use of direct-access files must include direct-access storage devices in its system configuration. Most likely,

REF

magnetic-disk storage units are employed. Magnetic-tape units do not provide capabilities for direct-access input/output. As with sequential operations, the programmer must know what logical unit numbers have been assigned to what devices. You should become familiar with programming conventions at your installation before using direct-access I/O.

QUEST

EXERCISES

1. (TUT) Distinguish between:
   formatted I/O, unformatted I/O, sequential I/O, direct-access I/O

2. (TUT)
   a) Explain the function and use of logical unit numbers in FORTRAN statements.
   b) Determine how logical unit numbers are assigned at the computer installation available to you.

3. (TUT) Write input/output statements to control the following operations:
   a) transfer of the current values of three floating-point variables, A, B, and C, from main storage to a punched-card file with format control
   b) transfer of values to be assigned to the first ten elements of array A, which can contain up to twenty integer values; assume input is from a magnetic-tape file, read without format control
   c) reposition the file on logical unit 8 to the position of the first logical record for subsequent read operations
   d) reposition the input file to the beginning of the record immediately preceding the current record of the file

4. (REF) Write statements to define the following direct-access files.
   a) a student personnel file comprising 4000 records, each up to 80 characters in length, to be written or read with format control
   b) a current project status file for management inquiry, consisting of 100 records, each up to 500 characters in length, to be written or read with or without format control
   c) a sort work file of 100 records, each up to 600 bytes in length, to be written and read without format control

5. (REF) When might use of the FIND statement be particularly advantageous in a program?

6. (REF) Explain how the associated variable of a direct-access file can be used.

PROGRAMMING PROBLEMS

1. (TUT) Write a program to copy the contents of 5000 80-column punched cards to magnetic tape to create a sequential accounts receivable master file.

2. (TUT) Write a program to add a date-of-last-payment field to the end of each record in the file that you created for 1 above.

3. (TUT) Write a program to print the current balance (in positions 21–30 of each record), together with customer number (positions 1–5) and name (positions 6–20), for every account whose date-of-last-payment precedes 01/01/73.

4. (TUT) Write a program to accept punched cards, each of which contains customer number and current payment, as input. Apply this input to update the sequential accounts receivable master file. Assume that the master file is in sequence by customer number. Include checks in your program to be certain that the punched-card input is in the sequence also.

5. (REF) Write a program to create a direct-access file for a large hospital. Accept 5000 cards as input, providing patient number, name, and address as initial entries in each record. Allow for up to 300 characters of information to be included in each record and for either formatted or unformatted accessing of the file.

6. (REF) Now write a program to print (dump) the contents of the master file created for 5 above, so that the contents of master file records can be verified.

7. (REF) Using direct-access I/O, write a simple editor to process a FORTRAN program as data. Assume one line of the FORTRAN program is stored in each record of the file. Allow commands which replace lines, print parts of the program, and replace parts of lines. For the latter, specify the part to be replaced as a string of characters, and specify the new section of code as a string of characters.

8. (REF) Write a command scanner that will identify certain keywords and change integer values expressed as characters into their corresponding internal forms. Change an input string into a vector of integers. Use one integer for each word, number, or string of blanks received as input. Make the numbers corresponding to your command names so large that they cannot be interpreted as valid integers. The list of command words and corresponding integers should be supplied by the user. This program should allow a form of format-free input for your other programs, in that the user will not have to type certain integers to request functions that can be performed by the programs.

9. (REF) Write an error message program to print messages retrieved from specified points in a direct-access file. The program should accept an integer that tells which message to print. You may assume that the file has been created previously, but your program should provide a facility for replacing an existing message on the file or adding a new message to the file.

10. (REF) To further enhance the program for 9 above, permit the user to input a value to be inserted in a message that is printed. Mark the place for the variable in the message with the character * for an integer, ¢ for a real value, and & for a logical value.

Responses to selected exercises are provided here to help you to check your understanding of the material presented. For some exercises, there is no one correct answer. Of course, the best way for you to check your responses to the programming problems is to compile, execute, and debug your programs with the aid of a computer.

CHAPTER 1.

2.a) Any character other than blank or 0 in column 6, the continuation field, implies that a line is a continuation line. Therefore, the first line of the PRINT statement will be treated as part of the preceding statement.

b) A comment line cannot appear immediately before a continuation line.

c) A comma must follow K.

CHAPTER 2.

3.a) REAL*4   d) REAL*4
  b) INTEGER*4   e) REAL*4
  c) REAL*4   f) REAL*4

6.   a, b, c, h, and j are valid declarations.

7.d) invalid because DOUBLE PRECISION conflicts with B*4

e) invalid because 6 cannot be specified as a size for REAL

f) invalid because 1 cannot be specified as a size for INTEGER

g) invalid because 2 cannot be specified as a size for LOGICAL

i) invalid because size, not dimensions, must follow REAL*

k) invalid because a WATFIV character variable cannot exceed 255 characters

8.a) REAL*8   d) REAL*4
  b) LOGICAL*1   e) COMPLEX*16
  c) COMPLEX*16   f) INTEGER*2

CHAPTER 3.

1.a) READ, R, P
   READ, I, J
  b) READ, R, P, I, J

2.   PRINT, '   X   Y   X∗Y'
       PRINT, X, Y, X∗Y

CHAPTER 4.

1.   a and e are valid integer constants; b and f are valid floating-point con-
       stants; c and d are invalid.

2.c)   Minus sign must follow E in exponent.
  d)   If exponent is given, E is required.

3.   a is valid integer; b, c, and d are valid real; and g and i are valid logical
       constants.

4.e)   Mantissa must precede E.
       f, h, k, and m will be treated as variable names.
  j)   I is not used in complex values in FORTRAN.
  l)   Can be used as literal constant in FORMAT statement but is not accept-
       able within the body of the program.

CHAPTER 5.

1.a)   A/(B+C)
  b)   B/(B∗C)
  c)   (A/B)∗C
  d)   2∗A∗∗4
  e)   (−B+4∗A∗C)/(−A)

8.   a, d, and f are valid.

10.b) For any value of I, either A(I,J) or B(I+2,J) would not be a valid
       subscript, given the DIMENSION statement above.
  c)   As noted for b above, except that J is the offending variable.
  e)   Right parenthesis is missing.
  g)   Two operators cannot appear consecutively.

CHAPTER 6.

3.a)   30   (b) 10   (c) 120   (d) 10

4.a)   DATA A/5∗0./
  b)   DATA B(3,1)/6/
  c)   DATA B(4,3), C/2∗1/
  d)   DATA B(4,1), B(4,2), B(4,3)/3∗20/
  e)   DATA (B(4,I),I=1,3)/3∗20/

7.   DIMENSION YIELD(10,20,30,16), RAIN(10,20,30,16),
       1FERTIL(10,20,30,16), SOILTP(20,30,16), TOPSIL(20,30,16)

       The first variable is time, the second and third are the 20 × 30 mile
       dimensions, and the last indicates 1/4 × 1/4 mile sections within each
       square mile.

8.   The suggested approach is as shown below. Note, however, that the

size of each array exceeds the permissible size in most FORTRAN implementations. A wiser approach involves use of direct-access files, which are explained in the reference section of chapter 12.

```
DIMENSION TBASE(288000), SBASE(19200), BBASE(307200)
EQUIVALENCE (TBASE,YIELD), (TBASE(96001),RAIN),
1(TBASE(192001),FERTIL), (BBASE,TBASE), (BBASE(288001),
1SBASE)
```

9.   `DATA RAIN/9600*4.5/, SOILTP/9600*1.0/, FERTIL/9600*0.0/,...`
Continue in the same way to take care of all zeroing. Note that filling the first year is convenient, because year is the first dimension listed, and the leftmost subscript is varied most rapidly in FORTRAN.

10.   `CHARACTER*10 MONTHS(12)/'JANUARY','FEBRUARY',...,'DECEMBER'/`

CHAPTER 7.

1.a)   `A = B * C`
      `D = B / C`
  b)   `IF (A.GT.X) GO TO 20`
        `B = X`
        `GO TO 30`
    `20   A = Y`
    `30   C = D`
  c) `IF (A.LE.B) A = B + C`
     `D = A - B`

2.   `IF ((A+B).GE.(C+D)) GO TO X`

7.   a and b are valid; c is invalid because a branch into the range of a DO is not allowed.

CHAPTER 8.

1.a) `SUBROUTINE LARGE (VECTOR,NELEMT,IFOUND)`

2.a) `INTEGER FUNCTION IFOUND (VECTOR,NELEMT)`

3.   `CALL LARGE (ARRAY,45,I)`
     `CALL LARGE (VECT,20,INDEX)`

4.   `I = IFOUND (ARRAY,45)`
     `INDEX = IFOUND (VECT,20)`

7.   `ENTRY LARSM (VECTOR,NELEMT,IFOUND,ISMALL)`

CHAPTER 9.

8. `AT 300`
   `TRACE ON`
   `DISPLAY`
   `END` or the AT statement of a succeeding packet

CHAPTER 10.

1.a) 99   FORMAT (5I5,5F5.2)
  b) 98   FORMAT (5(I1,F4.2))
  c) 97   FORMAT (3(I1,F4.2)/2(I1,F4.2))
  d) 96   FORMAT (5(I1,F4.2,2(D5.1)))
  e) 95   FORMAT (25A4)
  f) 94   FORMAT (−2P5F4.2,3(I2,0PF2.0))
  g) 93   FORMAT (3L6,2L1)
  h) 92   FORMAT (Z22)

CHAPTER 11.

3.a)   IF (A.EQ.47..OR.A.EQ.46..OR.(A.GT.99..AND.A.LT.101.))
           1PRINT, FOUND
     C   THE INNER PARENTHESES ARE OPTIONAL BUT ADVISABLE.
  b)   IF (L) PRINT, FOUND
  c)   IF (.NOT.L2.OR.(I.GT.5.AND.I.LT.9)) PRINT, FOUND
  d)   IF (L3.AND.L4) PRINT, FOUND

5.   LOGICAL L1, L2, L3, L4, L5
            READ (5,99) L1, L2, L3, L4, L5
     99   FORMAT (5L1)
            IF (.NOT.L1.AND..NOT.L2.AND..NOT.L3.AND.L4.AND.L5)
           1GO TO 100
            PRINT, 'FALSE'
            GO TO 101
     100   PRINT, 'TRUE'
     101   .
                .
                .

8.   REAL VAR/'AMT'/, VAR2*8, VAR3(3)

9.   CHARACTER VAR*3/'AMT'/, VAR2*8, VAR3*12

CHAPTER 12.

3.a)   WRITE (PUN,99) A, B, C
     99   FORMAT (3F5.2)
            where PUN contains the logical unit number assigned to the card punch.

  b)   READ (MAG) (A(I),I=1,10)
       where MAG contains the logical unit number assigned to the required
       magnetic-tape unit.

  c)   REWIND 8
       BACKSPACE 8

4.a)   DEFINE FILE 8 (4000,80,E,ASSOC)
  b)   DEFINE FILE 8 (100,500,L,ASSOC)
  c)   DEFINE FILE 8 (100,150,U,ASSOC)

WATFOR AND WATFIV

Differences between WATFOR and WATFIV are due mainly to the availability of additional features with WATFIV. Some are directly related to the FORTRAN language; others are related to control cards (described for WATFIV in appendix C) and system-dependent considerations. The language differences are listed below in the order that topics are discussed in this text.

1   The $ character follows Z in alphabetical ordering for first-letter specifications in IMPLICIT statements in WATFIV. WATFOR gives special treatment to the $ character.

2   WATFIV issues warning diagnostics if the proper ordering of statements is not established. Data declaration statements (type, DIMENSION, COMMON, and the like) should appear before statement function definitions, which should appear before the executable statements of a program.

3   If the value of the integer variable in a computed GO TO statement is zero or negative, WATFIV transfers control to the next executable statement. This interpretation is an extension to standard FORTRAN that is also implemented in IBM 360/370 FORTRAN. In WATFOR, an error message is printed and program execution is terminated.

4   DO loops may be nested to any level within the 255 DO statements per program limit under WATFIV.

5   WATFIV allows actual arguments passed to subprograms to be arrays, array elements, or single variables.

6   If a function subprogram has multiple entry points, WATFIV equivalences the function and entry-point names. WATFOR does not.

7   WATFOR does not permit use of the debugging statements ON ERROR GO TO and DUMPLIST.

8   WATFOR does not permit use of the NAMELIST statement.

Appendix

B

WATFIV Incompatibilities with WATFOR and FORTRAN G and H

9 An INTEGER∗2 variable cannot be used to represent a logical unit number in an input/output statement under WATFIV.

10 WATFOR does not permit the declaration of variables of CHARACTER type.

11 WATFOR does not permit direct-access I/O.

DIFFERENCES BETWEEN WATFIV AND IBM 360/370 FORTRAN G AND H

Differences between WATFIV and IBM 360/370 FORTRAN G and H compilers arise in three areas:

- extensions to the FORTRAN language implemented in WATFIV
- restrictions in language usage under WATFIV
- incompatibilities in the way statements are interpreted or acted upon

The differences in each of these areas that are apt to be encountered by those of you who are writing programs to be run on systems of either type are listed below.

EXTENSIONS

Extensions are features that are acceptable to WATFIV but are not likely to compile correctly when compilers other than WATFIV are used. Major extensions are:

1 WATFIV format-free input/output allows the programmer to easily read input or provide output in man-readable form without referring to FOR-MAT statements. The forms of WATFIV format-free input/output statements are:
READ, *list*
PRINT, *list*
PUNCH, *list*
READ (*unit*,∗[,END=*label1*] [,ERR=*label2*]) *list*
WRITE (*unit*,∗) *list*

2 Variables can be declared to be of CHARACTER type, and the values of character variables can be moved, compared, read as input, and written as output.

3 Multiple assignment statements of the form
v1 = *v2* = ... = *expression*
are permissible.

4 Subscripts may be used on the right-hand side of a statement function definition, for example,

FUNC (A,B,C) = (A+B)/ARR(1) ∗ C∗∗2

5 A value of COMPLEX, LOGICAL, or CHARACTER type can be used as the subscript of an array.

6 Implied DOs as used in I/O lists of input/output statements are also permitted in DATA statements, for example,

DATA (A(I),I=1,20,2)/10∗1.0/

7   Variables in either blank or labeled COMMON can be initialized in DATA or type statements, just as other variables can.

8   The last statement in the range of a DO may be a logical IF statement containing a GO TO statement of any form, PAUSE, STOP, RETURN, or arithmetic IF statement.

9   The DUMPLIST and ON ERROR GO TO debugging statements are available in WATFIV but not supported by other compilers.

10   The I/O list of a statement that controls output operations may contain expressions other than literal data, variables, and implied DOs. For example,

WRITE (6,30) A, B+C, FUNC(X)/2

is permissible. An expression in an I/O list should not start with a left parenthesis, however, because the compiler recognizes a left parenthesis as the first character of an implied DO.

11   Operations analogous to input/output, but moving data to or from an I/O area in main storage, rather than between main storage and an external medium, are permissible. The name of the I/O area replaces the logical unit number in a READ or WRITE statement controlling this core-to-core I/O.

Extensions of types other than 1, 2, and 11 in the list above are flagged as extensions on the source-program listing if the WARN parameter is specified on the $JOB ($COMPILE, in some systems) card or assumed by default. (See appendix C.) For WATFIV extensions not directly related to the FORTRAN language (for example, pertaining to punching statements onto cards), you should consult installation documentation.

RESTRICTIONS

Restrictions are minor rules of language usage that must be followed by WATFIV users but are not generally imposed in FORTRAN. Many of them are necessary because WATFIV is a one-pass compiler: All translation is done during one scan of source-program statements; there is no first pass to reserve storage locations and determine addresses, followed by a second pass to interpret statements with reference to tables of information already established.

1   Data declaration statements referring to variables used in NAMELIST or DEFINE FILE statements must precede the NAMELIST or DEFINE FILE statements.

2   COMMON or EQUIVALENCE statements referring to variables used in DATA or initializing type statements must precede those statements.

3   The name of a labeled COMMON must be unique; it cannot be used as the name of a simple variable, array variable, or statement function.

4   A variable name may appear in an EQUIVALENCE statement and in a subsequent type statement only if the type statement does not declare the size of the variable to be different from that otherwise assumed for it.

5   The concept of the extended range of a DO is not recognized. In FORTRAN this range is the set of executable statements in a program unit containing a

nest of DOs that are executed between the transfer out of the nest by a GO TO or IF within the range of the innermost DO and the transfer back into this range by a GO TO or IF not within the nest.

6 Not more than 255 DO statements can be used in one program.

7 The debug facility, described in this text as implemented in IBM 360/370 FORTRAN G, is not available in WATFIV.

8 The character sequence FORMAT is a reserved sequence when used as the first six nonblank characters of a statement. It must signal the beginning of a FORMAT statement.

9 The xxxFDUMP service subprogram with entry points DUMP and PDUMP is not available. (See appendix F.)

INCOMPATIBILITIES

By and large, most programs that are coded with awareness of the extensions and restrictions identified above produce virtually the same results when compiled under WATFOR, WATFIV, FORTRAN G, or FORTRAN H. Additional differences are minor and usually relate to either the treatment of FORTRAN-supplied subprograms or number conversions. Those within the scope of FORTRAN as covered in this text are identified below.

1 WATFIV terminates program execution if a floating-point underflow occurs. FORTRAN G and H set the result to zero and continue.

2 DO loops may be nested to any level within the 255 DO statements per program limit under WATFIV. The maximum level of nesting for DO loops and implied DOs is 25 under FORTRAN G. Limits of 25 for DO loops and 20 for implied DOs are established under FORTRAN H.

3 Upon completion of a DO loop, the value of the index variable is considered undefined according to the language rules for standard FORTRAN. However, most compilers allow the use of the index variable after a DO loop is exited. The value of the index variable after a normal exit is one less under WATFIV than under FORTRAN G or H. For example, upon completion of the looping action controlled by

DO 100 I=1,20

the value of I is 20 under WATFIV, but it is 21 under FORTRAN G or H.

4 WATFIV considers a program to be in error if it executes a statement of the form RETURN i in which the value of i is zero, negative, undefined, or greater than the number of statement-label arguments appearing in the argument list of the activating CALL statement.

5 Under WATFIV, the type and size of a system-supplied function subprogram (mathematical built-in function) must be declared explicitly if it differs from that otherwise assumed on the basis of a governing first-letter rule. For example, if the library subprogram to calculate the sine or cosine of a real variable of size 8 is used, the type statement shown below is appropriate. WATFIV supplies no automatic typing or sizing of system-supplied function subprograms.

REAL*8 DSIN, DCOS

Under IBM 360/370 FORTRAN G and H, a statement function can be used to cause selective automatic typing, for example,

SQRT(X) = DSQRT(X)

causes a desired function name substitution, so that each use of SQRT(X) in an expression causes execution of DSQRT(X). FORTRAN G requires that SQRT be typed as REAL*8, but FORTRAN H does not.

6   WATFIV evaluates all functions that require complicated approximations in double precision, even if the return value of such a function is a single-precision numeral.

7   FORTRAN G and H use two types of function subprograms: (1) in-line subprograms, which are inserted by the compiler at any point in the program where the subprogram is referred to, and (2) out-of-line subprograms, for which the compiler generates an external reference to a subprogram retained in an available system library. Under WATFIV, all functions are out-of-line.

8   With WATFIV, use of the T format code to move backwards in a line does not cause existing characters in the line to be replaced by blanks as they are in FORTRAN G and H.

9   Under WATFIV, REAL*4 values are printed with a maximum of seven significant digits, in correspondence with the definition of single-precision values. If a field descriptor dictates more, for example, E18.8, zeros are supplied in any unfilled positions to the right of the decimal point.

10 Separator characters are not required between field descriptors in a FORMAT statement under WATFIV. In IBM 360/370 FORTRAN, either one comma or any number of slashes must be used as a separator between field descriptors.

11 WATFIV does not allow repetition factors or group repeat counts in a FORMAT statement to be zero.

12 WATFIV uses only the high-order byte of a logical quantity in logical operations. For example, if L1 and L2 are declared to be LOGICAL*4 variables, the statement

L1 = L2

causes only the high-order byte of L2 to be moved.

The following control cards are available to the WATFIV user. They are included at appropriate points in the source deck that also includes the source-language statements of the WATFIV program. (See figure C.1.)

$JOB   Initiates compilation. This card is optional if only one program (main program plus subprograms) is being compiled. If two or more programs are being compiled, it is optional for the first program but must appear before the second and each subsequent program.

$PRINTOFF   Terminates printing of the source-program listing. The $PRINTOFF card is not printed.

$PRINTON   Resumes printing of the source-program listing if a preceding $PRINTOFF card is in effect or NOLIST (see below) was specified on the $JOB card. The $PRINTON card is printed.

$EJECT   Causes a skip to a new page.

$SPACE   Causes a skip to a new line.

$ENTRY   Initiates execution. This card is required. If data cards are included in the source deck, this card must precede the data cards.

$STOP   Terminates compilation. This card must be the last card in the input stream for the compiler.

The keywords $COMPILE and $DATA are used instead of $JOB and $ENTRY at Michigan Terminal System (MTS) installations.

The method of executing the WATFIV compiler is system-dependent as is the assignment of FORTRAN logical unit numbers to data files. An // EXEC card is used for the former in figure C.1. For details of this card and any other system-dependent control cards you should check documentation at your particular installation. The example below is a representative source deck. It shows how

Appendix

C

WATFIV Control Cards

$JOB...$ENTRY sequences can be repeated to batch the compilation and execution of WATFIV programs.

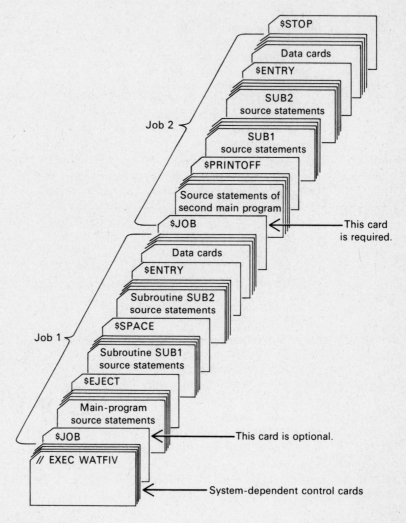

FIGURE C.1

The format of the $JOB (or $COMPILE) card is important, somewhat lengthy, and merits explanation. The following parameters may be punched, in any order, starting in any column after column 9 of the $JOB card. Default values assumed by the WATFIV compiler for omitted parameters are underlined or stated in the explanations that follow.

$$\text{KP} = \begin{Bmatrix} 26 \\ 29 \end{Bmatrix}, \text{TIME}=n, \text{PAGES}=n, \text{RUN} = \begin{Bmatrix} \text{CHECK} \\ \text{NOCHECK} \\ \text{FREE} \end{Bmatrix}, \begin{Bmatrix} \text{LIST} \\ \text{NOLIST} \end{Bmatrix}, \begin{Bmatrix} \text{NOLIBLIST} \\ \text{LIBLIST} \end{Bmatrix}, \begin{Bmatrix} \text{WARN} \\ \text{NOWARN} \end{Bmatrix}, \begin{Bmatrix} \text{EXT} \\ \text{NOEXT} \end{Bmatrix}, \text{SIZE}=k$$

$\text{KP} = \begin{Bmatrix} 26 \\ 29 \end{Bmatrix}$

26—source program was punched on a Model 026 (BCD) keypunch

29—source program was punched on a Model 029 (EBCDIC) keypunch

$\text{TIME}=n$

n is an integer constant representing the maximum number of seconds to be allowed for execution of the program. Usually, the default value for n is 30. This is a local time limit (discussed below).

$\text{PAGES}=n$

n is an integer constant representing the maximum number of pages of output to be produced by the program at execution-time. Usually, the default value for n is 20. This is a local page limit (discussed below).

$\text{RUN} = \begin{Bmatrix} \text{CHECK} \\ \text{NOCHECK} \\ \text{FREE} \end{Bmatrix}$

CHECK causes the compiler to check, at execution-time, for attempted uses of variables that have not been assigned values (undefined variables). Use of NOCHECK suppresses the check, resulting in somewhat shorter execution-time and somewhat less machine-language code. FREE is the same as CHECK, but the compiler initiates execution of the program even if it contains serious errors. If an executable statement that contained an error is encountered, execution is terminated.

$\begin{Bmatrix} \text{LIST} \\ \text{NOLIST} \end{Bmatrix}$

LIST causes the compiler to produce a source-program listing of the program that it compiles; NOLIST suppresses the listing.

$\begin{Bmatrix} \text{NOLIBLIST} \\ \text{LIBLIST} \end{Bmatrix}$

LIBLIST causes the compiler to produce a source-program listing of the subprograms retrieved from a library during compilation; NOLIBLIST suppresses the listing of library routines.

$\begin{Bmatrix} \text{WARN} \\ \text{NOWARN} \end{Bmatrix}$

WARN causes the compiler to print diagnostics on the source-program listing. NOWARN suppresses diagnostics for other than fatal errors. (Error severities are discussed in appendix D.)

$\begin{Bmatrix} \text{EXT} \\ \text{NOEXT} \end{Bmatrix}$

EXT causes the compiler to print extension diagnostics on the source-program listing. (See appendix D.) NOEXT suppresses extension diagnostics.

$\text{SIZE}=k$

This parameter is meaningful only for MTS installations. k is an integer constant indicating the number of 4096-byte pages of memory to be obtained for compiler work space. Generally, the default value for k is 25. The larger the value for k, the larger the programs that can be compiled (and the more expensive the compilation).

The parameters of the $JOB card are scanned from left to right. The first blank column, rather than comma, that follows a parameter terminates the scan. If a parameter is mispunched, the scan is terminated when that parameter is encountered. Default values are assumed for any parameters not yet processed. For example, the statement

$JOB PAGES = 200, NOWARN, TTME = 60, KP = 29, RUN = NOCHECK

causes 200 to be established as a maximum number for pages of output and suppresses diagnostics for other than fatal errors, but default values are assumed for all other parameters.

If any parameter is specified more than once on a $JOB card, the rightmost value for the parameter is used. For example, the statement

$JOB KP = 26, TIME = 60, LIST, KP = 29

specifies that EBCDIC punching was used for the source program.

If $PRINTOFF is in effect when an error is detected, the first card of the preceding source statement is printed before the diagnostic.

The values for TIME and PAGES specified on the $JOB card give local limits. They apply to a single program execution and cannot override global limits set either explicitly or implicitly by an // EXEC card (or its equivalent). If you want 30 seconds of execution-time for your program, the global time limit must be sufficiently greater to allow for loading of the WATFIV compiler and compilation of your program.

Diagnostics, or error messages, are designed to help the programmer understand what is happening to his program. They may occur at either of two times:

- at program compile-time, when the source statements written by the programmer are being translated by a compiler program into the machine language of the computer

- at program execution-time, when the machine-language version of the program is directing processing steps carried out by the computer

The WATFIV compiler generates compile-time diagnostics at three levels of severity: extension, warning, and error. Unless the programmer has specified otherwise, each diagnostic is printed on the source-program listing, immediately below the statement causing the diagnostic to be generated. The programmer may suppress printing of both extension and warning diagnostics, or of extension diagnostics, by specifying NOWARN or NOEXT, respectively, on the $JOB card for the program. (See appendix C.)

An extension message is generated when the WATFIV compiler detects an extension of the FORTRAN language allowed by WATFIV but not supported by most FORTRAN compilers. The message is issued so that the extension can be recognized and eliminated if the program is recompiled under a compiler not allowing the extension.

A warning message is issued when the compiler encounters a language violation for which it subsequently takes some reasonable action, hopefully, eliminating the error. If a variable name contains more than six characters, for example, the compiler issues a warning message, truncates the name to six characters, and continues compilation using the truncated name.

An error message is issued when the compiler encounters a language violation severe enough to prevent execution. In this case, unless the FREE parameter has been

Appendix

D

WATFOR/WATFIV

Diagnostics

specified on the $JOB card (appendix C), the compiler prevents execution of the program.

At program execution-time, the general rule is that all errors are fatal in the sense that WATFIV terminates the job containing the error and proceeds to the next job. The system generates a diagnostic message and a subprogram traceback is printed out. An example of such a traceback is shown below.

```
***ERROR***              VALUE OF V1 IS UNDEFINED
PROGRAM WAS EXECUTING LINE 15 IN ROUTINE SUB2    WHEN TERMINATION OCCURRED
PROGRAM WAS EXECUTING LINE 70 IN ROUTINE SUB1    WHEN TERMINATION OCCURRED
PROGRAM WAS EXECUTING LINE 95 IN ROUTINE M/PROG WHEN TERMINATION OCCURRED
```

The traceback gives the line number of the line at which the error occurred, the name of the subprogram containing the line, the name of the subprogram that called the subprogram, the line number of the activating call, and so on, all the way back to the main program (referred to as M/PROG). The line numbers in the traceback are references to compiler-generated line numbers appearing on the source-program listing and should not be confused with programmer-selected statement numbers assigned to statements by the programmer.

An exception to this general rule of error-handling occurs when an input/output error is detected but the programmer has included the ERR option in the READ statement controlling the I/O operation. In this case, an error message is given, but execution proceeds at the statement identified in the ERR option. Subsequent processing is governed accordingly.

An important goal of the designers of WATFIV was to supply under-standable, accurate diagnostics. Compilation continues, even when errors are detected, in an effort to detect any additional errors in the program. Hopefully, the number of runs required to obtain an error-free compilation and successful execution is lessened thereby. You should be aware, however, that an error in one statement may lead to apparent errors in subsequent statements. If you correct the first error, succeeding errors may disappear also. This is particularly true if the error occurs in a data declaration statement. The compiler scans each source statement from left to right, and usually abandons compilation of a statement if an error is encountered. Correct information that follows an error may be ignored. For example, when the statement

DIMENSION A(4), B(5,5(, C(20)

is compiled, A is established as a one-dimensional array having four elements. But the incorrect parenthesis in the declaration for B causes scanning of the statement to be terminated. References to elements of either B or C in subsequent statements may cause error messages to be generated.

A listing of WATFOR/WATFIV error messages follows. The messages are grouped in various categories, according to the kinds of errors described.

```
'ASSEMBLER LANGUAGE SUBPROGRAMMES'
AL-0   'MISSING END CARD ON ASSEMBLY LANGUAGE OBJECT DECK'
AL-1   'ENTRY-POINT OR CSECT NAME IN AN OBJECT DECK WAS PREVIOUSLY
       DEFINED.FIRST DEFINITION USED'
```

'BLOCK DATA STATEMENTS'
BD-0   'EXECUTABLE STATEMENTS ARE ILLEGAL IN BLOCK DATA SUBPROGRAMS'
BD-1   'IMPROPER BLOCK DATA STATEMENT'

'CARD FORMAT AND CONTENTS'
CC-0   'COLUMNS 1-5 OF CONTINUATION CARD ARE NOT BLANK.
        PROBABLE CAUSE:STATEMENT PUNCHED TO LEFT OF COLUMN 7'
CC-1   'LIMIT OF 5 CONTINUATION CARDS EXCEEDED'
CC-2   'INVALID CHARACTER IN FORTRAN STATEMENT.
        A '$' WAS INSERTED IN THE SOURCE LISTING'
CC-3   'FIRST CARD OF A PROGRAM IS A CONTINUATION CARD.
        PROBABLE CAUSE:STATEMENT PUNCHED TO LEFT OF COLUMN 7'
CC-4   'STATEMENT TOO LONG TO COMPILE (SCAN-STACK OVERFLOW)'
CC-5   'A BLANK CARD WAS ENCOUNTERED'
CC-6   'KEYPUNCH USED DIFFERS FROM KEYPUNCH SPECIFIED ON JOB CARD'
CC-7   'THE FIRST CHARACTER OF THE STATEMENT WAS NOT ALPHABETIC'
CC-8   'INVALID CHARACTER(S) ARE CONCATENATED WITH THE FORTRAN KEYWORD'
CC-9   'INVALID CHARACTERS IN COLUMNS 1-5.STATEMENT NUMBER IGNORED.
        PROBABLE CAUSE:STATEMENT PUNCHED TO LEFT OF COLUMN 7'

'COMMON'
CM-0   'THE VARIABLE IS ALREADY IN COMMON'
CM-1   'OTHER COMPILERS MAY NOT ALLOW COMMONED VARIABLES TO BE INITIALIZED IN
        OTHER THAN A BLOCK DATA SUBPROGRAM'
CM-2   'ILLEGAL USE OF A COMMON BLOCK OR NAMELIST NAME'

'FORTRAN TYPE CONSTANTS'
CN-0   'MIXED REAL*4,REAL*8 IN COMPLEX CONSTANT;REAL*8 ASSUMED FOR BOTH'
CN-1   'AN INTEGER CONSTANT MAY NOT BE GREATER THAN 2,147,483,647 (2**31-1)'
CN-2   'EXPONENT ON A REAL CONSTANT IS GREATER THAN 2 DIGITS'
CN-3   'A REAL CONSTANT HAS MORE THAN 16 DIGITS.IT WAS TRUNCATED TO 16'
CN-4   'INVALID HEXADECIMAL CONSTANT'
CN-5   'ILLEGAL USE OF A DECIMAL POINT'
CN-6   'CONSTANT WITH MORE THAN 7 DIGITS BUT E-TYPE EXPONENT,ASSUMED TO BE
        REAL*4'
CN-7   'CONSTANT OR STATEMENT NUMBER GREATER THAN 99999'
CN-8   'AN EXPONENT OVERFLOW OR UNDERFLOW OCCURRED WHILE CONVERTING A CONSTANT
        IN A SOURCE STATEMENT'

'COMPILER ERRORS'
CP-0   'COMPILER ERROR - LANDR/ARITH'
CP-1   'COMPILER ERROR.LIKELY CAUSE:MORE THAN 255 DO STATEMENTS'
CP-4   'COMPILER ERROR - INTERRUPT AT COMPILE TIME,RETURN TO SYSTEM'

'CHARACTER VARIABLE'
CV-0   'A CHARACTER VARIABLE IS USED WITH A RELATIONAL OPERATOR'
CV-1   'LENGTH OF A CHARACTER VALUE ON RIGHT OF EQUAL SIGN EXCEEDS THAT ON
        LEFT. TRUNCATION WILL OCCUR'
CV-2   'UNFORMATTED CORE-TO-CORE I/O NOT IMPLEMENTED'

'DATA STATEMENT'
DA-0   'REPLICATION FACTOR IS ZERO OR GREATER THAN 32767.
        IT IS ASSUMED TO BE 32767'
DA-1   'MORE VARIABLES THAN CONSTANTS'
DA-2   'ATTEMPT TO INITIALIZE A SUBPROGRAM PARAMETER IN A DATA STATEMENT'
DA-3   'OTHER COMPILERS MAY NOT ALLOW NON-CONSTANT SUBSCRIPTS IN DATA
        STATEMENTS'
DA-4   'TYPE OF VARIABLE AND CONSTANT DO NOT AGREE. (MESSAGE ISSUED ONCE FOR
        AN ARRAY)'
DA-5   'MORE CONSTANTS THAN VARIABLES'
DA-6   'A VARIABLE WAS PREVIOUSLY INITIALIZED.THE LATEST VALUE IS USED.
        CHECK COMMONED AND EQUIVALENCED VARIABLES'

```
DA-7    'OTHER COMPILERS MAY NOT ALLOW INITIALIZATION OF BLANK COMMON'
DA-8    'A LITERAL CONSTANT HAS BEEN TRUNCATED'
DA-9    'OTHER COMPILERS MAY NOT ALLOW IMPLIED DO-LOOPS IN DATA STATEMENTS'

'DEFINE FILE STATEMENTS'
DF-0    'THE UNIT NUMBER IS MISSING'
DF-1    'INVALID FORMAT TYPE'
DF-2    'THE ASSOCIATED VARIABLE IS NOT A SIMPLE INTEGER VARIABLE'
DF-3    'NUMBER OF RECORDS OR RECORD SIZE IS ZERO OR GREATER THAN 32767'

'DIMENSION STATEMENTS'
DM-0    'NO DIMENSIONS ARE SPECIFIED FOR A VARIABLE IN A DIMENSION STATEMENT'
DM-1    'THE VARIABLE HAS ALREADY BEEN DIMENSIONED'
DM-2    'CALL-BY-LOCATION PARAMETERS MAY NOT BE DIMENSIONED'
DM-3    'THE DECLARED SIZE OF ARRAY EXCEEDS SPACE PROVIDED BY CALLING ARGUMENT'

'DO LOOPS'
DO-0    'THIS STATEMENT CANNOT BE THE OBJECT OF A DO-LOOP'
DO-1    'ILLEGAL TRANSFER INTO THE RANGE OF A DO-LOOP'
DO-2    'THE OBJECT OF THIS DO-LOOP HAS ALREADY APPEARED'
DO-3    'IMPROPERLY NESTED DO-LOOPS'
DO-4    'ATTEMPT TO REDEFINE A DO-LOOP PARAMETER WITHIN THE RANGE OF THE LOOP'
DO-5    'INVALID DO-LOOP PARAMETER'
DO-6    'ILLEGAL TRANSFER TO A STATEMENT WHICH IS INSIDE THE RANGE OF A DO-LOOP'
DO-7    'A DO-LOOP PARAMETER IS UNDEFINED OR OUT OF RANGE'
DO-8    'BECAUSE OF ONE OF THE PARAMETERS,THIS DO-LOOP WILL TERMINATE AFTER THE
         FIRST TIME THROUGH'
DO-9    'A DO-LOOP PARAMETER MAY NOT BE REDEFINED IN AN INPUT LIST'
DO-A    'OTHER COMPILERS MAY NOT ALLOW THIS STATEMENT TO END A DO-LOOP'

'EQUIVALENCE AND/OR COMMON'
EC-0    'EQUIVALENCED VARIABLE APPEARS IN A COMMON STATEMENT'
EC-1    'A COMMON BLOCK HAS A DIFFERENT LENGTH THAN IN A PREVIOUS
         SUBPROGRAM:GREATER LENGTH USED'
EC-2    'COMMON AND/OR EQUIVALENCE CAUSES INVALID ALIGNMENT.
         EXECUTION SLOWED.REMEDY:ORDER VARIABLES BY DECREASING LENGTH'
EC-3    'EQUIVALENCE EXTENDS COMMON DOWNWARDS'
EC-4    'A SUBPROGRAM PARAMETER APPEARS IN A COMMON OR EQUIVALENCE STATEMENT'
EC-5    'A VARIABLE WAS USED WITH SUBSCRIPTS IN AN EQUIVALENCE STATEMENT BUT HAS
         NOT BEEN PROPERLY DIMENSIONED'

'END STATEMENTS'
EN-0    'MISSING END STATEMENT:END STATEMENT GENERATED'
EN-1    'AN END STATEMENT WAS USED TO TERMINATE EXECUTION'
EN-2    'AN END STATEMENT CANNOT HAVE A STATEMENT NUMBER. STATEMENT NUMBER
         IGNORED'
EN-3    'END STATEMENT NOT PRECEDED BY A TRANSFER'

'EQUAL SIGNS'
EQ-0    'ILLEGAL QUANTITY ON LEFT OF EQUALS SIGN'
EQ-1    'ILLEGAL USE OF EQUAL SIGN'
EQ-2    'OTHER COMPILERS MAY NOT ALLOW MULTIPLE ASSIGNMENT STATEMENTS'
EQ-3    'MULTIPLE ASSIGNMENT IS NOT IMPLEMENTED FOR CHARACTER VARIABLES'

'EQUIVALENCE STATEMENTS'
EV-0    'ATTEMPT TO EQUIVALENCE A VARIABLE TO ITSELF'
EV-2    'A MULTI-SUBSCRIPTED EQUIVALENCED VARIABLE HAS BEEN INCORRECTLY
         RE-EQUIVALENCED.REMEDY:DIMENSION THE VARIABLE FIRST'

'POWERS AND EXPONENTIATION'
EX-0    'ILLEGAL COMPLEX EXPONENTIATION'
EX-1    'I**J WHERE I=J=0'
```

```
EX-2    'I**J WHERE I=0, J.LT.0'
EX-3    '0.0**Y WHERE Y.LE.0.0'
EX-4    '0.0**J WHERE J=0'
EX-5    'C.0**J WHERE J.LT.0'
EX-6    'X**Y WHERE X.LT.0.0, Y.NE.0.0'


'ENTRY STATEMENT'
EY-0    'ENTRY-PCINT NAME WAS PREVIOUSLY DEFINED'
EY-1    'PREVIOUS DEFINITION OF FUNCTION NAME IN AN ENTRY IS INCORRECT'
EY-2    'THE USAGE CF A SUBPROGRAM PARAMETER IS INCONSISTENT WITH A PREVIOUS
        ENTRY-PCINT'
EY-3    'A PARAMETER HAS APPEARED IN A EXECUTABLE STATEMENT BUT IS NOT A
        SUBPROGRAM PARAMETER'
EY-4    'ENTRY STATEMENTS ARE INVALID IN THE MAIN PRCGRAM'
EY-5    'ENTRY STATEMENT INVALID INSIDE A DO-LOOP'


'FORMAT'
  SOME FORMAT ERROR MESSAGES GIVE CHARACTERS IN WHICH ERROR WAS DETECTED
FM-0    'IMPROPER CHARACTER SEQUENCE OR INVALIC CHARACTER IN INPUT DATA'
FM-1    'NO STATEMENT NUMBER ON A FORMAT STATEMENT'
FM-2    'FORMAT CCDE AND DATA TYPE DO NOT MATCH'
FM-4    'FORMAT PROVIDES NO CONVERSION SPECIFICATION FOR A VALUE IN I/O LIST'
FM-5    'AN INTEGER IN THE INPUT DATA IS TCO LARGE.
        (MAXIMUM=2,147,483,647=2**31-1)'
FM-6    'A REAL NUMBER IN THE INPUT DATA IS OUT OF MACHINE RANGE (1.E-78,1.E+75)'
FM-7    'UNREFERENCED FORMAT STATEMENT'
FT-0    'FIRST CHARACTER OF VARIABLE FORMAT IS NCT A LEFT PARENTHESIS'
FT-1    'INVALID CHARACTER ENCOUNTERED IN FORMAT'
FT-2    'INVALID FORM FOLLOWING A FORMAT CODE'
FT-3    'INVALID FIELD OR GROUP COUNT'
FT-4    'A FIELD CR GROUP COUNT GREATER THAN 255'
FT-5    'NO CLOSING PARENTHESIS ON VARIABLE FORMAT'
FT-6    'NO CLCSING QUOTE IN A HOLLERITH FIELD'
FT-7    'INVALID USE OF COMMA'
FT-8    'FORMAT STATEMENT TCC IONG TO COMPILE (SCAN-STACK OVERFLOW)'
FT-9    'INVALID USE OF P FORMAT CODE'
FT-A    'INVALID USE CF PERIOD(.)'
FT-B    'MORE THAN THREE LEVELS OF PARENTHESES'
FT-C    'INVALID CHARACTER BEFORE A RIGHT PARENTHESIS'
FT-D    'MISSING CR ZERO LENGTH HOLLERITH ENCOUNTERED'
FT-E    'NO CLCSING RIGHT PARENTHESIS'
FT-F    'CHARACTERS FOLLOW CLOSING RIGHT PARENTHESIS'
FT-G    'WRONG QUCTE USED FCR KEY-PUNCH SPECIFIED'
FT-H    'LENGTH OF HOLLERITH EXCEEDS 255'


'FUNCTICNS AND SUBROUTINES'
FN-1    'A PARAMETER APPEARS MCRE THAN CNCE IN A SUBPRCGRAM OR STATEMENT
        FUNCTION DEFINITION'
FN-2    'SUBSCRIPTS CN RIGHT-HAND SIDE OF STATEMENT FUNCTION.
        PROBABLE CAUSE:VARIABLE TO LEFT CF EQUAL SIGN NOT DIMENSIONED'
FN-3    'MULTIPLE RETURNS ARE INVALIC IN FUNCTION SUBPROGRAMS'
FN-4    'ILLEGAL LENGTH MODIFIER'
FN-5    'INVALID PARAMETER'
FN-6    'A PARAMETER HAS THE SAME NAME AS THE SUBPROGRAM'


'GC TO STATEMENTS'
GC-0    'THIS STATEMENT COULD TRANSFER TC ITSELF'
GC-1    'THIS STATEMENT TRANSFERS TO A NCN-EXECUTABLE STATEMENT'
GC-2    'ATTEMPT TO DEFINE ASSIGNED GOTO INDEX IN AN ARITHMETIC STATEMENT'
GC-3    'ASSIGNED GCTO INDEX MAY BE USED ONLY IN ASSIGNED GOTO AND ASSIGN
        STATEMENTS'
```

```
GC-4    'THE INDEX OF AN ASSIGNED GOTO IS UNDEFINED CR OUT OF RANGE,OR INDEX OF
        COMPUTED GOTO IS UNDEFINED'
GC-5    'ASSIGNED GCTO INDEX MAY NCT BE AN INTEGER*2 VARIABLE'

'HOLLERITH CONSTANTS'
HO-0    'ZERO LENGTH SPECIFIED FOR H-TYPE HOLLERITH'
HO-1    'ZERO LENGTH QUOTE-TYPE HOLLERITH'
HO-2    'NO CLOSING QUOTE OR NEXT CARD NCT A CONTINUATION CARD'
HO-3    'UNEXPECTED HOLLERITH CR STATEMENT NUMBER CONSTANT'

'IF STATEMENTS (ARITHMETIC AND LOGICAL)'
IF-0    'AN INVALID STATEMENT FOLLOWS THE LOGICAL IF'
IF-1    'ARITHMETIC OR INVALID EXPRESSICN IN LOGICAL IF'
IF-2    'LOGICAL,COMPLEX OR INVALID EXPRESSION IN ARITHMETIC IF'

'IMPLICIT STATEMENT'
IM-0    'INVALID DATA TYPE'
IM-1    'INVALID CPTICNAL LENGTH'
IM-3    'IMPROPER ALPHABETIC SEQUENCE IN CHARACTER RANGE'
IM-4    'A SPECIFICATION IS NOT A SINGLE CHARACTER.THE FIRST CHARACTER IS USED'
IM-5    'IMPLICIT STATEMENT DOES NOT PRECEDE OTHER SPECIFICATION STATEMENTS'
IM-6    'ATTEMPT TO DECLARE THE TYPE OF A CHARACTER MORE THAN CNCE'
IM-7    'ONLY CNE IMPLICIT STATEMENT PER PROGRAM SEGMENT ALLOWED. THIS ONE
        IGNORED'

'INPUT/CUTPUT'
IC-0    'I/O STATEMENT REFERENCES A STATEMENT WHICH IS NOT A FCRMAT STATEMENT'
IC-1    'A VARIABLE FORMAT MUST BE AN ARRAY NAME'
IC-2    'INVALID ELEMENT IN INFUT LIST OR CATA LIST'
IC-3    'CTHER COMPILERS MAY NCT ALLOW EXPRESSIONS IN OUTPUT LISTS'
IC-4    'ILLEGAL USE CF END= OR ERR= PARAMETERS'
IC-5    'INVALID UNIT NUMBER'
IC-6    'INVALID FORMAT'
IC-7    'CNLY CONSTANTS,SIMPLE INTEGER*4 VARIABLES,AND CHARACTER VARIABLES ARE
        ALLOWED AS UNIT'
IC-8    'ATTEMPT TO PERFORM I/O IN A FUNCTION WHICH IS CALLED IN AN OUTPUT
        STATEMENT'
IC-9    'UNFORMATTED WRITE STATEMENT MUST HAVE A LIST'

'JCB CCNTROL CARDS'
JE-0    'CONTROL CARD ENCOUNTERED DURING COMPILATION;
        PRCBABLE CAUSE:MISSING $DATA CARD'
JE-1    'MIS-PUNCHED JOB OPTION'

'JCB TERMINATION'
KO-0    'SOURCE ERROR ENCOUNTERED WHILE EXECUTING WITH RUN=FREE'
KC-1    'LIMIT EXCEEDED FOR FIXED-POINT DIVISION BY ZERO'
KC-2    'LIMIT EXCEEDED FOR FLCATING-POINT DIVISION BY ZERO'
KC-3    'EXPONENT OVERFLOW LIMIT EXCEEDED'
KO-4    'EXPONENT UNDERFLOW LIMIT EXCEEDED'
KO-5    'FIXED-PCINT CVERFLOW LIMIT EXCEEDED'
KO-6    'JOB-TIME EXCEEDED'
KC-7    'COMPILER ERROR - EXECUTICN TIME:RETURN TO SYSTEM'
KO-8    'TRACEBACK ERROR. TRACEBACK TERMINATED'
KC-9    'CANNOT OPEN WATFIV.ERRTEXTS. RUN TERMINATED'
KC-A    'I/O ERROR ON TEXT FILE'

'LOGICAL OPERATICNS'
LG-0    '.NOT. WAS USED AS A BINARY OPERATOR'

'LIBRARY ROUTINES'
LI-0    'ARGUMENT OUT OF RANGE DGAMMA OR GAMMA. (1.382E-76 .LT. X .LT. 57.57)'
```

```
LI-1    'ABSOLUTE VALUE OF ARGUMENT .GT. 174.673, SINH,COSH,DSINH,DCOSH'
LI-2    'SENSE LIGHT OTHER THAN 0,1,2,3,4 FOR SLITE OR 1,2,3,4 FOR SLITET'
LI-3    'REAL PORTICN OF ARGUMENT .GT. 174.673, CEXP OR CDEXP'
LI-4    'ABS(AIMAG(Z)) .GT. 174.673 FOR CSIN, CCOS, CDSIN OR CDCOS OF Z'
LI-5    'ABS(REAL(Z)) .GE. 3.537E15 FOR CSIN, CCOS, CDSIN OR CDCOS OF Z'
LI-6    'ABS(AIMAG(Z)) .GE. 3.537E15 FOR CEXP OR CDEXP OF Z'
LI-7    'ARGUMENT .GT. 174.673, EXP OR DEXP'
LI-8    'ARGUMENT IS ZERO, CLOG, CLOG10, CDLOG OR CDLG10'
LI-9    'ARGUMENT IS NEGATIVE OR ZERO, ALOG, ALOG10, DLOG OR DLOG10'
LI-A    'ABS(X) .GE. 3.537E15 FOR SIN, COS, DSIN OR DCOS OF X'
LI-B    'ABSOLUTE VALUE OF ARGUMENT .GT. 1, FOR ARSIN, ARCOS, DARSIN OR DARCOS'
LI-C    'ARGUMENT IS NEGATIVE, SQRT OR DSQRT'
LI-D    'BOTH ARGUMENTS OF DATAN2 OR ATAN2 ARE ZERO'
LI-E    'ARGUMENT TCO CLOSE TO A SINGULARITY, TAN, COTAN, DTAN OR DCOTAN'
LI-F    'ARGUMENT OUT OF RANGE DLGAMA OR ALGAMA. (0.0 .LT. X .LT. 4.29E73)'
LI-G    'ABSCLUTE VALUE OF ARGUMENT .GE. 3.537E15, TAN, COTAN, DTAN, DCOTAN'
LI-H    'LESS THAN TWO ARGUMENTS FOR ONE OF MINO,MIN1,AMINO,ETC.'


'MIXED MCDE'
MD-0    'RELATIONAL OPERATOR HAS LOGICAL OPERAND'
MD-1    'RELATIONAL OPERATOR HAS COMPLEX OPERAND'
MD-2    'MIXED MODE - LOGICAL OR CHARACTER WITH ARITHMETIC'
MD-3    'OTHER COMPILERS MAY NOT ALLOW SUBSCRIPTS OF TYPE COMPLEX,LOGICAL OR
        CHARACTER'


'MEMORY CVERFLCW'
MO-0    'INSUFFICIENT MEMORY TO COMPILE THIS PROGRAM.REMAINDER WILL BE ERROR
        CHECKED CNLY'
MO-1    'INSUFFICIENT MEMORY TO ASSIGN ARRAY STORAGE. JOB ABANDONED'
MO-2    'SYMBOL TABLE EXCEEDS AVAILABLE SPACE,JOB ABANDONED'
MO-3    'DATA AREA OF SUBPROGRAM EXCEEDS 24K -- SEGMENT SUBPROGRAM'
MO-4    'INSUFFICIENT MEMORY TC ALLOCATE COMPILER WORK AREA OR WATLIB BUFFER'


'NAMELIST STATEMENTS'
NL-0    'NAMELIST ENTRY MUST BE A VARIABLE,NOT A SUBPROGRAM PARAMETER'
NL-1    'NAMELIST NAME PREVIOUSLY DEFINED'
NL-2    'VARIAELE NAME TOO LCNG'
NL-3    'VARIABLE NAME NOT FOUND IN NAMELIST'
NL-4    'INVALID SYNTAX IN NAMELIST INPUT'
NL-6    'VARIAELE INCORRECTLY SUBSCRIPTED'
NI-7    'SUBSCRIPT CUT OF RANGE'


'PARENTHESES'
PC-0    'UNMATCHED PARENTHESIS'
PC-1    'INVALID PARENTHESIS NESTING IN I/O LIST'


'PAUSE, STOP STATEMENTS'
PS-0    'OPERATOR MESSAGES NOT ALLOWED:SIMPLE STOP ASSUMED FOR STOP,
        CCNTINUE ASSUMED FOR PAUSE'


'RETURN STATEMENT'
RE-1    'RETURN I, WHERE I IS CUT OF RANGE OR UNDEFINED'
RE-2    'MULTIPLE RETURN NOT VALID IN FUNCTION SUBPROGRAM'
RE-3    'VARIAELE IS NOT A SIMPLE INTEGER'
RE-4    'A MULTIPLE RETURN IS NOT VALID IN THE MAIN PROGRAM'


'ARITHMETIC AND LOGICAL STATEMENT FUNCTIONS'
    PROBABLE CAUSE OF SF ERRORS - VARIABLE CN LEFT OF = WAS NOT DIMENSIONED
SF-1    'A PREVIOUSLY REFERENCED STATEMENT NUMBER APPEARS ON A STATEMENT
        FUNCTION DEFINITION'
SF-2    'STATEMENT FUNCTION IS THE OBJECT OF A LOGICAL IF STATEMENT'
```

```
SF-3    'RECURSIVE STATEMENT FUNCTION DEFINITION:NAME APPEARS ON BOTH SIDES OF
        EQUAL SIGN.LIKELY CAUSE:VARIABLE NOT DIMENSIONED'
SF-4    'A STATEMENT FUNCTION DEFINITION APPEARS AFTER THE FIRST EXECUTABLE
        STATEMENT'
SF-5    'ILLEGAL USE OF A STATEMENT FUNCTION NAME'

'SUBPROGRAMS'
SR-0    'MISSING SUBPROGRAM'
SR-1    'SUBPROGRAM REDEFINES A CONSTANT,EXPRESSION,DO-PARAMETER OR ASSIGNED
        GOTO INDEX'
SR-2    'THE SUBPROGRAM WAS ASSIGNED DIFFERENT TYPES IN DIFFERENT PROGRAM
        SEGMENTS'
SR-3    'ATTEMPT TO USE A SUBPROGRAM RECURSIVELY'
SR-4    'INVALID TYPE OF ARGUMENT IN REFERENCE TO A SUBPROGRAM'
SR-5    'WRONG NUMBER OF ARGUMENTS IN A REFERENCE TO A SUBPROGRAM'
SR-6    'A SUBPROGRAM WAS PREVIOUSLY DEFINED. THE FIRST DEFINITION IS USED'
SR-7    'NO MAIN PROGRAM'
SR-8    'ILLEGAL OR MISSING SUBPROGRAM NAME'
SR-9    'LIBRARY PROGRAM WAS NOT ASSIGNED THE CORRECT TYPE'
SR-A    'METHOD FOR ENTERING SUBPROGRAM PRODUCES UNDEFINED VALUE FOR
        CALL-BY-LOCATION PARAMETER'

'SUBSCRIPTS'
SS-0    'ZERO SUBSCRIPT OR DIMENSION NOT ALLOWED'
SS-1    'ARRAY SUBSCRIPT EXCEEDS DIMENSION'
SS-2    'INVALID SUBSCRIPT FORM'
SS-3    'SUBSCRIPT IS OUT OF RANGE'

'STATEMENTS AND STATEMENT NUMBERS'
ST-0    'MISSING STATEMENT NUMBER'
ST-1    'STATEMENT NUMBER GREATER THAN 99999'
ST-2    'STATEMENT NUMBER HAS ALREADY BEEN DEFINED'
ST-3    'UNDECODEABLE STATEMENT'
ST-4    'UNNUMBERED EXECUTABLE STATEMENT FOLLOWS A TRANSFER'
ST-5    'STATEMENT NUMBER IN A TRANSFER IS A NON-EXECUTABLE STATEMENT'
ST-6    'ONLY CALL STATEMENTS MAY CONTAIN STATEMENT NUMBER ARGUMENTS'
ST-7    'STATEMENT SPECIFIED IN A TRANSFER STATEMENT IS A FORMAT STATEMENT'
ST-8    'MISSING FORMAT STATEMENT'
ST-9    'SPECIFICATION STATEMENT DOES NOT PRECEDE STATEMENT FUNCTION DEFINITIONS
        OR EXECUTABLE STATEMENTS'
ST-A    'UNREFERENCED STATEMENT FOLLOWS A TRANSFER'

'SUBSCRIPTED VARIABLES'
SV-0    'THE WRONG NUMBER OF SUBSCRIPTS WERE SPECIFIED FOR A VARIABLE'
SV-1    'AN ARRAY OR SUBPROGRAM NAME IS USED INCORRECTLY WITHOUT A LIST'
SV-2    'MORE THAN 7 DIMENSIONS ARE NOT ALLOWED'
SV-3    'DIMENSION OR SUBSCRIPT TOO LARGE (MAXIMUM 10**8-1)'
SV-4    'A VARIABLE USED WITH VARIABLE DIMENSIONS IS NOT A SUBPROGRAM PARAMETER'
SV-5    'A VARIABLE DIMENSION IS NOT ONE OF SIMPLE INTEGER VARIABLE,SUBPROGRAM
        PARAMETER,IN COMMON'

'SYNTAX ERRORS'
SX-0    'MISSING OPERATOR'
SX-1    'EXPECTING OPERATOR'
SX-2    'EXPECTING SYMBOL'
SX-3    'EXPECTING SYMBOL OR OPERATOR'
SX-4    'EXPECTING CONSTANT'
SX-5    'EXPECTING SYMBOL OR CONSTANT'
SX-6    'EXPECTING STATEMENT NUMBER'
SX-7    'EXPECTING SIMPLE INTEGER VARIABLE'
SX-8    'EXPECTING SIMPLE INTEGER VARIABLE OR CONSTANT'
SX-9    'ILLEGAL SEQUENCE OF OPERATORS IN EXPRESSION'
```

```
SX-A    'EXPECTING END-OF-STATEMENT'

'TYPE STATEMENTS'
TY-0    'THE VARIABLE HAS ALREADY BEEN EXPLICITLY TYPED'
TY-1    'THE LENGTH OF THE EQUIVALENCED VARIABLE MAY NOT BE CHANGED.
        REMEDY: INTERCHANGE TYPE AND EQUIVALENCE STATEMENTS'

'I/O OPERATIONS'
UN-0    'CONTROL CARD ENCOUNTERED ON UNIT 5 AT EXECUTION.
        PROBABLE CAUSE:MISSING DATA OR INCORRECT FORMAT'
UN-1    'END OF FILE ENCOUNTERED (IBM CODE IHC217)'
UN-2    'I/O ERROR (IBM CODE IHC218)'
UN-3    'NO DD STATEMENT WAS SUPPLIED (IBM CODE IHC219)'
UN-4    'REWIND,ENDFILE,BACKSPACE REFERENCES UNIT 5, 6 OR 7'
UN-5    'ATTEMPT TO READ ON UNIT 5 AFTER IT HAS HAD END-OF-FILE'
UN-6    'AN INVALID VARIABLE UNIT NUMBER WAS DETECTED (IBM CODE IHC220)'
UN-7    'PAGE-LIMIT EXCEEDED'
UN-8    'ATTEMPT TO DO DIRECT ACCESS I/O ON A SEQUENTIAL FILE OR VICE VERSA.
        POSSIBLE MISSING DEFINE FILE STATEMENT (IBM CODE IHC231)'
UN-9    'WRITE REFERENCES 5 OR READ REFERENCES 6 OR 7'
UN-A    'DEFINE FILE REFERENCES A UNIT PREVIOUSLY USED FOR SEQUENTIAL I/O (IBM
        CODE IHC235)'
UN-B    'RECORD SIZE FOR UNIT EXCEEDS 32767,OR DIFFERS FROM DD STATEMENT
        SPECIFICATION (IBM CODES IHC233,IHC237)'
UN-C    'FOR DIRECT ACCESS I/O THE RELATIVE RECORD POSITION IS NEGATIVE,ZERO,OR
        TOO LARGE (IBM CODE IHC232)'
UN-D    'AN ATTEMPT WAS MADE TO READ MORE INFORMATION THAN LOGICAL RECORD
        CONTAINS (IBM CODE IHC236)'
UN-E    'FORMATTED LINE EXCEEDS BUFFER LENGTH (IBM CODE IHC212)'
UN-F    'I/O ERROR - SEARCHING LIBRARY DIRECTORY'
UN-G    'I/O ERROR - READING LIBRARY'
UN-H    'ATTEMPT TO DEFINE THE OBJECT ERROR FILE AS A DIRECT ACCESS FILE
        (IBM CODE IHC234)'
UN-I    'RECFM IS NOT V(B)S FOR I/O WITHOUT FORMAT CONTROL " (IBM CODE IHC214)'
UN-J    'MISSING DD CARD FOR WATLIB.NO LIBRARY ASSUMED'
UN-K    'ATTEMPT TO READ OR WRITE PAST THE END OF CHARACTER VARIABLE BUFFER'
UN-L    'ATTEMPT TO READ ON AN UNCREATED DIRECT ACCESS FILE (IHC236)'

'UNDEFINED VARIABLES'
UV-0    'VARIABLE IS UNDEFINED'
UV-3    'SUBSCRIPT IS UNDEFINED'
UV-4    'SUBPROGRAM IS UNDEFINED'
UV-5    'ARGUMENT IS UNDEFINED'
UV-6    'UNDECODABLE CHARACTERS IN VARIABLE FORMAT'

'VARIABLE NAMES'
VA-0    'A NAME IS TOO LONG.IT HAS BEEN TRUNCATED TO SIX CHARACTERS'
VA-1    'ATTEMPT TO USE AN ASSIGNED OR INITIALIZED VARIABLE OR DO-PARAMETER IN A
        SPECIFICATION STATEMENT'
VA-2    'ILLEGAL USE OF A SUBROUTINE NAME'
VA-3    'ILLEGAL USE OF A VARIABLE NAME'
VA-4    'ATTEMPT TO USE THE PREVIOUSLY DEFINED NAME AS A FUNCTION OR AN ARRAY'
VA-5    'ATTEMPT TO USE A PREVIOUSLY DEFINED NAME AS A SUBROUTINE'
VA-6    'ATTEMPT TO USE A PREVIOUSLY DEFINED NAME AS A SUBPROGRAM'
VA-7    'ATTEMPT TO USE A PREVIOUSLY DEFINED NAME AS A COMMON BLOCK'
VA-8    'ATTEMPT TO USE A FUNCTION NAME AS A VARIABLE'
VA-9    'ATTEMPT TO USE A PREVIOUSLY DEFINED NAME AS A VARIABLE'
VA-A    'ILLEGAL USE OF A PREVIOUSLY DEFINED NAME'

'EXTERNAL STATEMENT'
XT-0    'A VARIABLE HAS ALREADY APPEARED IN AN EXTERNAL STATEMENT'
```

In 1966 the American National Standards Institute (ANSI, now ANS) adopted a list of standards for the FORTRAN language. Since that time, the list has undergone some revision. The following features of IBM's FORTRAN G and H are not included in the ANS recommendations. They are listed in the order in which topics are discussed in this text.

IMPLICIT

initial data values in type statements

length of variables as part of type specification

function names in type statements

INTEGER*2, COMPLEX*16, and LOGICAL*2 data types

hexadecimal constants

multiple exponentiation without parentheses to indicate order of computation

mixed-mode expressions

generalized subscripts

more than three dimensions in an array

execution-time dimensioning by means of values for dimensions obtained from COMMON (in addition to dimensioning by means of arguments in a CALL statement or function reference)

PAUSE 'message'

length specification in FUNCTION statement

literal as actual argument in function reference (as well as in CALL statement)

call by location for subprogram arguments

ENTRY

RETURN *i*

END and ERR options for READ

literal enclosed in single quotes

Appendix

E

ANS FORTRAN

G format code can be used with integer or logical data as well as with real values

T and Z format codes

READ *b, list*

PRINT *b, list*

PUNCH *b, list*

NAMELIST

direct-access input/output

The forms of READ, PRINT, and PUNCH above are retained in FORTRAN G and H primarily to provide compatibility with prior FORTRAN implementations. In these forms, *b* is a FORMAT statement number or array name used for execution-time dimensioning and *list* is an I/O list as described in chapter 10 of this text. A system-dependent logical unit number is assumed for each as a default.

Generally, a system-supplied FORTRAN library comprises two types of subprograms: mathematical subprograms and service subprograms. The mathematical subprograms are analogous to subprograms defined by FUNCTION statements in a FORTRAN source program. Each execution of one of these subprograms yields one result, or return value, for the calling program. The service subprograms correspond to subprograms defined by SUBROUTINE statements. These subprograms may or may not return values to calling programs.

MATHEMATICAL SUBPROGRAMS

The mathematical subprograms included in a FORTRAN library perform computations required frequently in FORTRAN programming. They are called in either of two ways: (1) explicitly, when the programmer writes an appropriate entry-point name in a source-program statement, and (2) implicitly, when certain notation (e.g., exponentiation) is used in a program. Subprograms in the first of these categories, as available in IBM 360/370 FORTRAN G and H, are summarized in Tables F.1 through F.4. In the subprogram names, xxx is IHC for IBM's Operating System, BOA for IBM's Model 44 Programming System, and ILF for IBM's Disk Operating System. Additional details of these subprograms and of implicitly called mathematical subprograms are given in system documentation prepared for user installations.

Appendix

F

FORTRAN- Supplied Subprograms

TABLE F.1. Logarithmic and Exponential Subprograms

General Function	Subprogram Name	Definition	Entry Name	Argument(s)			Function Value Type
				No.	Type	Range	
Common and natural logarithm	xxxCLLOG	$y = PV \log_e(z)$ See Note 1	CDLOG	1	COMPLEX *16	$z \neq 0 + 0i$ See Note 2	COMPLEX *16
	xxxCSLOG	$y = PV \log_e(z)$ See Note 1	CLOG	1	COMPLEX *8	$z \neq 0 + 0i$ See Note 2	COMPLEX *8
	xxxLLOG	$y = \log_e x$ or $y = \ln x$	DLOG	1	REAL*8	$x > 0$	REAL*8
		$y = \log_{10} x$	DLOG10	1	REAL*8	$x > 0$	REAL*8
	xxxSLOG	$y = \log_e x$ or $y = \ln x$	ALOG	1	REAL*4	$x > 0$	REAL*4
		$y = \log_{10} x$	ALOG10	1	REAL*4	$x > 0$	REAL*4
Exponential	xxxCLEXP	$y = e^z$ See Note 3	CDEXP	1	COMPLEX *16	$x_1 \leq 174.673$ $\lvert x_2 \rvert < (2^{50} \cdot \pi)$	COMPLEX *16
	xxxCSEXP	$y = e^z$ See Note 3	CEXP	1	COMPLEX *8	$x_1 \leq 174.673$ $\lvert x_2 \rvert < (2^{50} \cdot \pi)$	COMPLEX *8
	xxxLEXP	$y = e^x$	DEXP	1	REAL*8	$x \leq 174.673$	REAL*8
	xxxSEXP	$y = e^x$	EXP	1	REAL*4	$x \leq 174.673$	REAL*4
Square root	xxxCLSQT	$y = \sqrt{z}$	CDSQRT	1	COMPLEX *16	any complex argument See Note 2	COMPLEX *16
	xxxCSSQT	$y = \sqrt{z}$	CSQRT	1	COMPLEX *8	any complex argument See Note 2	COMPLEX *8
	xxxLSQRT	$y = \sqrt{x}$	DSQRT	1	REAL*8	$x \geq 0$	REAL*8
	xxxSSQRT	$y = \sqrt{x}$	SQRT	1	REAL*4	$x \geq 0$	REAL*4

Notes:
1. Where PV means principal value. The answer given is from that point where the imaginary part (y_2) lies between $-\pi$ and $+\pi$. More specifically, $-\pi < y_2 \leq \pi$, unless $x_1 < 0$ and $x_2 = -0$, in which case, $y_2 = -\pi$.
2. Floating-point overflow can occur.
3. Where z is a complex number of the form $x_1 + x_2 i$.

TABLE F.2.   Trigonometric Subprograms

General Function	Subprogram Name	Definition	Entry Name	Argument(s)			Function Value Type
				No.	Type	Range	
Arcsine and arccosine	xxxLASCN	$y = \arcsin(x)$	DARSIN	1	REAL*8	$\lvert x \rvert \leq 1$	REAL*8 (in radians)
		$y = \arccos(x)$	DARCOS	1	REAL*8	$\lvert x \rvert \leq 1$	REAL*8 (in radians)
	xxxSASCN	$y = \arcsin(x)$	ARSIN	1	REAL*4	$\lvert x \rvert \leq 1$	REAL*4 (in radians)
		$y = \arccos(x)$	ARCOS	1	REAL*4	$\lvert x \rvert \leq 1$	REAL*4 (in radians)
Arctangent	xxxLATN2	$y = \arctan(x)$	DATAN	1	REAL*8	any real argument	REAL*8 (in radians)
		$y = \arctan\left(\dfrac{x_1}{x_2}\right)$	DATAN2	2	REAL*8	any real arguments (except 0, 0)	REAL*8 (in radians)
	xxxSATN2	$y = \arctan(x)$	ATAN	1	REAL*4	any real argument	REAL*4 (in radians)
		$y = \arctan\left(\dfrac{x_1}{x_2}\right)$	ATAN2	2	REAL*4	any real arguments (except 0, 0)	REAL*4 (in radians)
Sine and cosine	xxxCLSCN	$y = \sin(z)$ See Note 1	CDSIN	1	COMPLEX *16 (in radians)	$\lvert x_1 \rvert < (2^{50} \cdot \pi)$ $\lvert x_2 \rvert \leq 174.673$	COMPLEX *16
		$y = \cos(z)$ See Note 1	CDCOS	1	COMPLEX *16 (in radians)	$\lvert x_1 \rvert < (2^{50} \cdot \pi)$ $\lvert x_2 \rvert \leq 174.673$	COMPLEX *16
	xxxCSSCN	$y = \sin(z)$ See Note 1	CSIN	1	COMPLEX *8 (in radians)	$\lvert x_1 \rvert < (2^{18} \cdot \pi)$ $\lvert x_2 \rvert \leq 174.673$	COMPLEX *8
		$y = \cos(z)$ See Note 1	CCOS	1	COMPLEX *8 (in radians)	$\lvert x_1 \rvert < (2^{18} \cdot \pi)$ $\lvert x_2 \rvert \leq 174.673$	COMPLEX *8
	xxxLSCN	$y = \sin(x)$	DSIN	1	REAL*8 (in radians)	$\lvert x \rvert < (2^{50} \cdot \pi)$	REAL*8
		$y = \cos(x)$	DCOS	1	REAL*8 (in radians)	$\lvert x \rvert < (2^{50} \cdot \pi)$	REAL*8
	xxxSSCN	$y = \sin(x)$	SIN	1	REAL*4 (in radians)	$\lvert x \rvert < (2^{18} \cdot \pi)$	REAL*4
		$y = \cos(x)$	COS	1	REAL*4 (in radians)	$\lvert x \rvert < (2^{18} \cdot \pi)$	REAL*4

TABLE F.2—*continued*

General Function	Subprogram Name	Definition	Entry Name	Argument(s)			Function Value Type
				No.	Type	Range	
Tangent and cotangent	xxxLTNCT	$y = \tan(x)$	DTAN	1	REAL*8 (in radians)	$|x| < (2^{50} \cdot \pi)$ See Note 2	REAL*8
		$y = \cotan(x)$	DCOTAN	1	REAL*8 (in radians)	$|x| < (2^{50} \cdot \pi)$ See Note 2	REAL*8
	xxxSTNCT	$y = \tan(x)$	TAN	1	REAL*4 (in radians)	$|x| < (2^{18} \cdot \pi)$ See Note 2	REAL*4
		$y = \cotan(x)$	COTAN	1	REAL*4 (in radians)	$|x| < (2^{18} \cdot \pi)$ See Note 2	REAL*4

Notes:
1. Where z is a complex number of the form $x_1 + x_2 i$.
2. The argument for the cotangent functions may not be near a multiple of π; the argument for the tangent functions may not be near an odd multiple of $\pi/2$.

TABLE F.3.   Hyperbolic Function Subprograms

General Function	Subprogram Name	Definition	Entry Name	Argument(s)			Function Value Type
				No.	Type	Range	
Hyperbolic sine and cosine	xxxLSCNH	$y = \dfrac{e^x - e^{-x}}{2}$	DSINH	1	REAL*8	$|x| < 174.673$	REAL*8
		$y = \dfrac{e^x + e^{-x}}{2}$	DCOSH	1	REAL*8	$|x| < 174.673$	REAL*8
	xxxSSCNH	$y = \dfrac{e^x - e^{-x}}{2}$	SINH	1	REAL*4	$|x| < 174.673$	REAL*4
		$y = \dfrac{e^x + e^{-x}}{2}$	COSH	1	REAL*4	$|x| < 174.673$	REAL*4
Hyperbolic tangent	xxxLTANH	$y = \dfrac{e^x - e^{-x}}{e^x + e^{-x}}$	DTANH	1	REAL*8	any real argument	REAL*8
	xxxSTANH	$y = \dfrac{e^x - e^{-x}}{e^x + e^{-x}}$	TANH	1	REAL*4	any real argument	REAL*4

TABLE F.4.   Miscellaneous Mathematical Subprograms

General Function	Subprogram Name	Definition	Entry Name	Argument(s)			Function Value Type
				No.	Type	Range	
Absolute value	ABSOLUTE	$y = \lvert z \rvert$	IABS	1	INTEGER*4	any integer argument	INTE-GER*4
		$y = \lvert z \rvert$	ABS	1	REAL*4	any real argument	REAL*4
		$y = \lvert z \rvert$	DABS	1	REAL*8	any real argument	REAL*8
	xxxCLABS	$y = \lvert z \rvert$ $= (x_1{}^2 + x_2{}^2)^{1/2}$	CDABS	1	COMPLEX*16	any complex argument See Note 1	REAL*8
	xxxCSABS	$y = \lvert z \rvert$ $= (x_1{}^2 + x_2{}^2)^{1/2}$	CABS	1	COMPLEX*8	any complex argument See Note 1	REAL*4
Error function	xxxLERF	$y = \dfrac{2}{\sqrt{\pi}} \displaystyle\int_0^x e^{-u^2}\, du$	DERF	1	REAL*8	any real argument	REAL*8
		$y = \dfrac{2}{\sqrt{\pi}} \displaystyle\int_x^\infty e^{-u^2}\, du$ $y = 1 - \text{erf}(x)$	DERFC	1	REAL*8	any real argument	REAL*8
	xxxSERF	$y = \dfrac{2}{\sqrt{\pi}} \displaystyle\int_0^x e^{-u^2}\, du$	ERF	1	REAL*4	any real argument	REAL*4
		$y = \dfrac{2}{\sqrt{\pi}} \displaystyle\int_x^\infty e^{-u^2}\, du$ $y = 1 - \text{erf}(x)$	ERFC	1	REAL*4	any real argument	REAL*4
Gamma and log-gamma	xxxLGAMA	$y = \displaystyle\int_0^\infty u^{x-1} e^{-u}\, du$	DGAMMA	1	REAL*8	$x > 2^{-252}$ and $x < 57.5744$	REAL*8
		$y = \log_e \Gamma(x)$ or $y = \log_e \displaystyle\int_0^\infty u^{x-1} e^{-u}\, du$	DLGAMA	1	REAL*8	$x > 0$ and $x < 4.2913 \cdot 10^{73}$	REAL*8
	xxxSGAMA	$y = \displaystyle\int_0^\infty u^{x-1} e^{-u}\, du$	GAMMA	1	REAL*4	$x > 2^{-252}$ and $x < 57.5744$	REAL*4
		$y = \log_e \Gamma(x)$ or $y = \log_e \displaystyle\int_0^\infty u^{x-1} e^{-u}\, du$	ALGAMA	1	REAL*4	$x > 0$ and $x < 4.2913 \cdot 10^{73}$	REAL*4

TABLE F.4—*continued*

General Function	Subprogram Name	Definition	Entry Name	Argument(s)			Function Value Type
				No.	Type	Range	
Maximum and minimum values	xxxFMAXD	$y = \max(x_1, \ldots, x_n)$	DMAXI	≥ 2	REAL*8	any real arguments	REAL*8
		$y = \min(x_1, \ldots, x_n)$	DMINI	≥ 2	REAL*8	any real arguments	REAL*8
	xxxFMAXI	$y = \max(x_1, \ldots, x_n)$	AMAX0	≥ 2	INTEGER *4	any integer arguments	REAL*4
			MAX0	≥ 2	INTEGER *4	any integer arguments	INTE-GER*4
		$y = \min(x_1, \ldots, x_n)$	AMIN0	≥ 2	INTEGER *4	any integer arguments	REAL*4
			MIN0	≥ 2	INTEGER *4	any integer arguments	INTE-GER*4
	xxxFMAXR	$y = \max(x_1, \ldots, x_n)$	AMAX1	≥ 2	REAL*4	any real arguments	REAL*4
			MAX1	≥ 2	REAL*4	any real arguments	INTE-GER*4
		$y = \min(x_1, \ldots, x_n)$	AMIN1	≥ 2	REAL*4	any real arguments	REAL*4
			MIN1	≥ 2	REAL*4	any real arguments	INTE-GER*4
Modular arithmetic	IHCFMODI	$y = x_1$ (modulo x_2) See Note 2	MOD	2	INTEGER	$x_2 \neq 0$ See Note 3	INTE-GER*4
	IHCFMODR	$y = x_1$ (modulo x_2) See Note 2	AMOD	2	REAL*4	$x_2 \neq 0$ See Note 3	REAL*4
		$y = x_1$ (modulo x_2) See Note 2	DMOD	2	REAL*8	$x_2 \neq 0$ See Note 3	REAL*8
Truncation	IHCFAINT	$y = (\text{sign } x) \cdot n$ where n is the largest integer $\leq \lvert x \rvert$	AINT	1	REAL*4	any real argument	REAL*4
	IHCFIFIX	$y = (\text{sign } x) \cdot n$ where n is the largest integer $\leq \lvert x \rvert$	IDINT	1	REAL*8	any real argument	INTE-GER
			INT	1	REAL*4	any real argument	INTE-GER

TABLE F.4—*continued*

General Function	Subprogram Name	Definition	Entry Name	Argument(s)			Function Value Type
				No.	Type	Range	
Type conversion	SNGLDBLE	y = significant part of REAL*8 value	SNGL	1	REAL*8	any real argument	REAL*4
		y = REAL*8 form of REAL*4 value	DBLE	1	REAL*4	any real argument	REAL*8
	REALIMAG	y = real part of a complex value	REAL	1	COM-PLEX*8	any complex argument	REAL*4
		y = imaginary part of a complex value	AIMAG	1	COM-PLEX*8	any complex argument	REAL*4
	xxxCMPLX	y = complex form of 2 real values	CMPLX	2	REAL*4	any real arguments	COM-PLEX*8
		y = complex form of 2 real values	DCMPLX	2	REAL*8	any real arguments	COM-PLEX*16
	xxxCONJG	y = conjugate of complex value	CONJG	1	COM-PLEX*8	any complex argument	COM-PLEX*8
		y = conjugate of complex value	DCONJG	1	COM-PLEX*16	any complex argument	COM-PLEX*16

Notes:
1. Floating-point overflow can occur.

2. The expression x_1 (modulo x_2) is defined as $x_1 - \left[\dfrac{x_1}{x_2}\right] \cdot x_2$, where the brackets indicate that an integer is used. The largest integer whose magnitude does not exceed the magnitude of $\dfrac{x_1}{x_2}$ is used. The sign of the integer is the same as the sign of $\dfrac{x_1}{x_2}$.

3. If $x_2 = 0$, the modulus function is mathematically undefined. A divide exception is recognized and an interruption occurs.

SERVICE SUBPROGRAMS

The service subprograms included in an IBM 360/370 FORTRAN G or H library are divided into two groups: (1) machine indicator test subprograms and (2) utility subprograms.

The machine indicator test subprograms test the status of pseudo indicators and may return a value to the calling program. When an indicator is zero, it is off; when an indicator is other than zero, it is on. The machine indicator test subprograms are:

- xxxFSLIT with entry-point names SLITE and SLITET which is used to alter, test, and/or record the status of pseudo sense lights

- xxxFOVER with entry-point name OVERFL which tests for an exponent overflow or underflow exception and returns a value that indicates the existing condition

- xxxFDVCH with entry-point name DVCHK which tests for a divide-check exception and returns a value that indicates the existing condition

The utility subprograms perform two operations:

- xxxFEXIT with entry-point name EXIT terminates execution of a FORTRAN program and returns control to an operating-system program
- xxxFDUMP with entry-point names DUMP and PDUMP dumps a specified area of storage, with execution terminated or resumed, respectively, depending on the entry point used

In the subprogram names given above, xxx is IHC for IBM's Operating System, BOA for IBM's Model 44 Programming System, and ILF for IBM's Disk Operating System. The entry-point names, which are the same in all systems, are the names that must be used in CALL statements referring to these subprograms. The forms of the CALL statements are summarized below.

CALL SLITE (i)

where i has a value of 0, indicating that all sense lights are to be turned off; or of 1, 2, 3, or 4, indicating that the corresponding sense light is to be turned on.

CALL SLITET (i,j)

where i has a value of 1, 2, 3, or 4, indicating which sense light is to be tested; and j is set to 1 if the sense light was on, or to 2 if it was off.

CALL OVERFL (j)

where j is set to 1 if a floating-point overflow condition exists; to 2 if no overflow or underflow condition exists; or to 3 if a floating-point underflow condition exists.

CALL DVCHK (j)

where j is set to 1 if the divide-check indicator was on, or to 2 if it was off.

CALL EXIT

CALL DUMP ($a_1,b_1,f_1,\ldots,a_n,b_n,f_n$)

where a and b are variables that give the limits of storage to be dumped; and f indicates the dump format as follows:

f	Format	f	Format
0	Hexadecimal	5	REAL*4
1	LOGICAL*1	6	REAL*8
2	LOGICAL*4	7	COMPLEX*8
3	INTEGER*2	8	COMPLEX*16
4	INTEGER*4	9	Literal

CALL PDUMP ($a_1,b_1,f_1,\ldots,a_n,b_n,f_n$)

where a, b, and f have the meanings described for DUMP above.

ADDITIONAL SUBPROGRAMS SUPPORTED BY WATFIV

WATFIV supports four subprograms not available in IBM 360/370 FORTRAN. Each accepts, as arguments, any type of variable that occupies four bytes of storage (INTEGER*4, REAL*4, LOGICAL*4, or CHARACTER*4). All 32 bits of each argument are used in computing the result, a REAL*4 value. The name, description, and number of arguments for each of these function subprograms are given below.

Function Name	Description	Arguments
AND	logical AND of arguments	2 or more 4-byte values
OR	logical OR of arguments	2 or more 4-byte values
EOR	exclusive OR of arguments	2 or more 4-byte values
COMPL	logical 1s complement of argument	1 4-byte value

WATFIV also provides TRAPS, a subroutine subprogram that can be used in conjunction with the DVCHK and OVERFL subroutine subprograms to monitor the occurrence of fixed overflow, exponent overflow, exponent under- flow, fixed-point divide, and floating-point divide exceptions in a program. TRAPS can be called and recalled, giving up to five integer constants and variables as arguments, to set interrupt counters governing program termination as a result of occurrence of any of these exceptions. The WATFIV compiler interrupt routine decrements the appropriate counter when an interrupt occurs. When any counter reaches zero, execution is terminated. (If TRAPS is not used, the first occurrence of an exponent overflow or underflow, or fixed-point or floating-point divide, terminates program execution.)

CALL TRAPS $(0,3,4,-2,1)$

The statement above sets interrupt counters so that the program is ter- minated upon occurrence of exceptions as follows:

* third exponent overflow
* fourth exponent underflow
* second fixed-point divide
* first floating-point divide

after execution of this CALL statement

An argument value of zero ensures that the current value of the interrupt counter for the exception is not changed as a result of the CALL statement. An argument value of one may be omitted if no succeeding argument values need be specified. The absolute values of arguments are used. Hence, either of the statements below is equivalent to the CALL statement above.

CALL TRAPS $(0,3,4,-2)$
CALL TRAPS $(0,-3,4,2,1)$

Index

The text was set in 9 point Univers 55 by Holmes Typography, Inc. of San Jose, California, and printed by Segerdahl-Halford, Inc. of Chicago, Illinois.

Project Editor : Carol Harris
Sponsoring Editor : Stephen Mitchell
Designer : Michael Rogondino